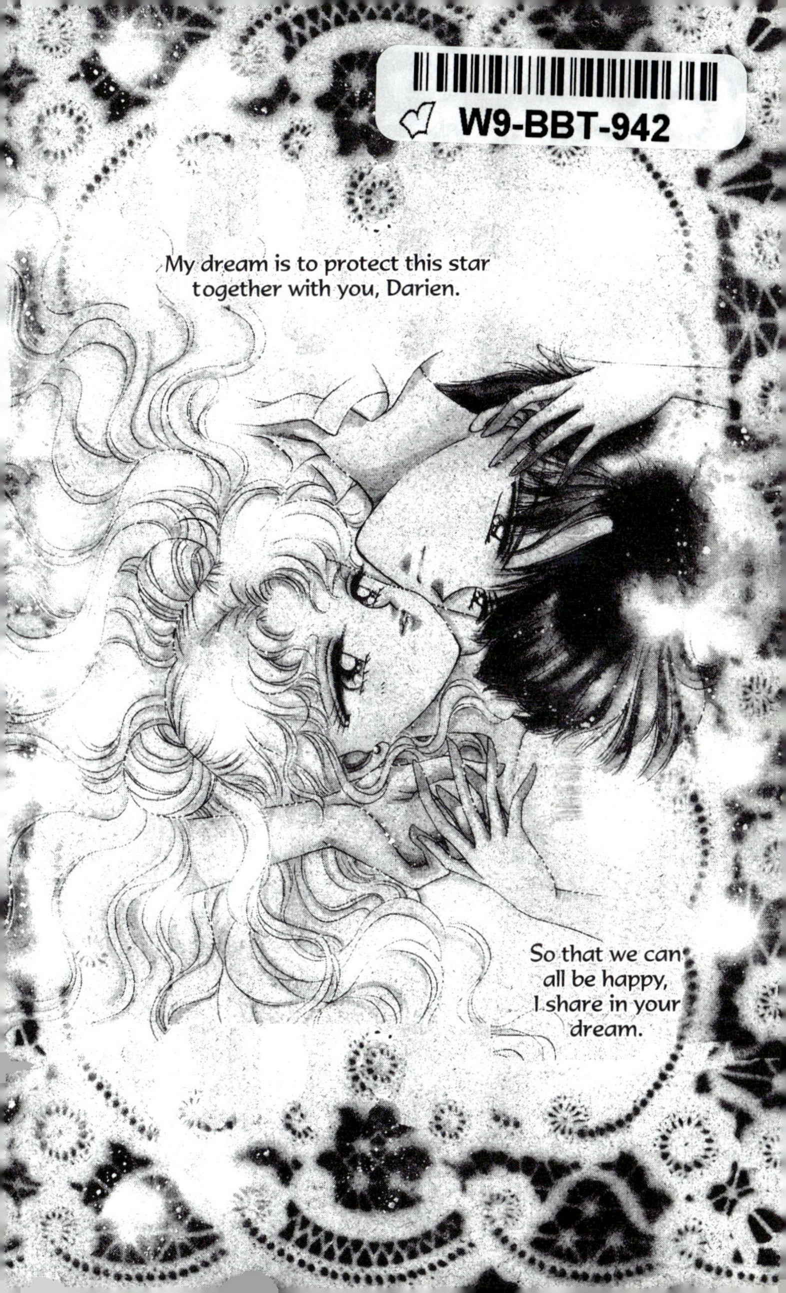
My dream is to protect this star together with you, Darien.
So that we can all be happy, I share in your dream.

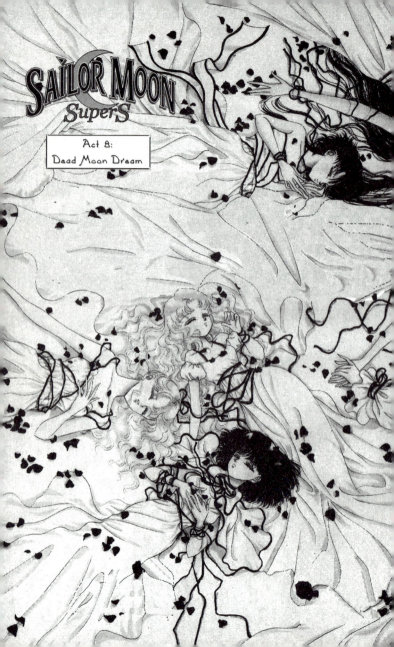

SAILOR MOON SuperS

Act 8:
Dead Moon Dream

2/2/09

SAILOR MOON™ SuperS

④

by Naoko Takeuchi

Dead Moon Dream.. 4

Earth & Moon Dream...91

TOKYOPOP PRESS

CHIX COMIX
Pocket Edition

TOKYOPOP Press Presents
Sailor Moon SuperS 4 by Naoko Takeuchi
Chix Comix Pocket Edition is an imprint of Mixx Entertainment, Inc.
ISBN: 1-892213-39-7
First Printing August 2000

10   9   8   7   6   5   4   3   2   1

This volume contains the SAILOR MOON SuperS installments from
Smile No. 2.4 through No. 2.6 in their entirety.

Translator - Anita Sengupta. Retouch Artist - Wilbert Lacuna.
Graphics Assistant - Steven Kindernay. Graphic Designer - Akemi Imafuku.
Associate Editor - Jake Forbes. Editor - Mary Coco.
Production Manager - Fred Lui. Director of Publishing - Henry Kornman.

Email: info@mixxonline.com
Come visit us at www.TOKYOPOP.com.

Mixx Entertainment, Inc.
Los Angeles - Tokyo

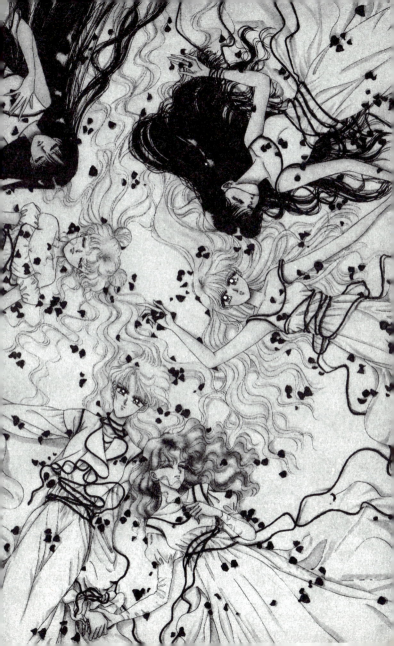

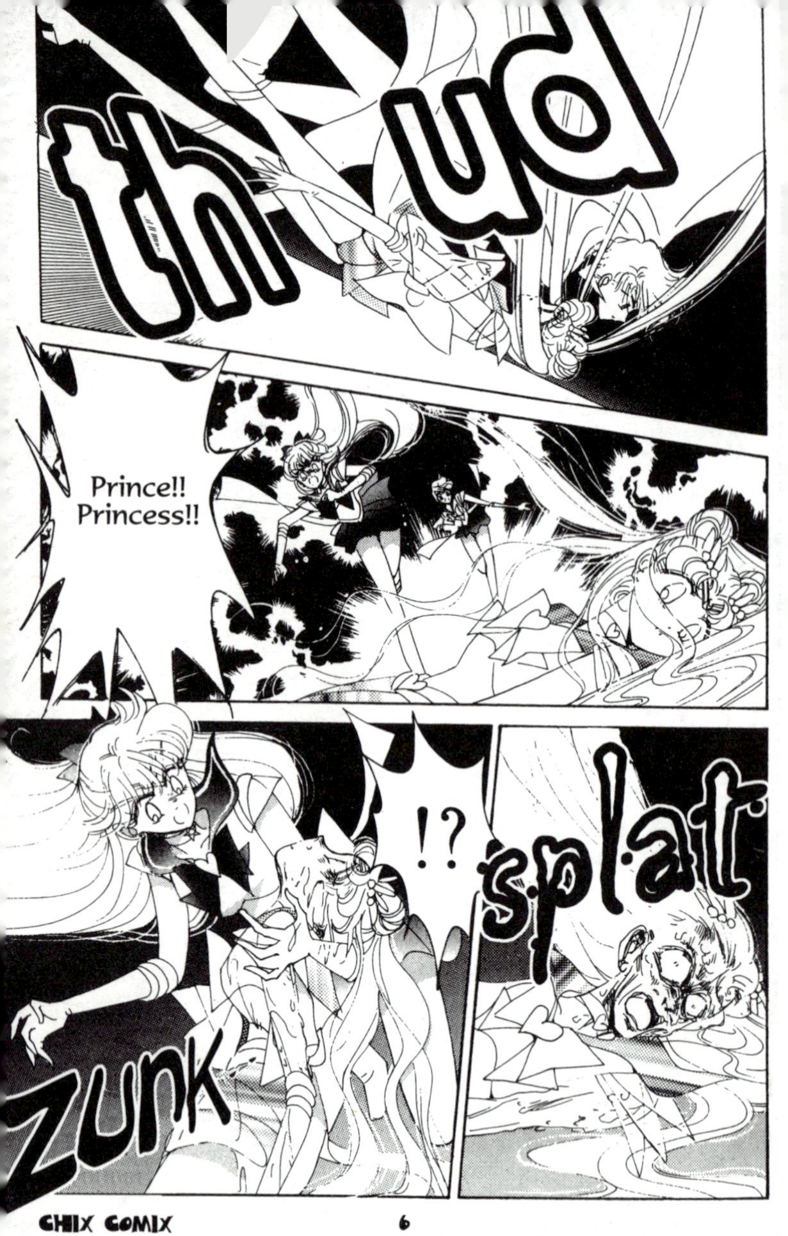
thud
Prince!!
Princess!!
zunk
!?
splat

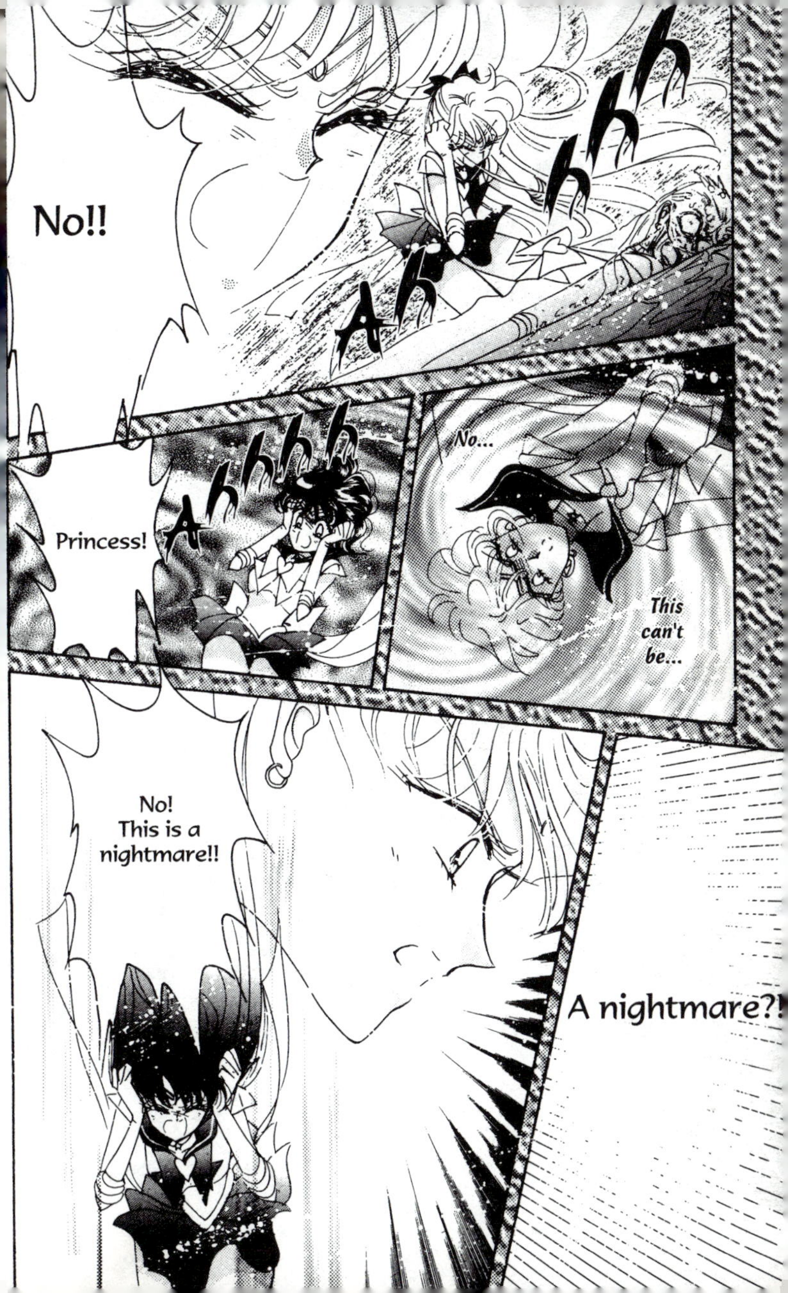
No!!
Ahhhhh
Princess!
Ahhhhh
No...
This can't be...
No! This is a nightmare!!
A nightmare?!

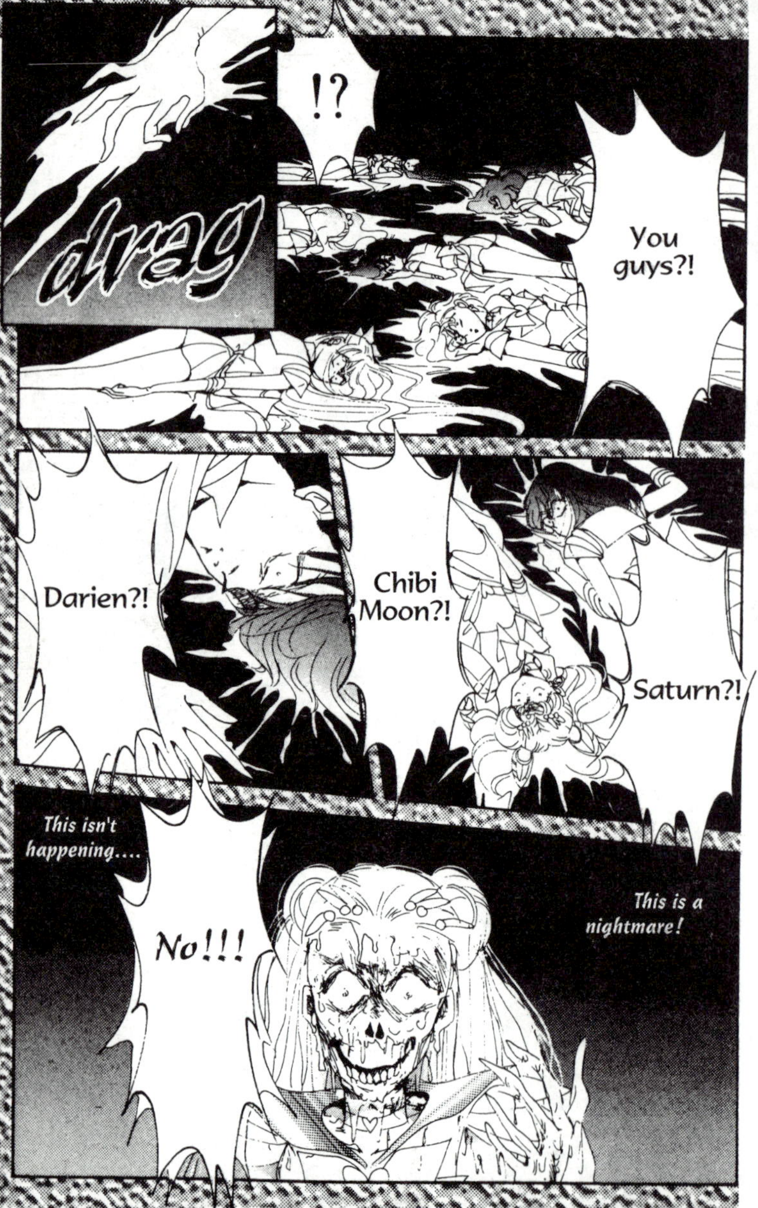

drag
!?
You guys?!
Darien?!
Chibi Moon?!
Saturn?!
This isn't happening....
No!!!
This is a nightmare!

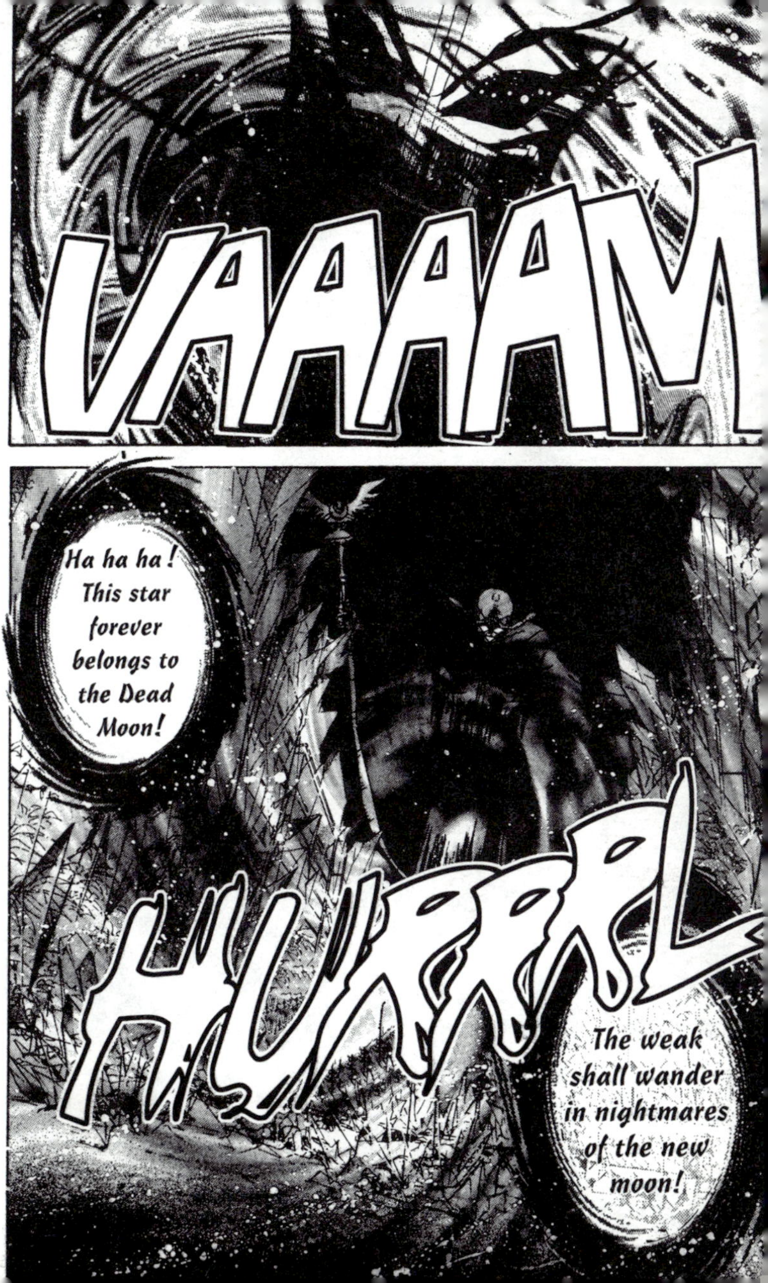
VAAAAM
Ha ha ha! This star forever belongs to the Dead Moon!
HURRRL
The weak shall wander in nightmares of the new moon!

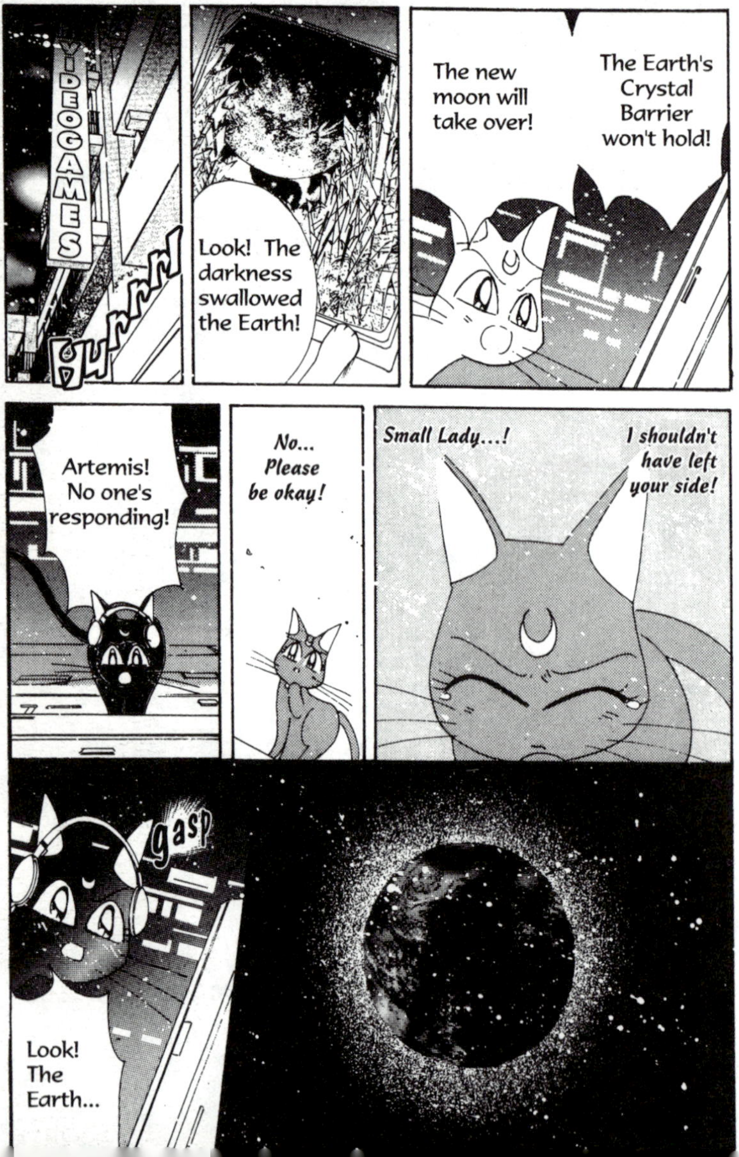
VIDEOGAMES
Look! The darkness swallowed the Earth!
The new moon will take over!
The Earth's Crystal Barrier won't hold!
Artemis! No one's responding!
No... Please be okay!
Small Lady...!
I shouldn't have left your side!
gasp
Look! The Earth...

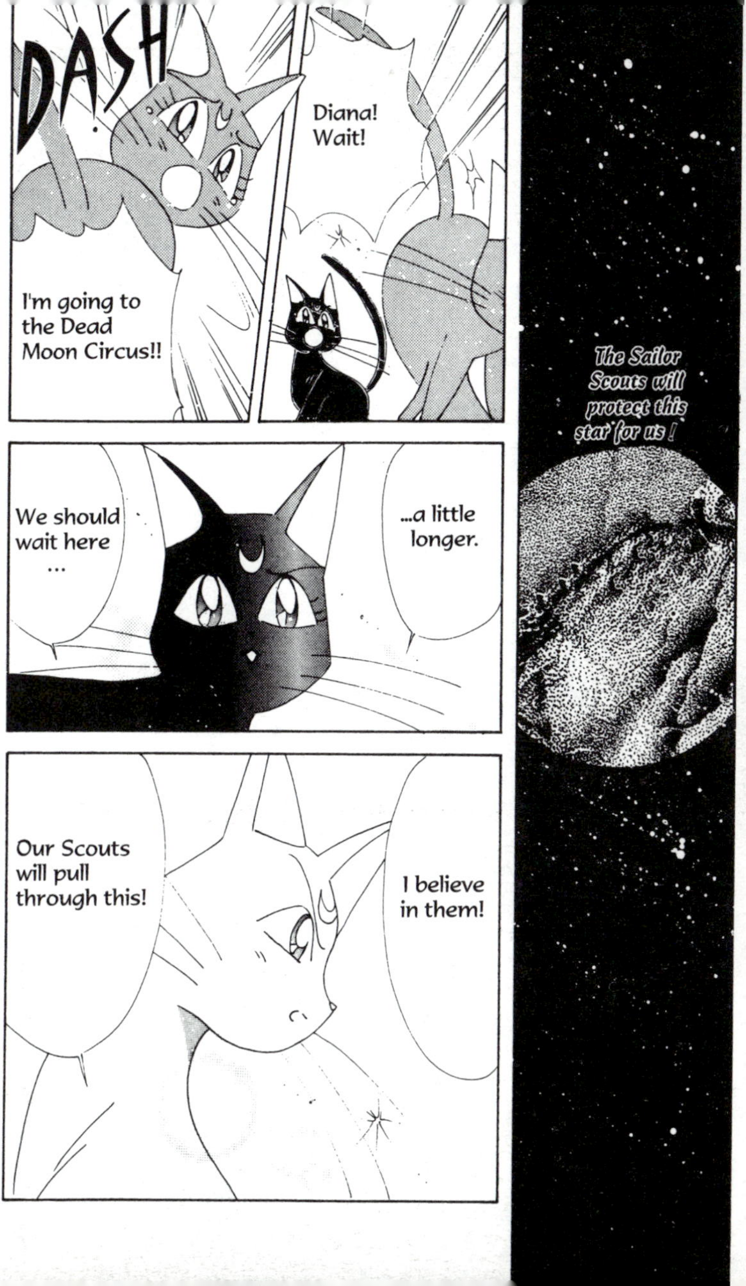
DASH
I'm going to the Dead Moon Circus!!
Diana! Wait!
We should wait here ...
...a little longer.
Our Scouts will pull through this!
I believe in them!
The Sailor Scouts will protect this star for us!

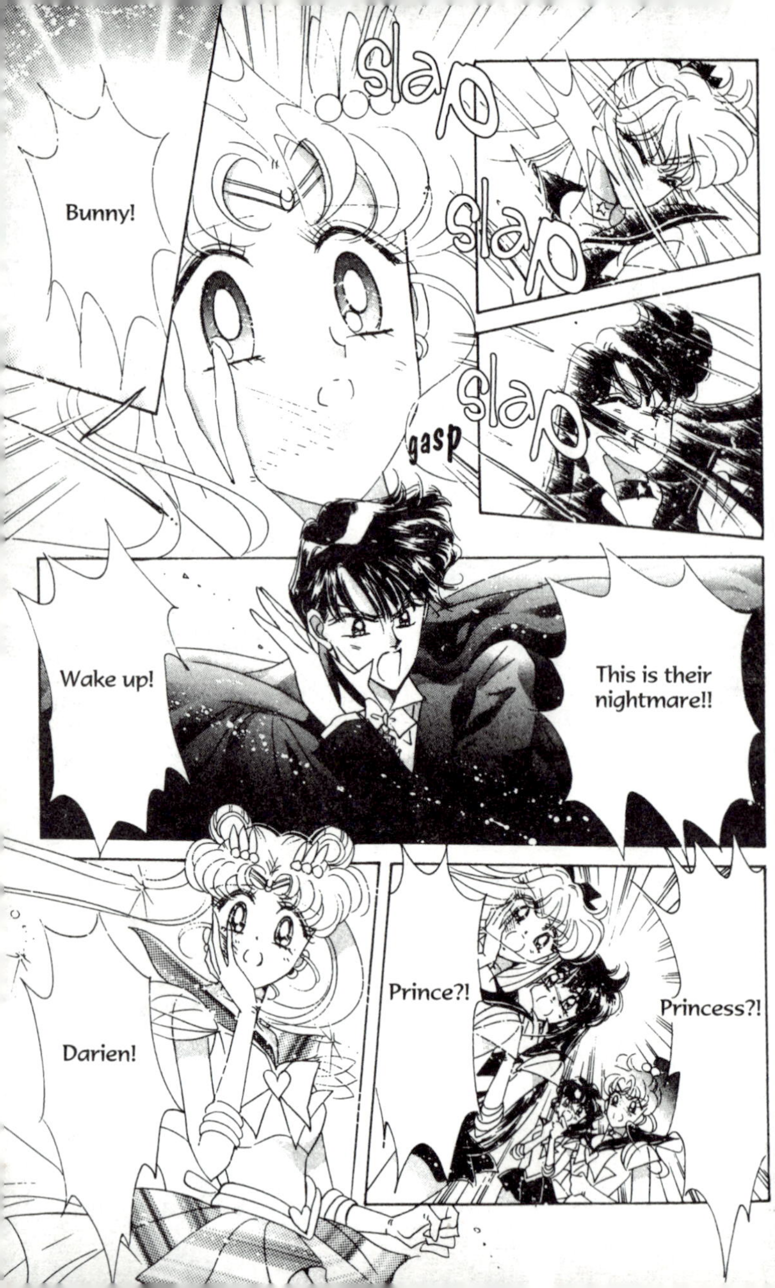
Bunny!
...slap
slap
slap
gasp
Wake up!
This is their nightmare!!
Darien!
Prince?!
Princess?!

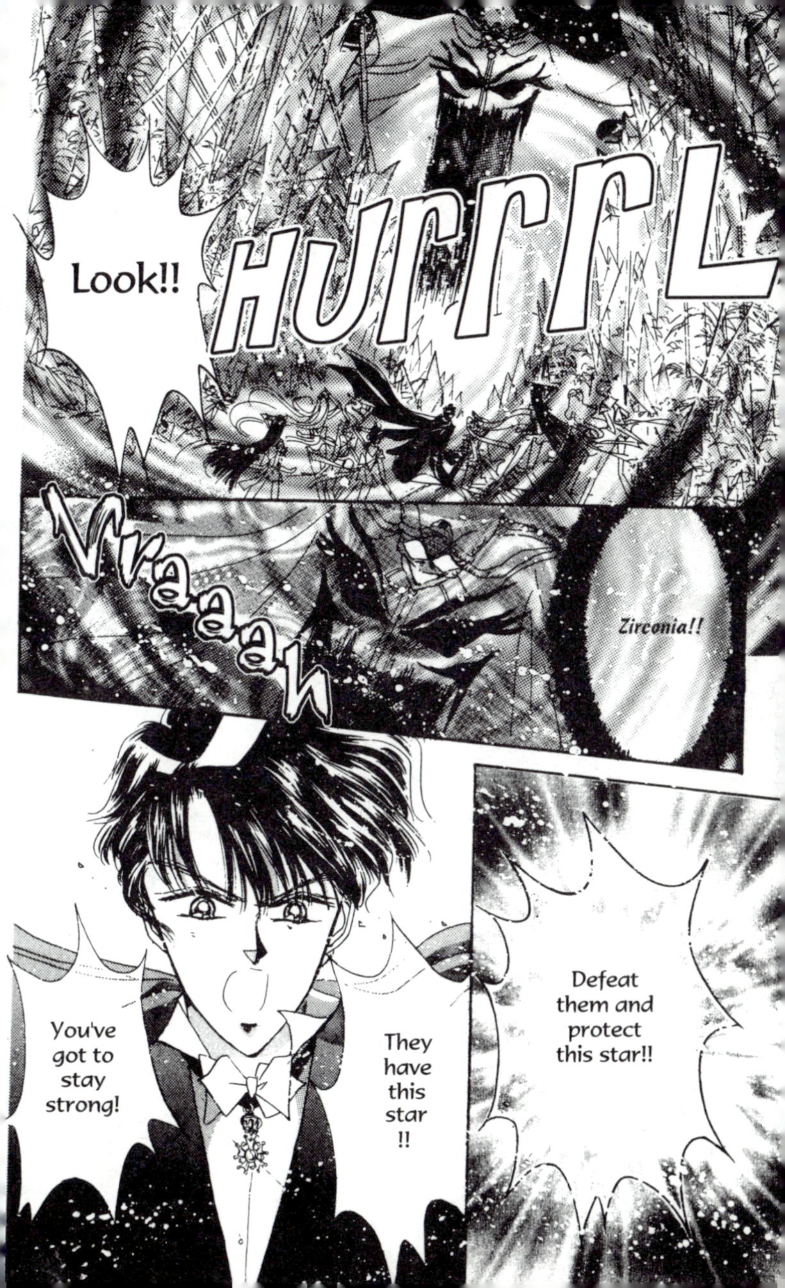
Look!!
HURRRL
Vraaaan
Zirconia!!
You've got to stay strong!
They have this star !!
Defeat them and protect this star!!

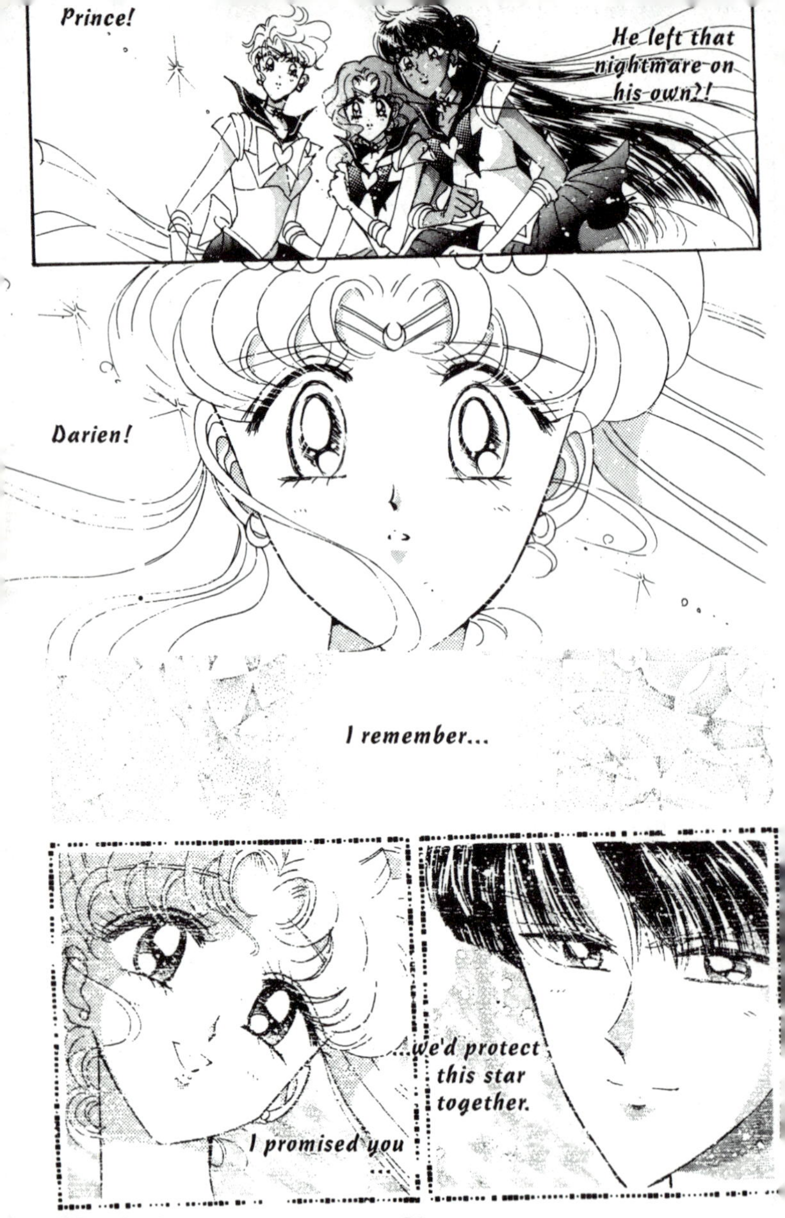
Prince!
He left that nightmare on his own?!
Darien!
I remember...
I promised you
...
...we'd protect this star together.

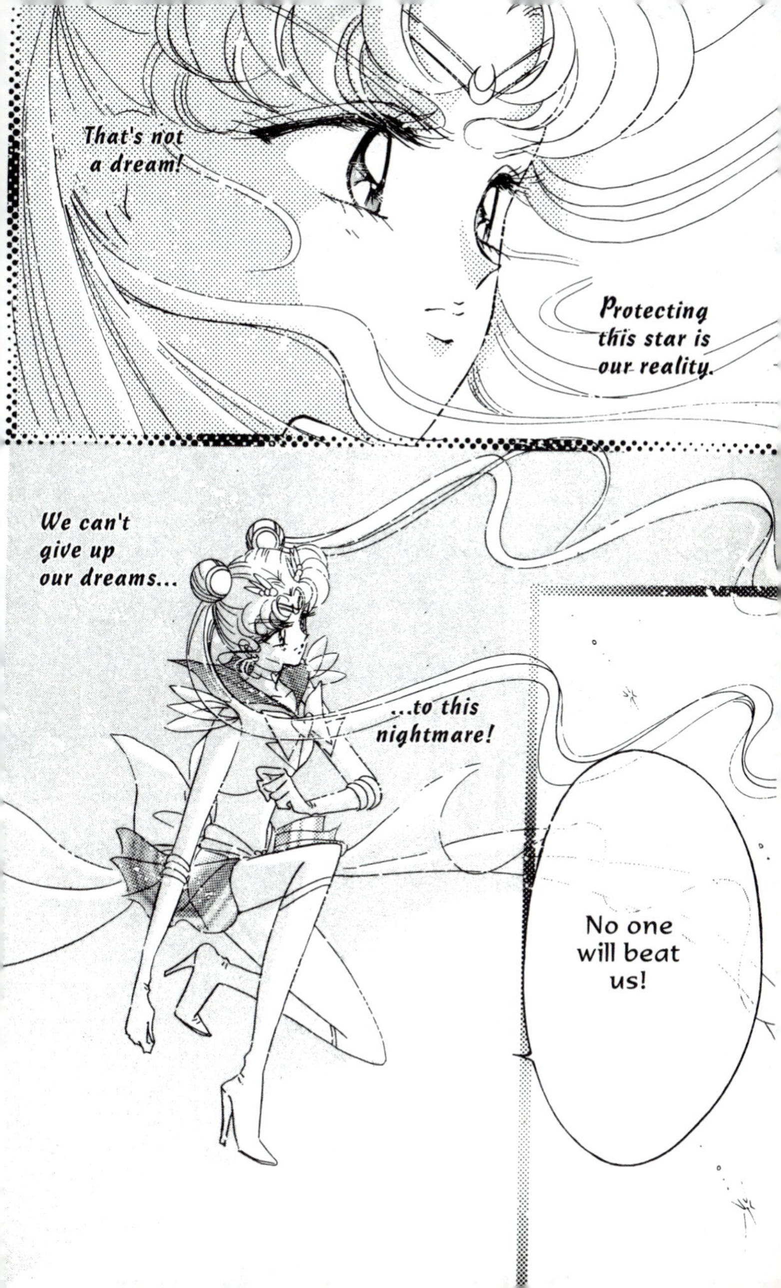
That's not a dream!
Protecting this star is our reality.
We can't give up our dreams...
...to this nightmare!
No one will beat us!

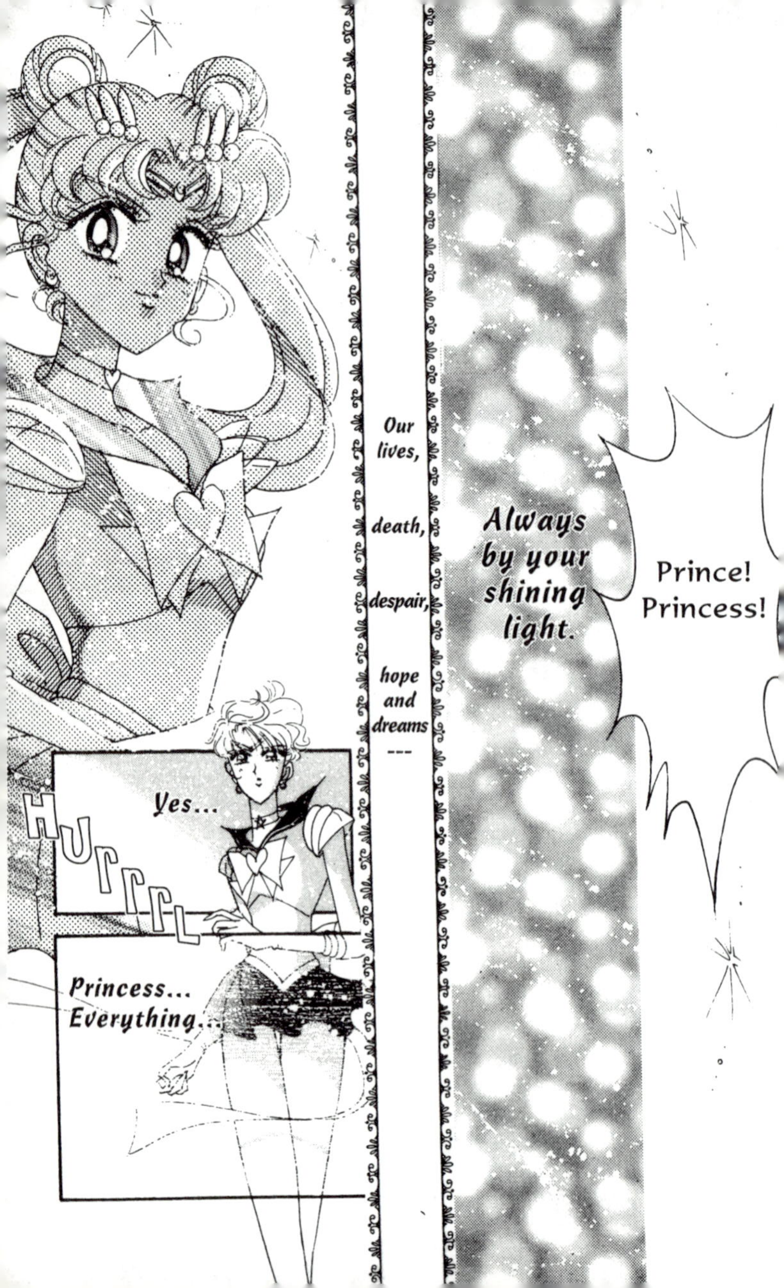
Yes...
HUrrrL
Princess... Everything...
Our lives,
death,
despair,
hope and dreams ---
Always by your shining light.
Prince! Princess!

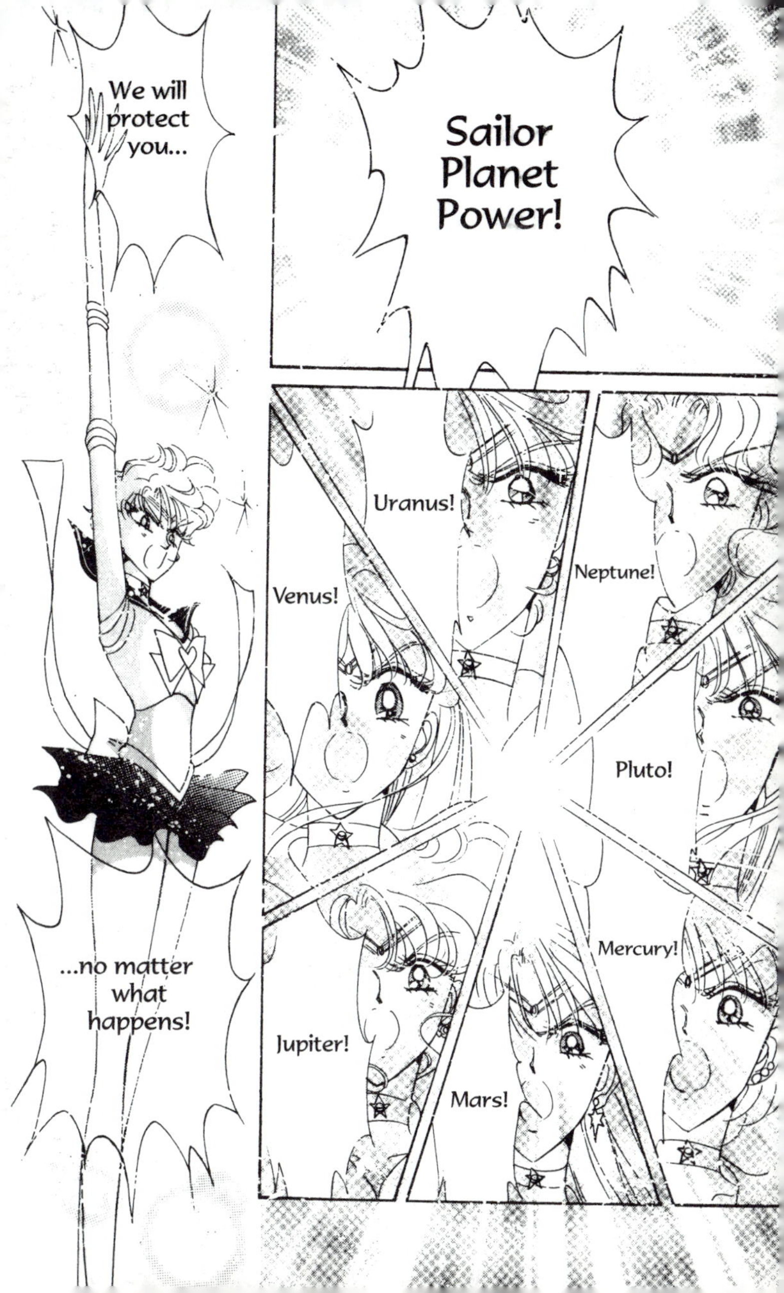
We will protect you...
...no matter what happens!
Sailor Planet Power!
Uranus!
Neptune!
Venus!
Pluto!
Mercury!
Jupiter!
Mars!

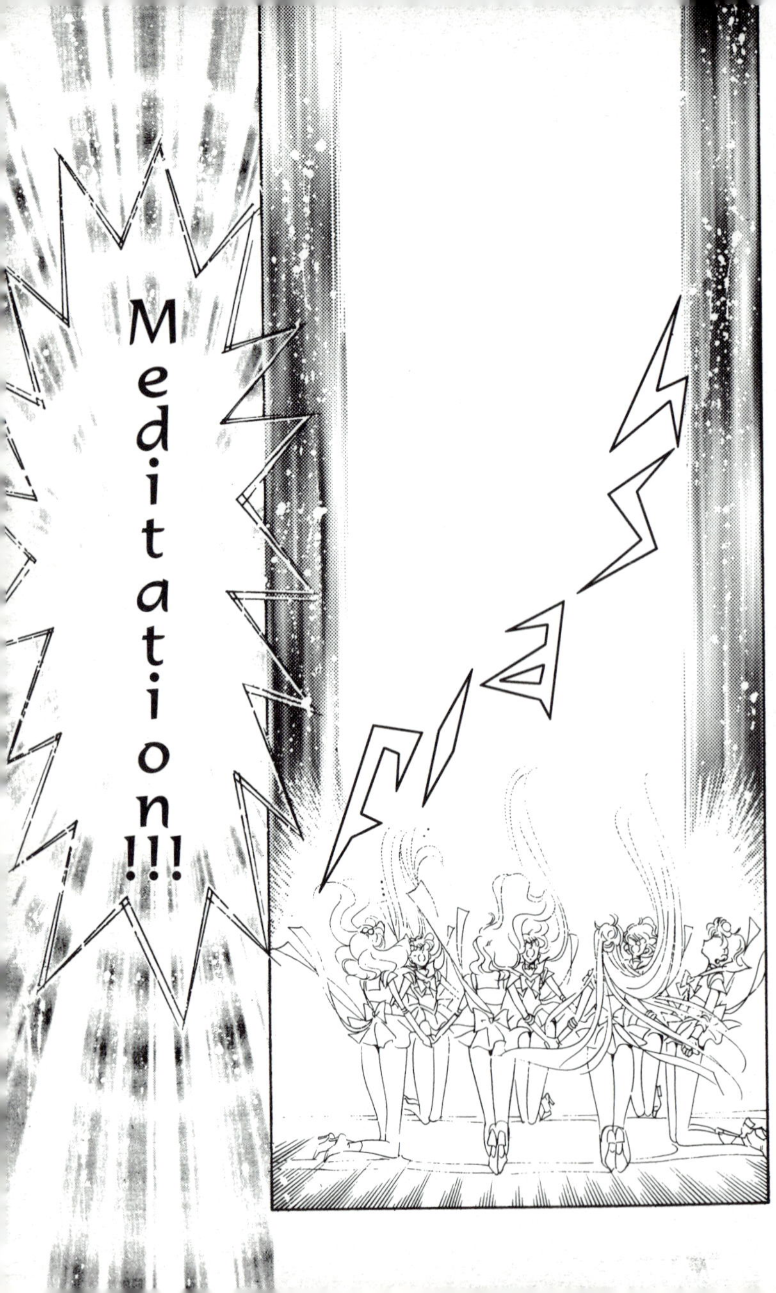
Meditation!!!

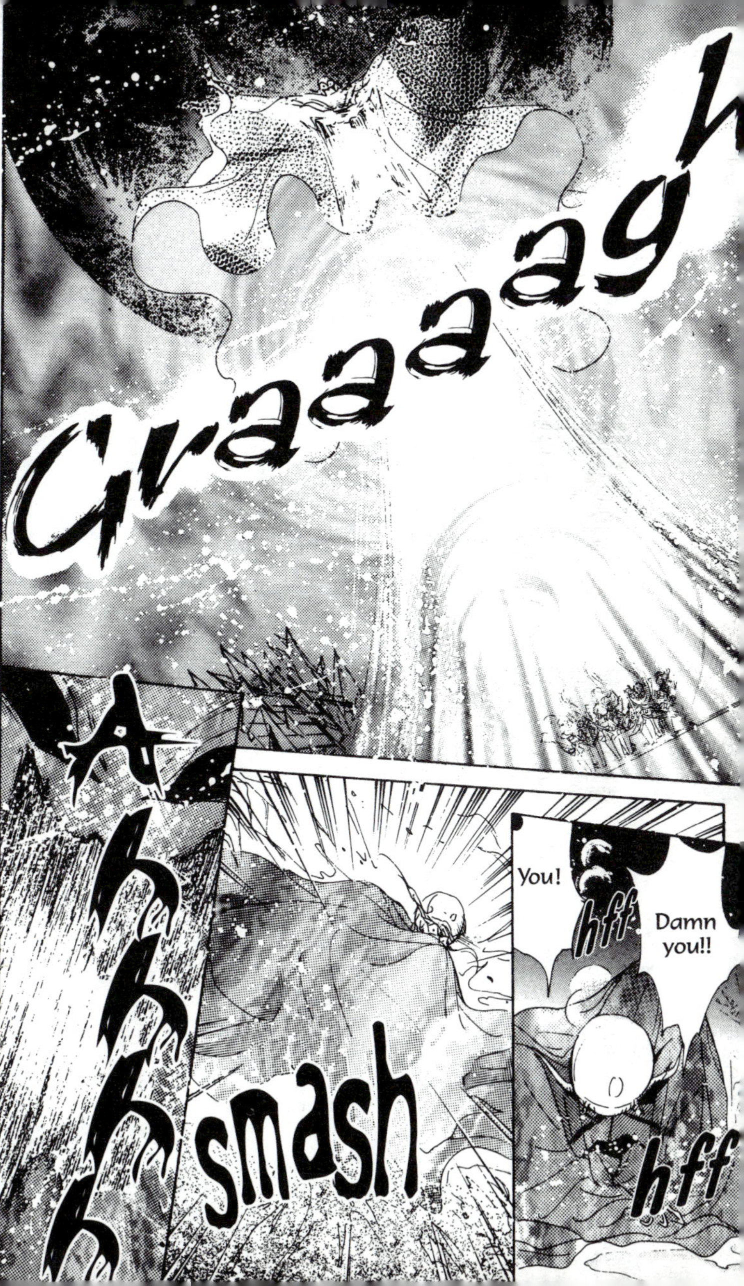

Graaaagh
Ahhhh
smash
You!
hff
Damn you!!
hff

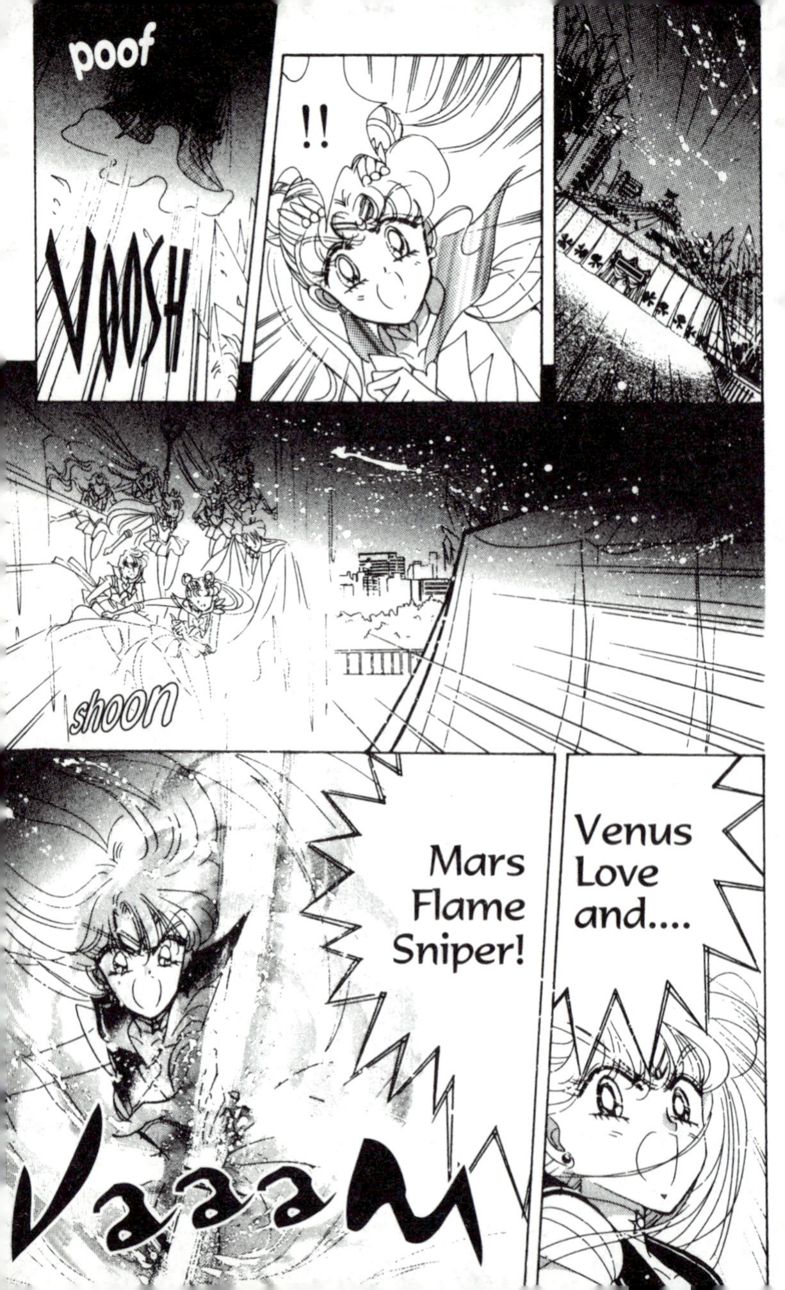
poof
VOOSH
!!
shoon
Vaaam
Mars Flame Sniper!
Venus Love and....

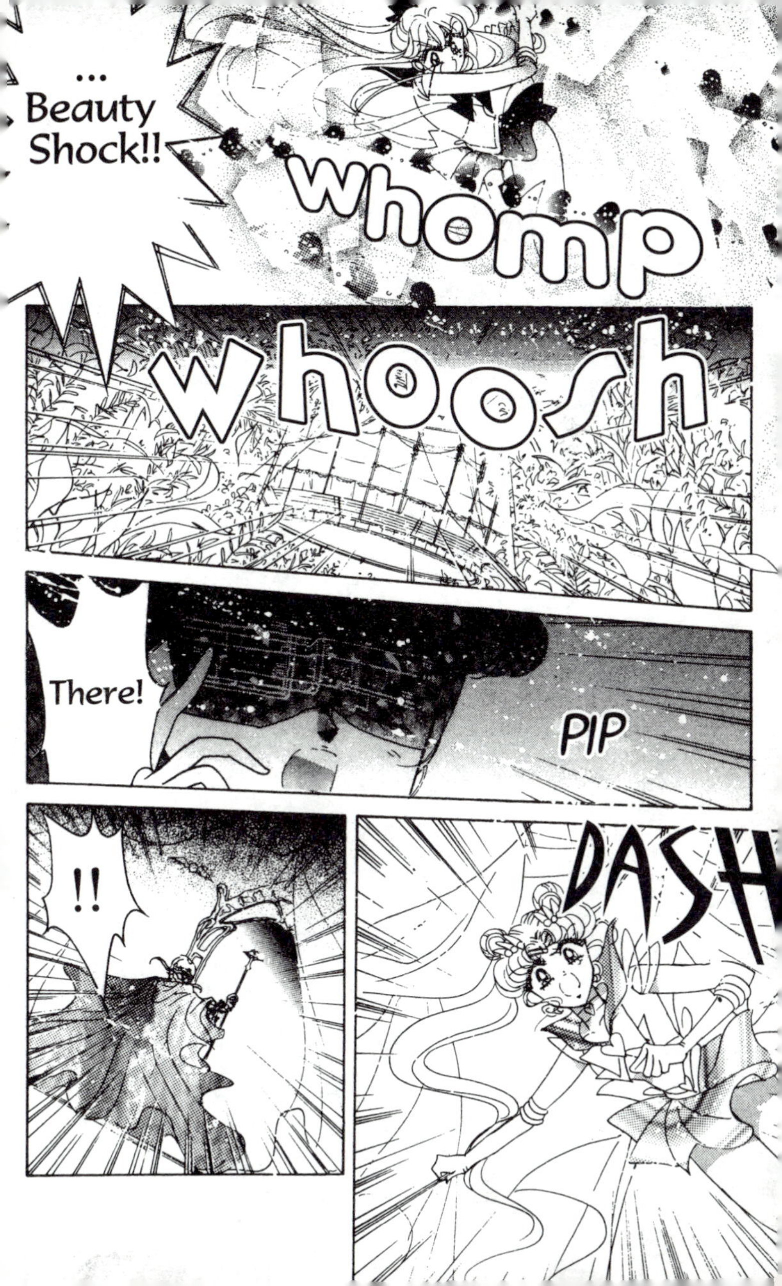
... Beauty Shock!!
whomp
whoosh
There!
PIP
!!
DASH

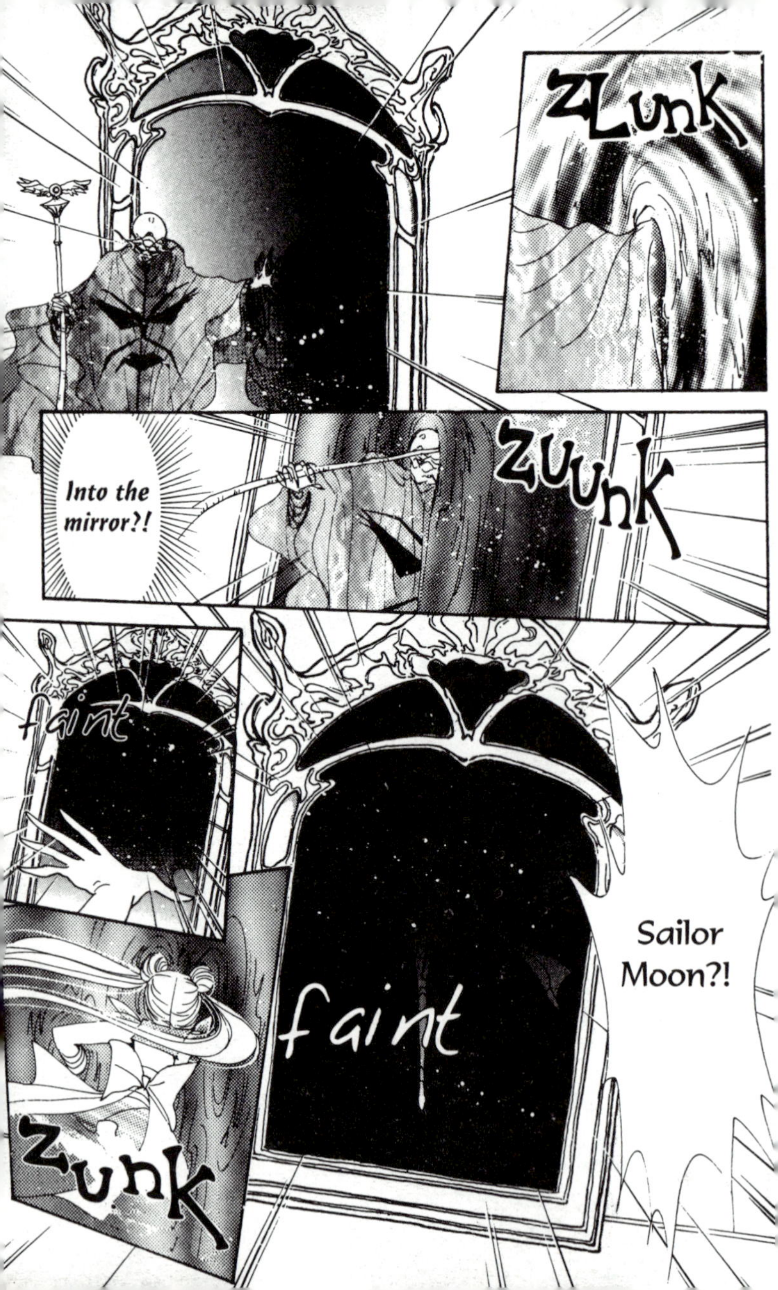
ZLUNK
Into the mirror?!
ZUUNK
faint
faint
Sailor Moon?!
ZUNK

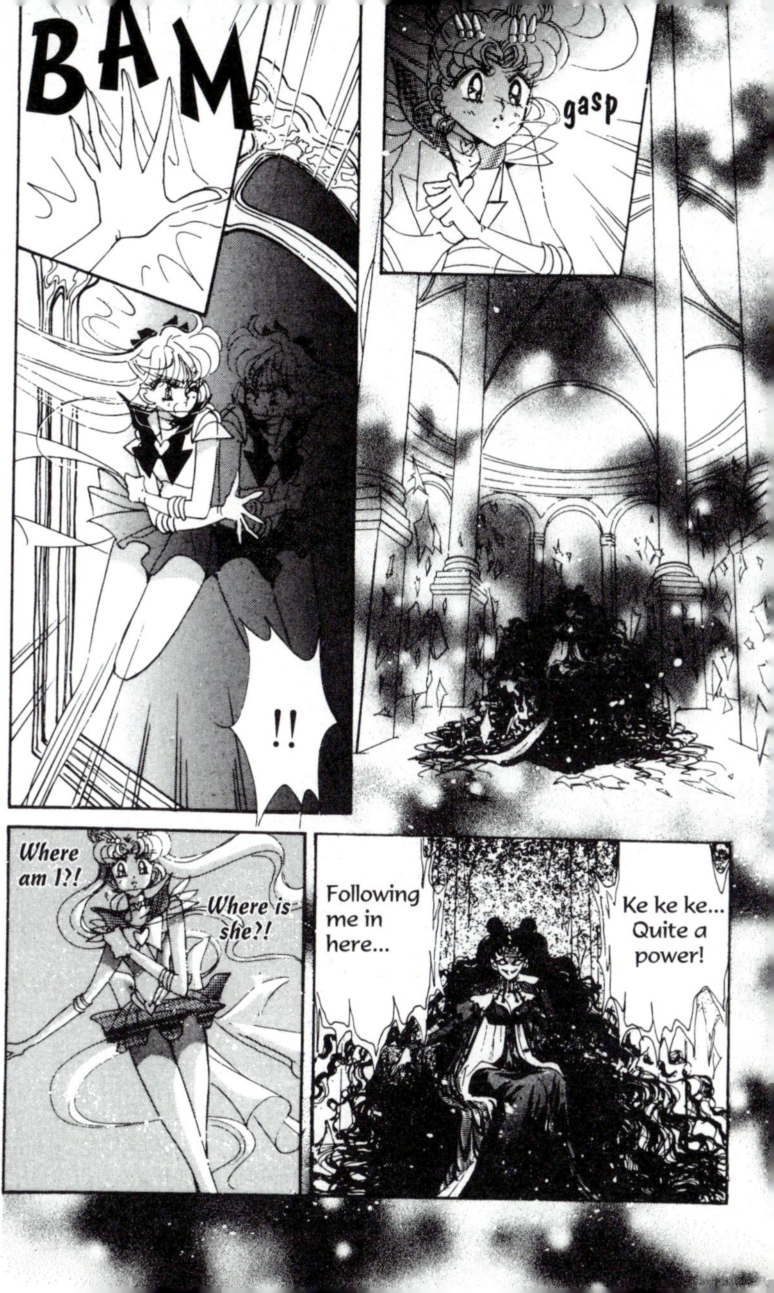
BAM
gasp
!!
Where am I?!
Where is she?!
Following me in here...
Ke ke ke... Quite a power!

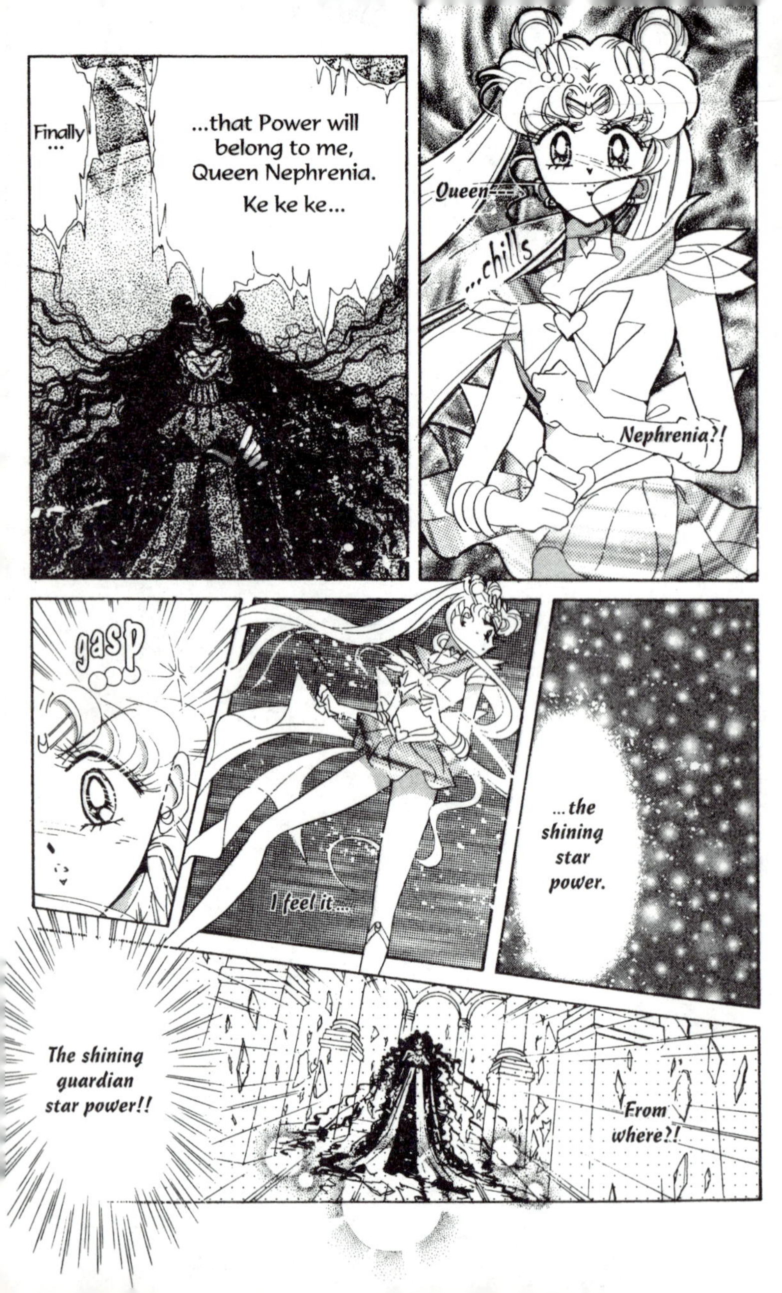
Finally ...
...that Power will belong to me, Queen Nephrenia.
Ke ke ke...
Queen---
...chills
Nephrenia?!
gasp
I feel it...
...the shining star power.
The shining guardian star power!!
From where?!

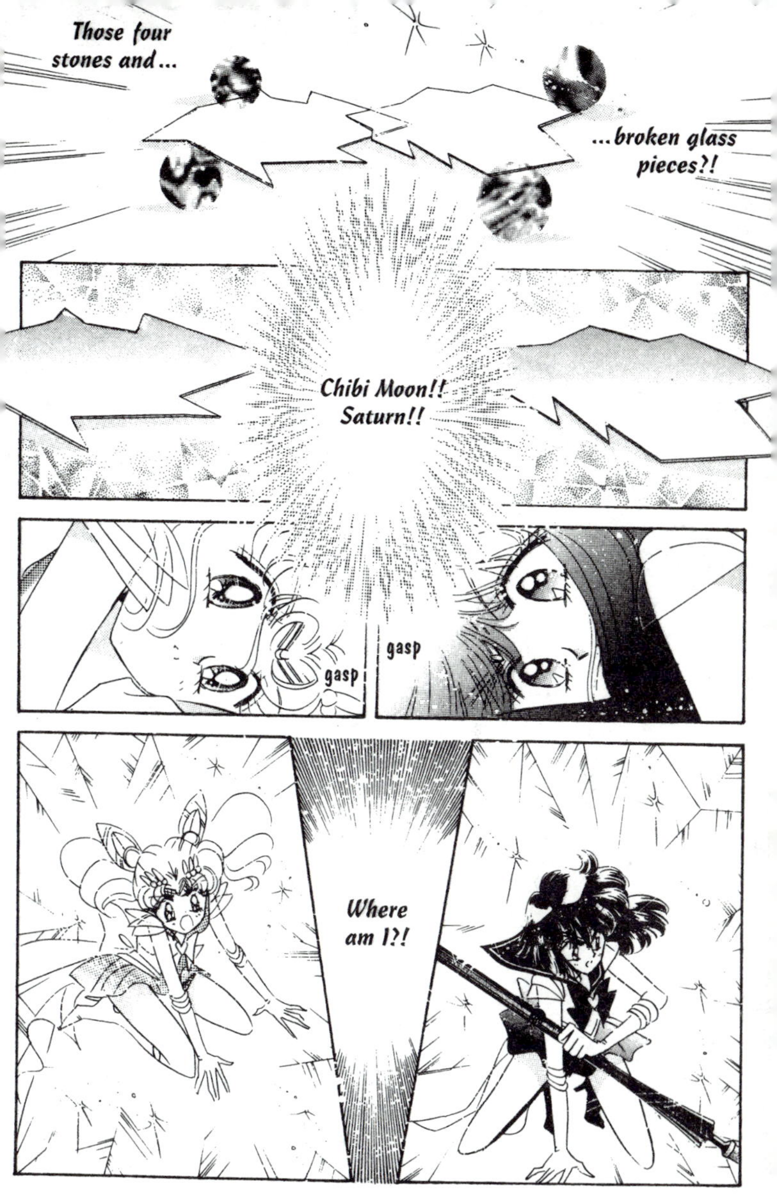
Those four stones and...
...broken glass pieces?!
Chibi Moon!! Saturn!!
gasp
gasp
Where am I?!

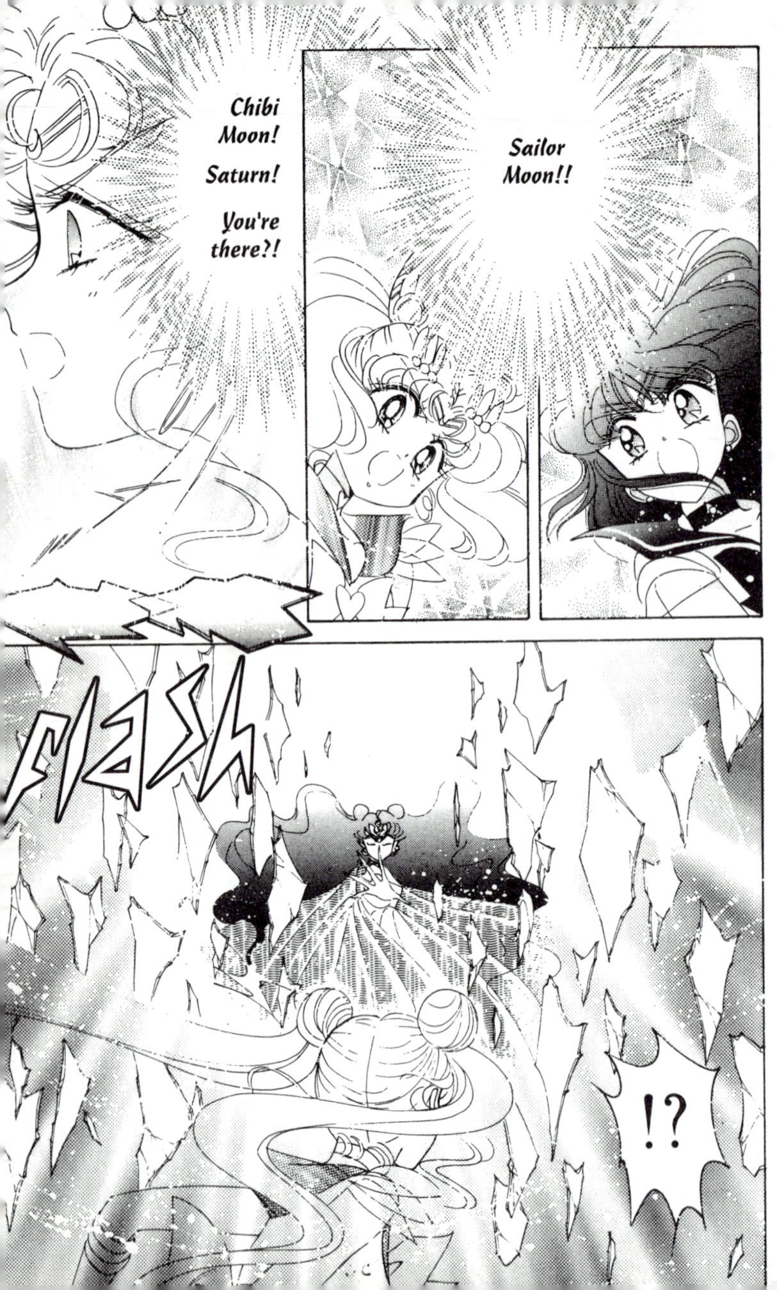
Chibi
Moon!
Saturn!
You're
there?!
Sailor
Moon!!
Flash
!?

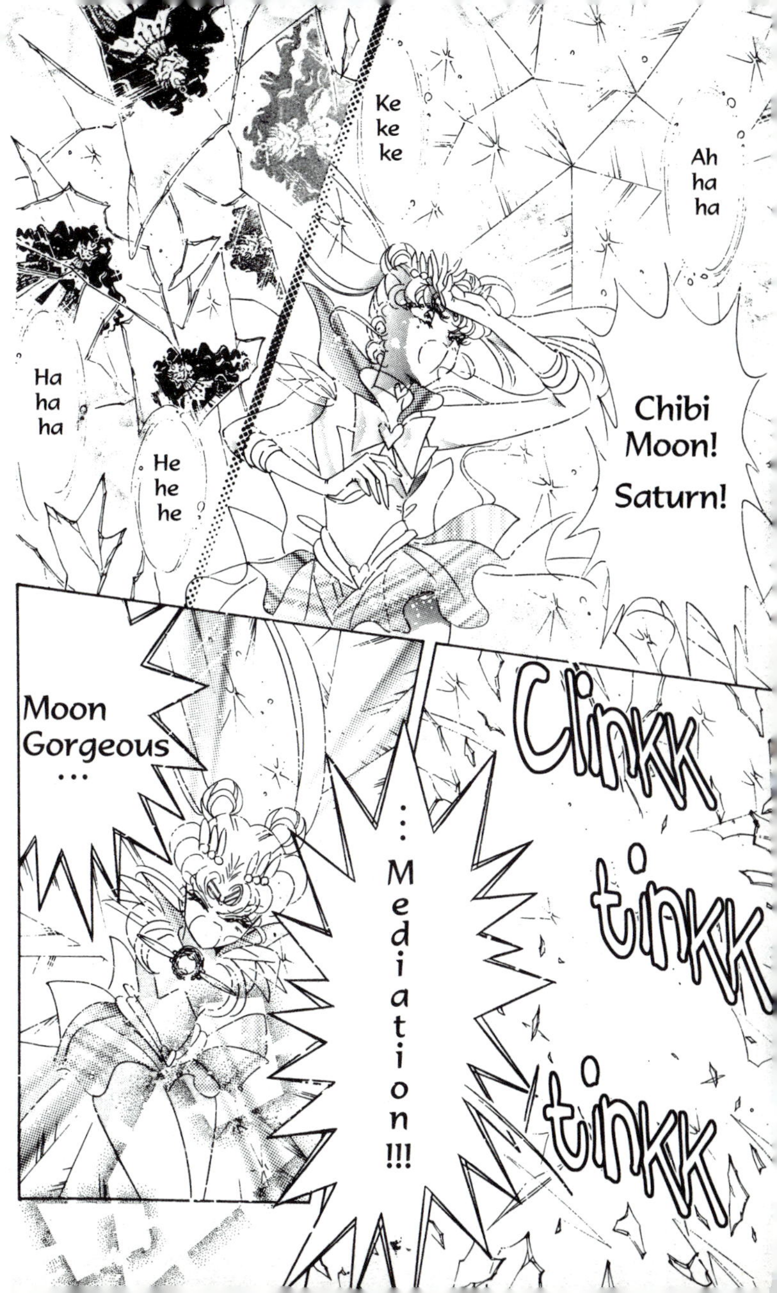

Ke ke ke
Ah ha ha
Ha ha ha
He he he
Chibi Moon! Saturn!
Moon Gorgeous ...
... Mediation !!!
Clinkk
tinkk
tinkk

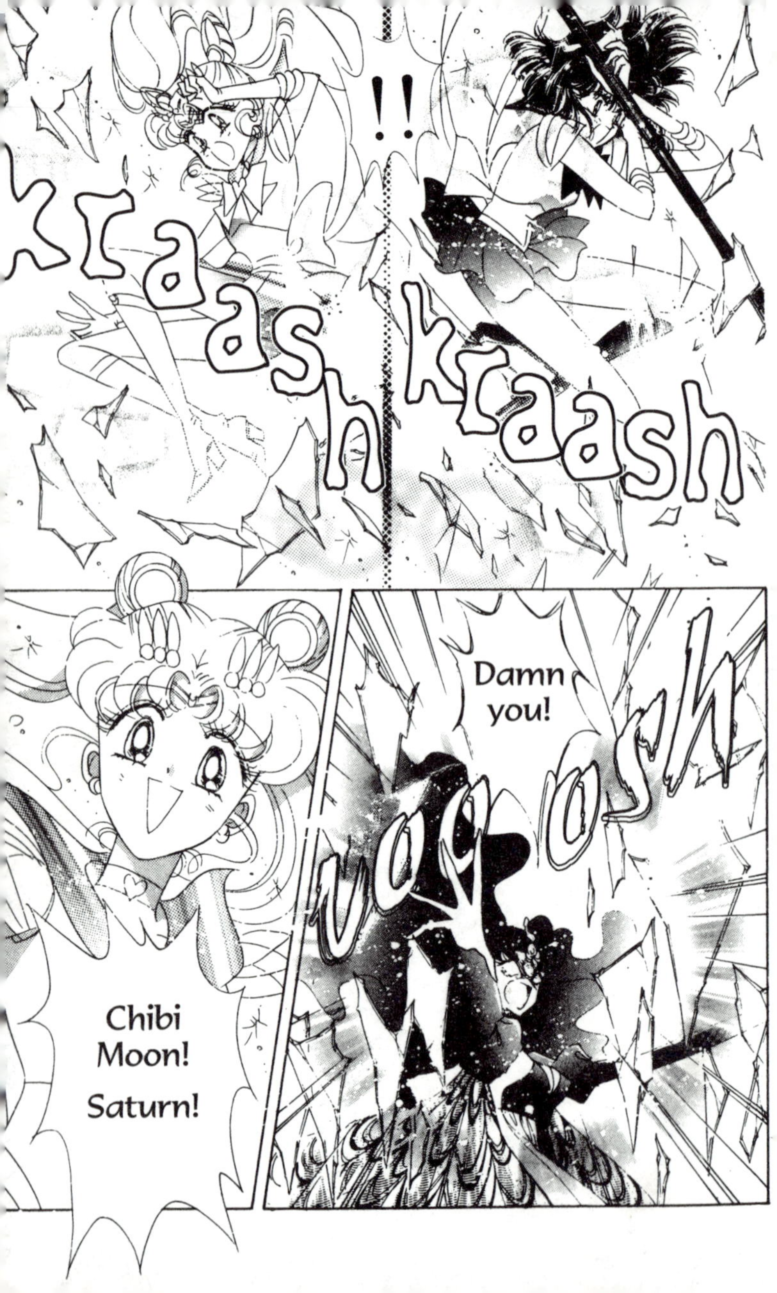
!!
kraash
kraash
Chibi Moon! Saturn!
Damn you!
voooosh

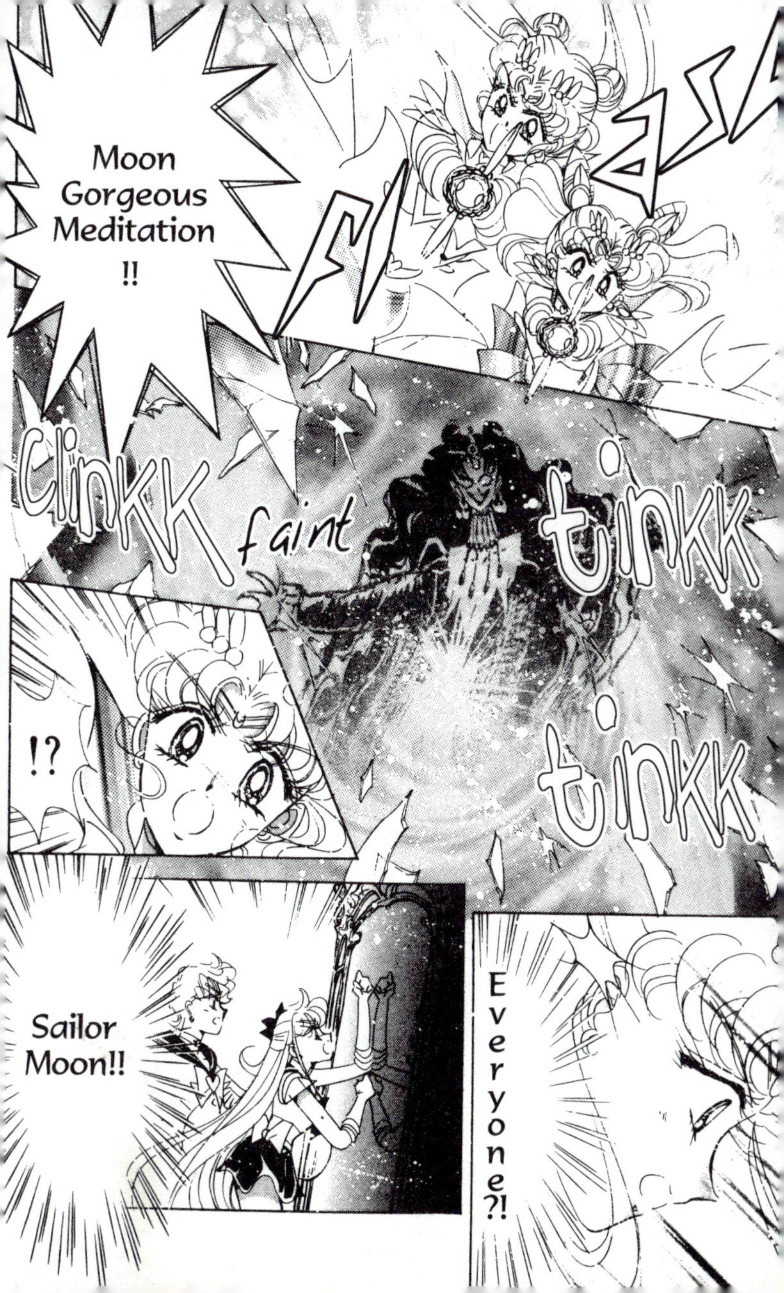
Moon Gorgeous Meditation !!
FLASH
CLINKK
faint
tinkk
!?
tinkk
Sailor Moon!!
Everyone?!

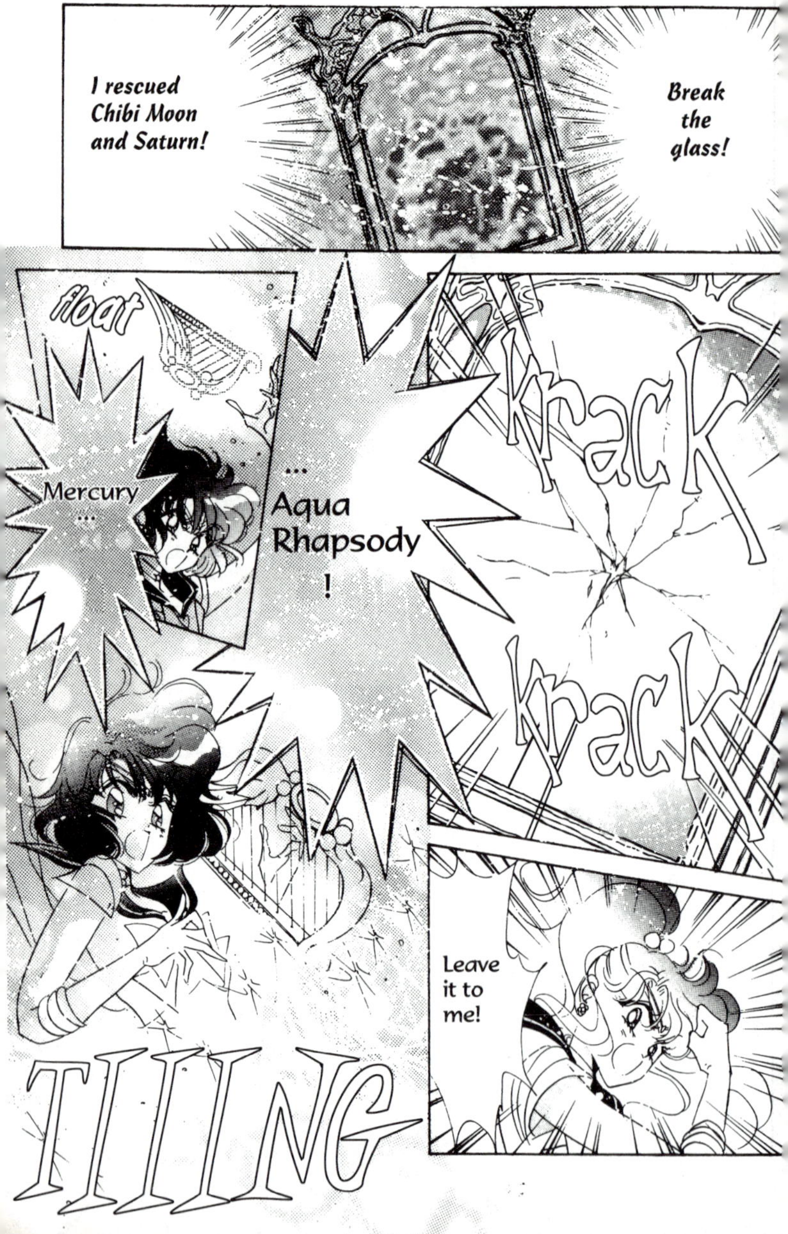

I rescued Chibi Moon and Saturn!
Break the glass!
float
Mercury ...
... Aqua Rhapsody !
krack
krack
Leave it to me!
TIIING

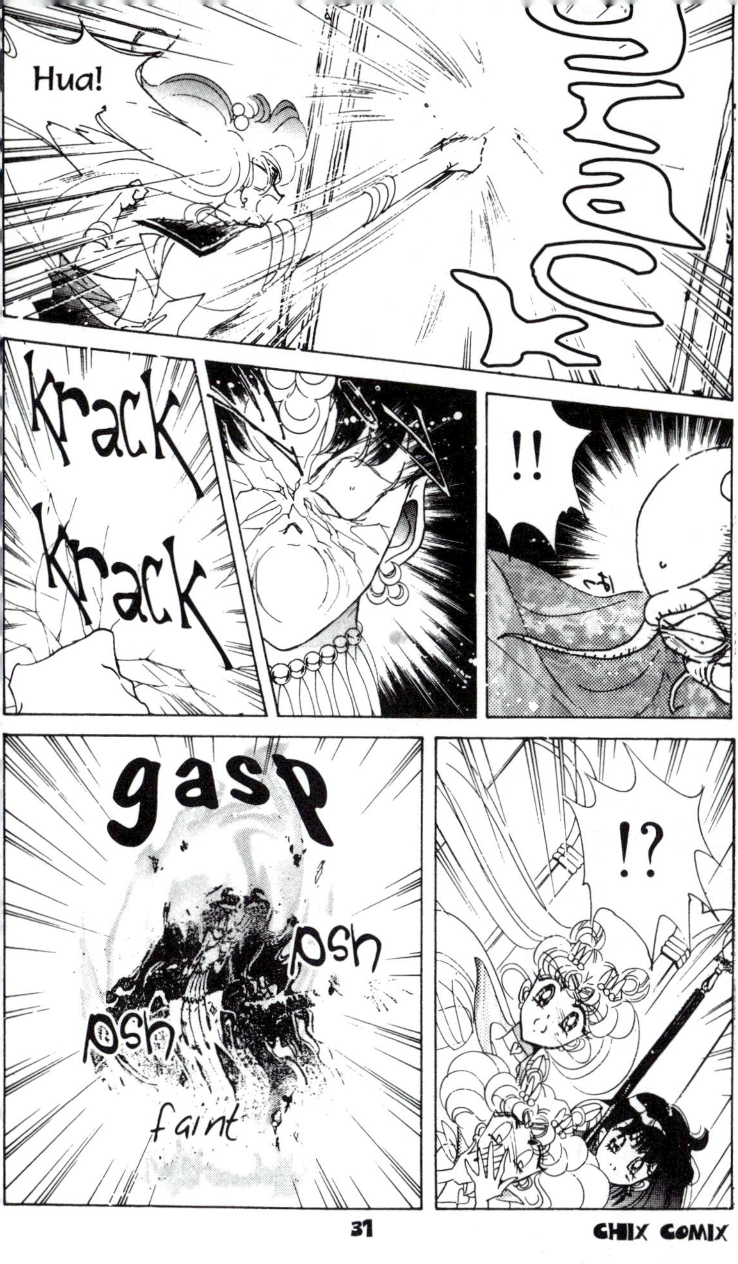
Hua!
krack
krack
!!
gasp
psh
psh
faint
!?

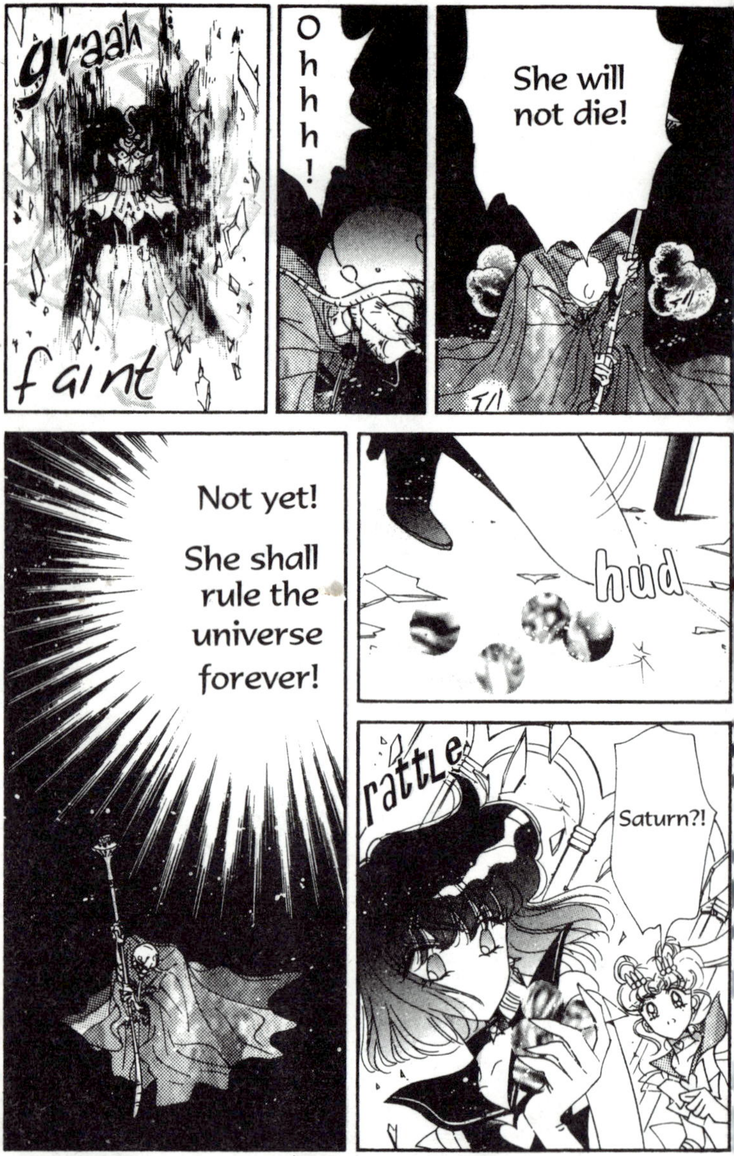
graah
faint
Ohhh!
She will not die!
Not yet!
She shall rule the universe forever!
hud
rattle
Saturn?!

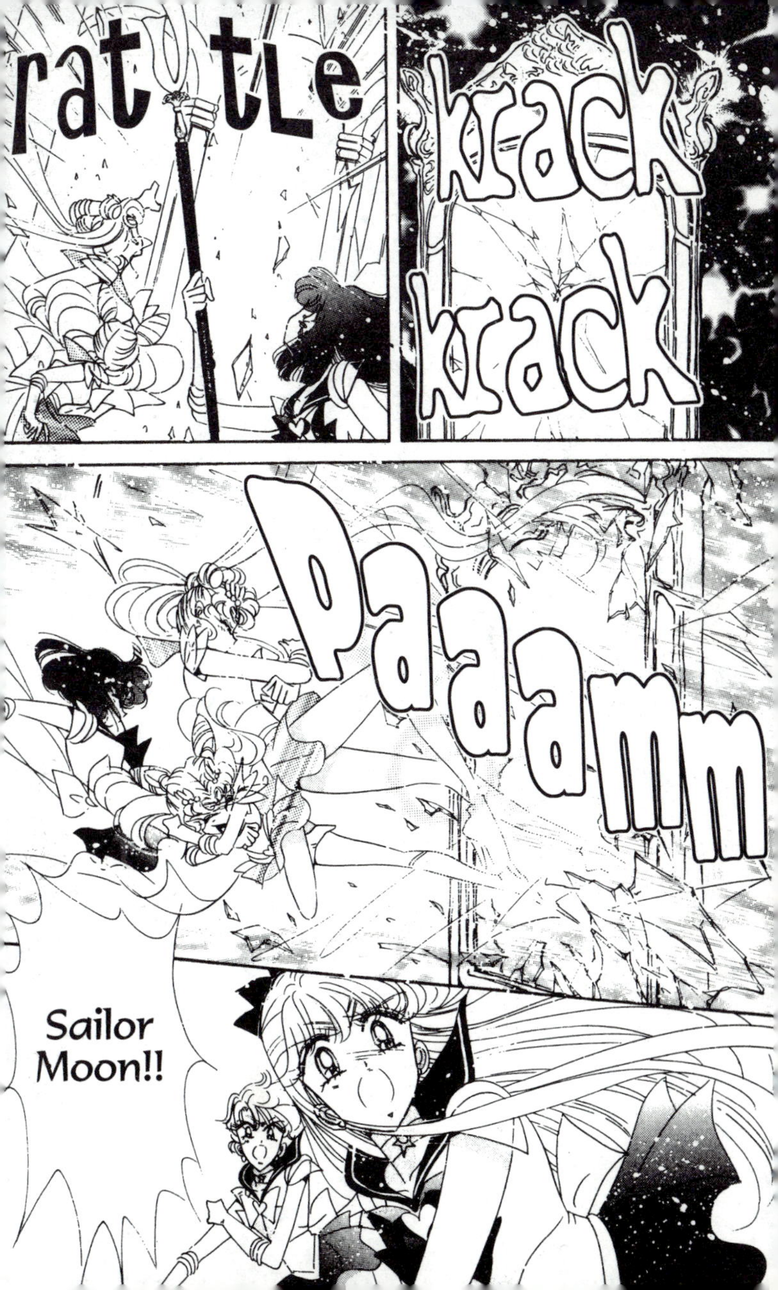
rattle
krack
krack
Paaaamm
Sailor Moon!!

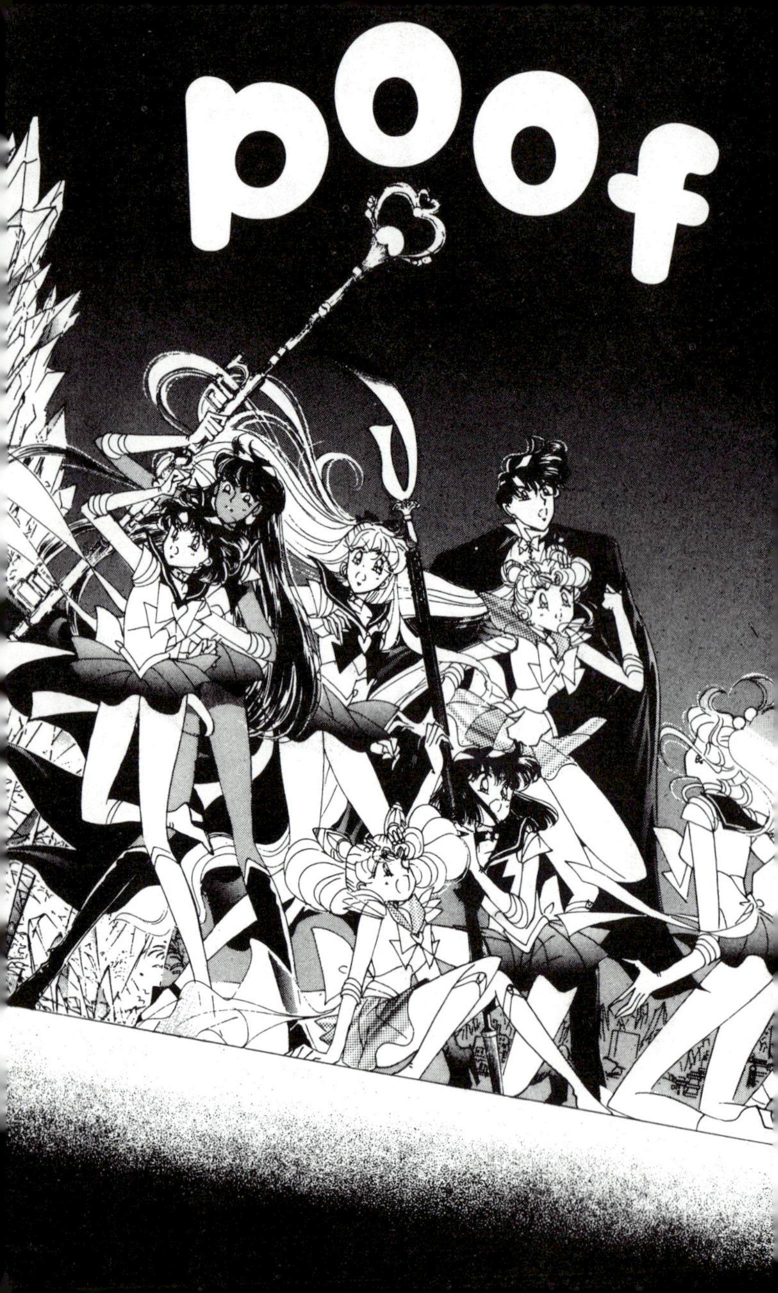
poof

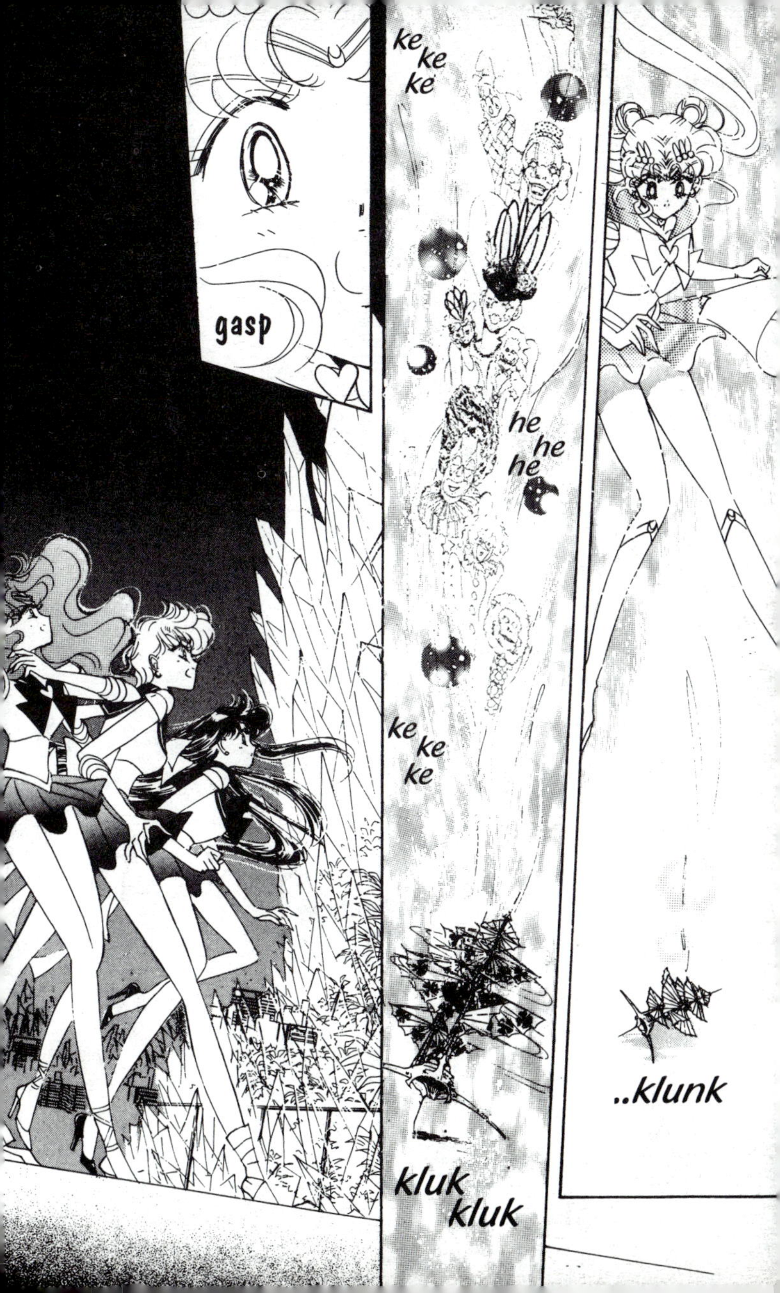
gasp
ke ke ke
he he he
ke ke ke
kluk kluk
..klunk

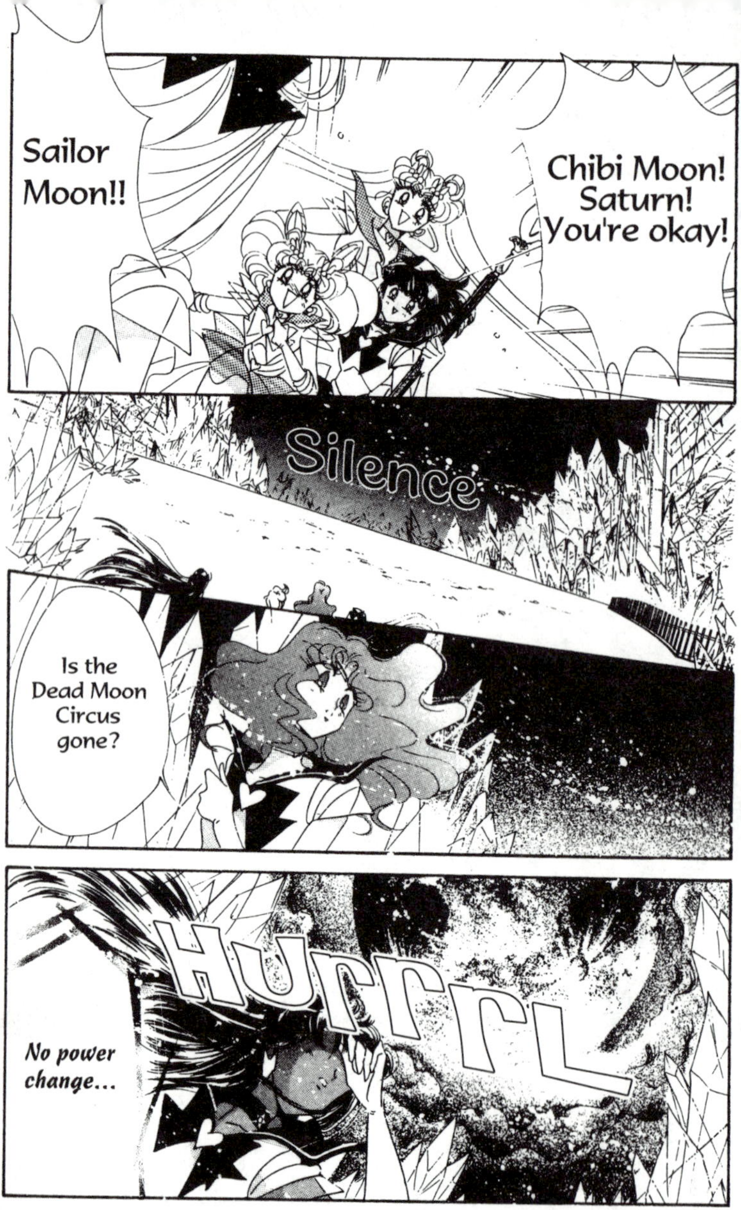
Sailor Moon!!
Chibi Moon! Saturn! You're okay!
Silence
Is the Dead Moon Circus gone?
HURRRL
No power change...

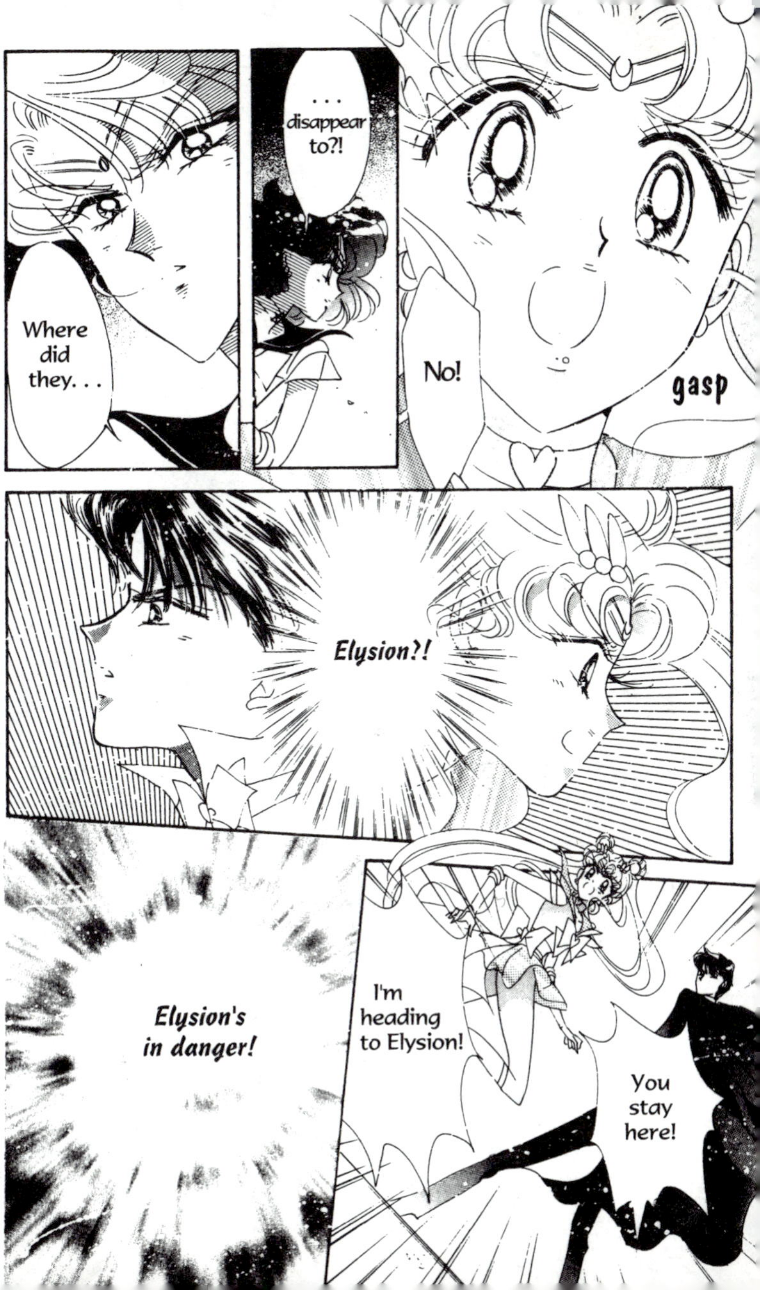
Where did they. . .
. . . disappear to?!
No!
gasp
Elysion?!
Elysion's in danger!
I'm heading to Elysion!
You stay here!

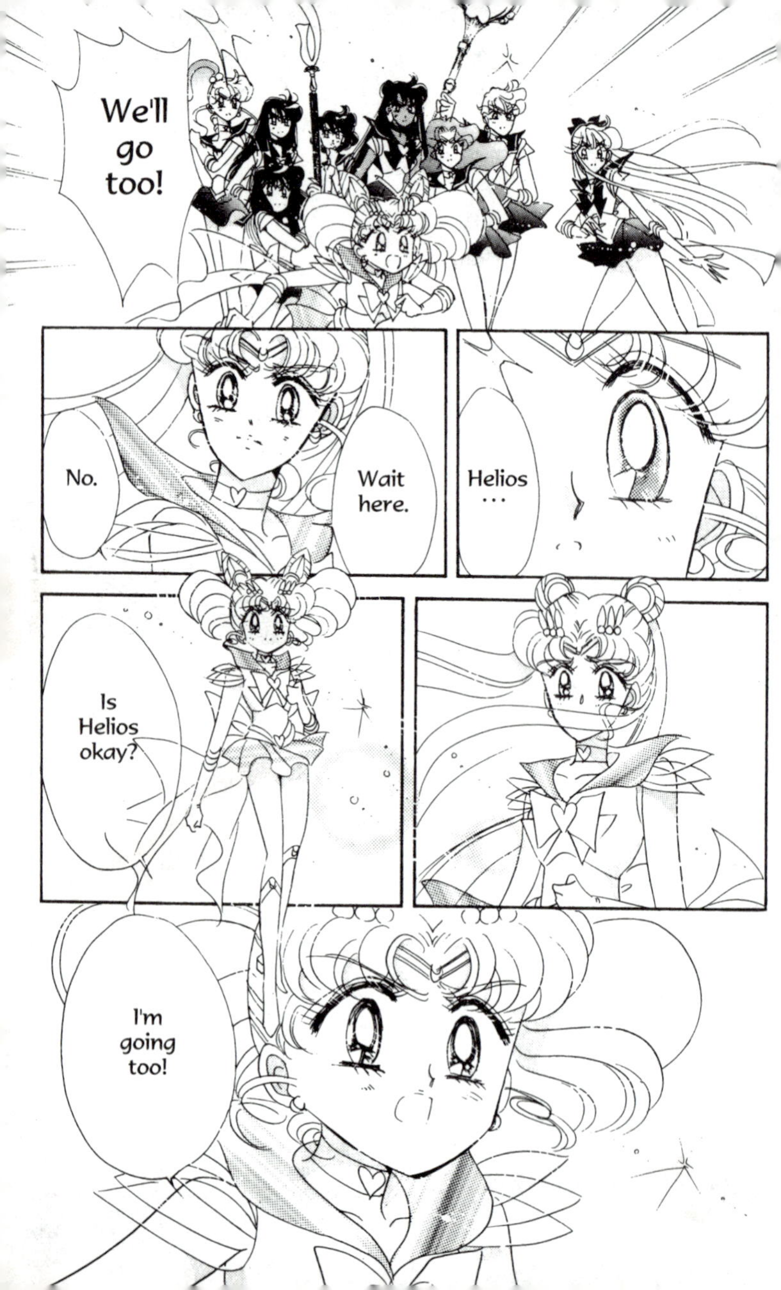
We'll go too!
No.
Wait here.
Helios ...
Is Helios okay?
I'm going too!

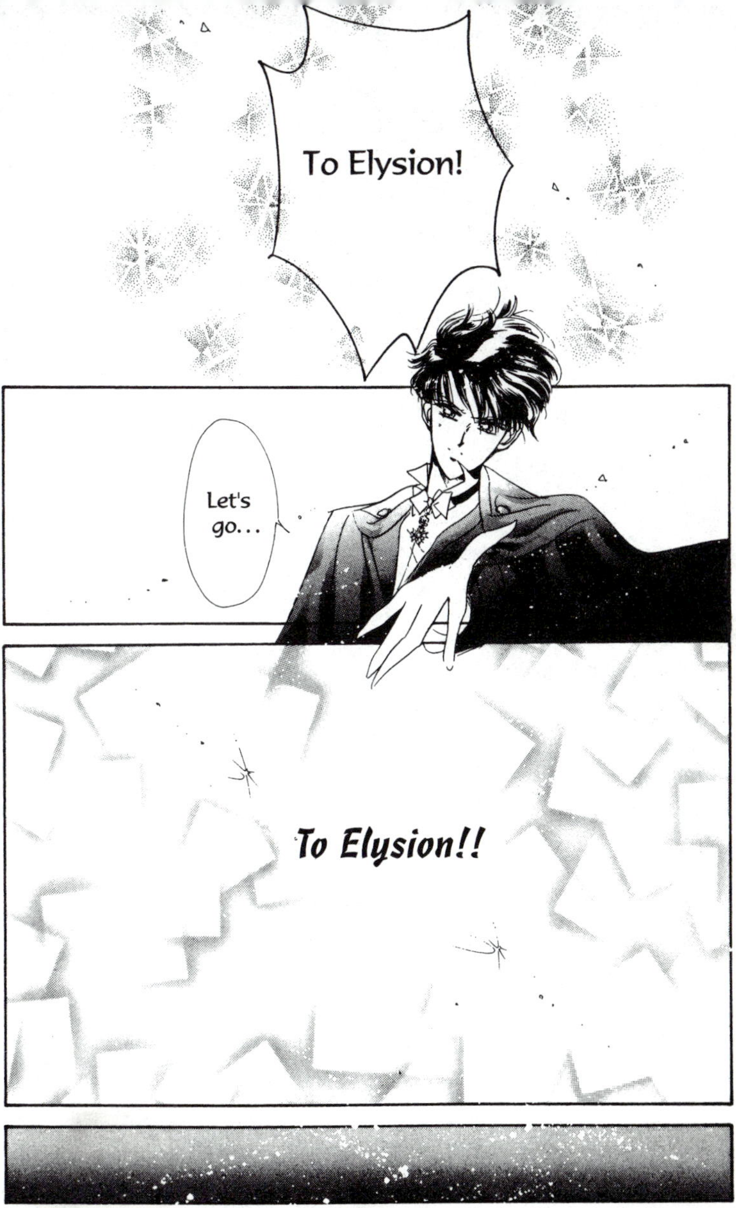
To Elysion!
Let's go...
To Elysion!!

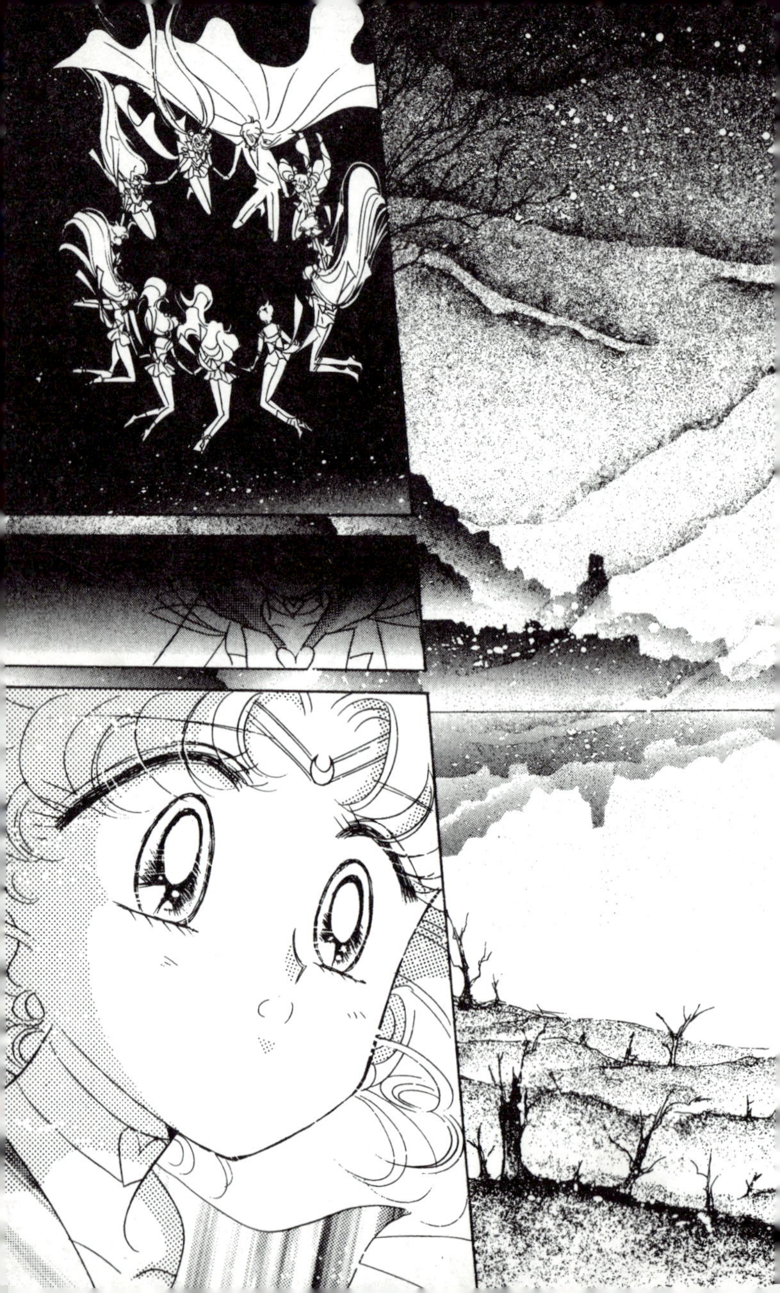

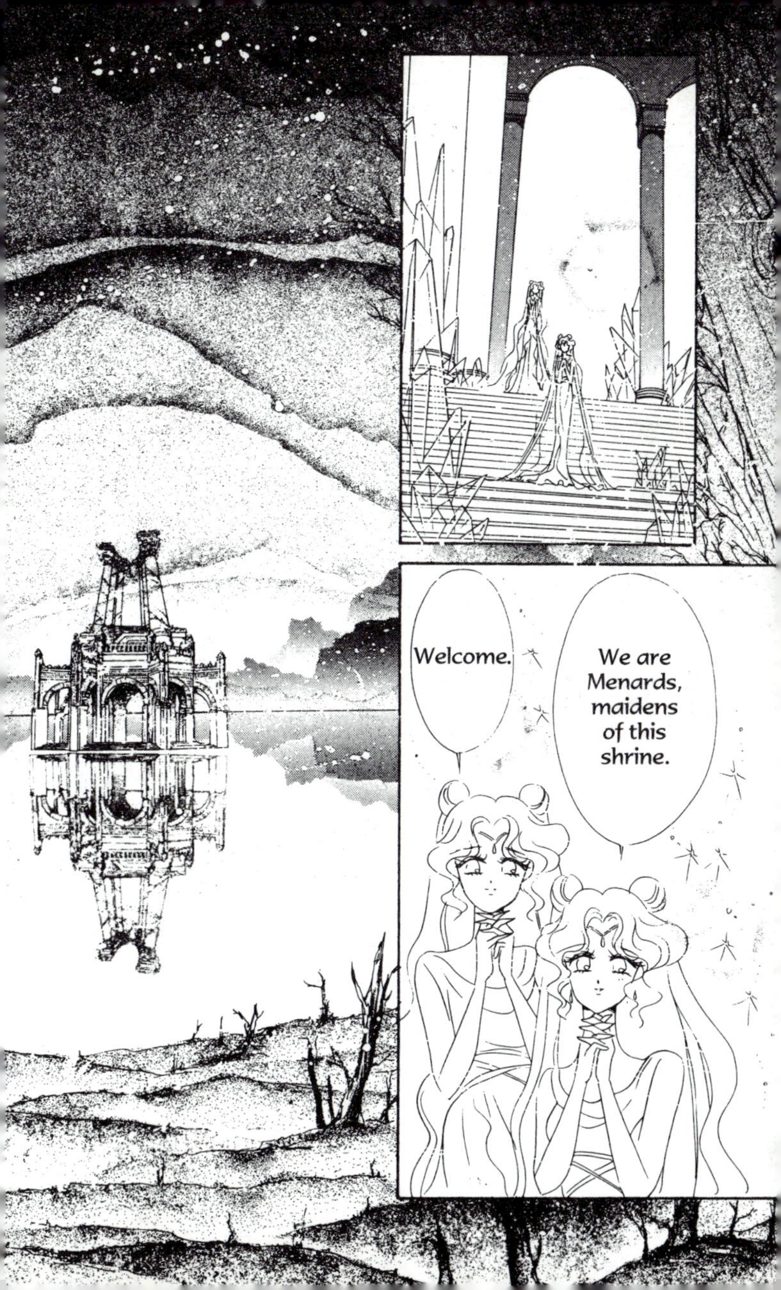
Welcome.
We are Menards, maidens of this shrine.

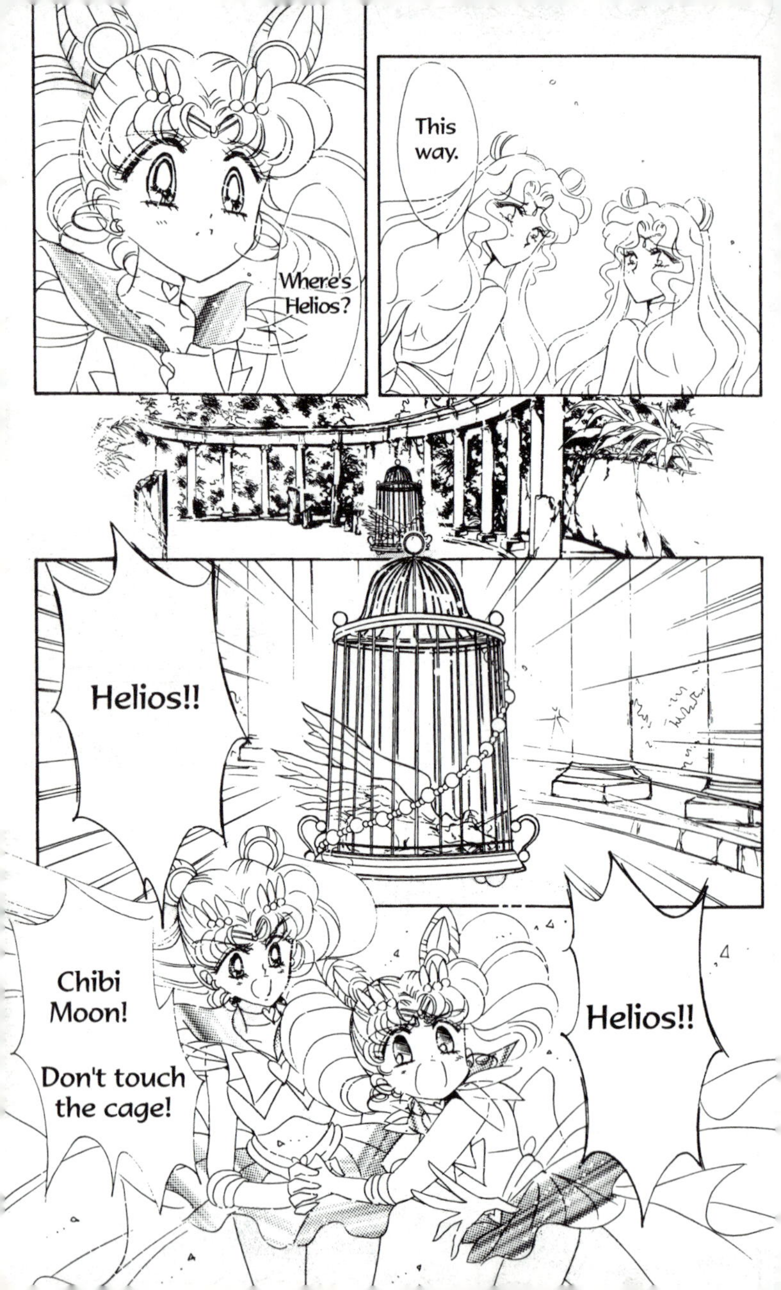
Where's Helios?
This way.
Helios!!
Chibi Moon!
Don't touch the cage!
Helios!!

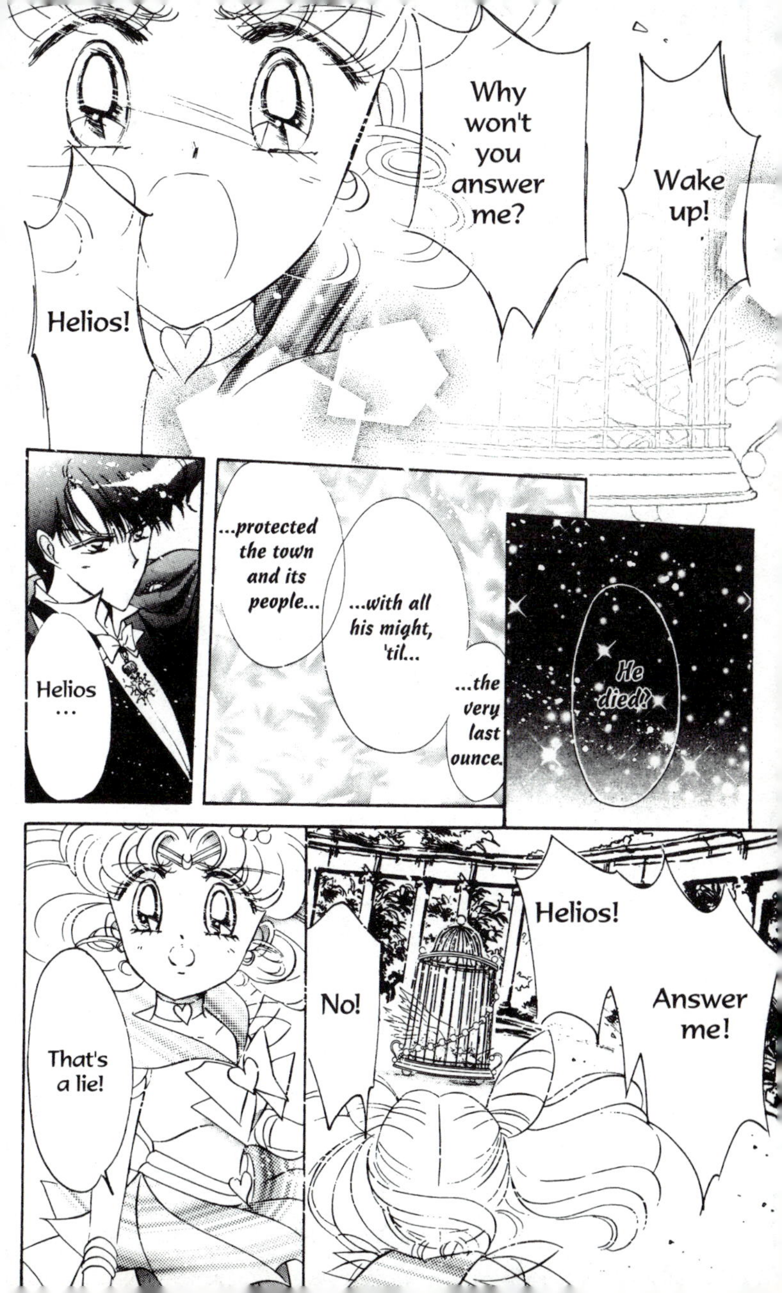
Helios!
Why won't you answer me?
Wake up!
Helios...
...protected the town and its people...
...with all his might, 'til...
...the very last ounce.
He died!?
That's a lie!
No!
Helios!
Answer me!

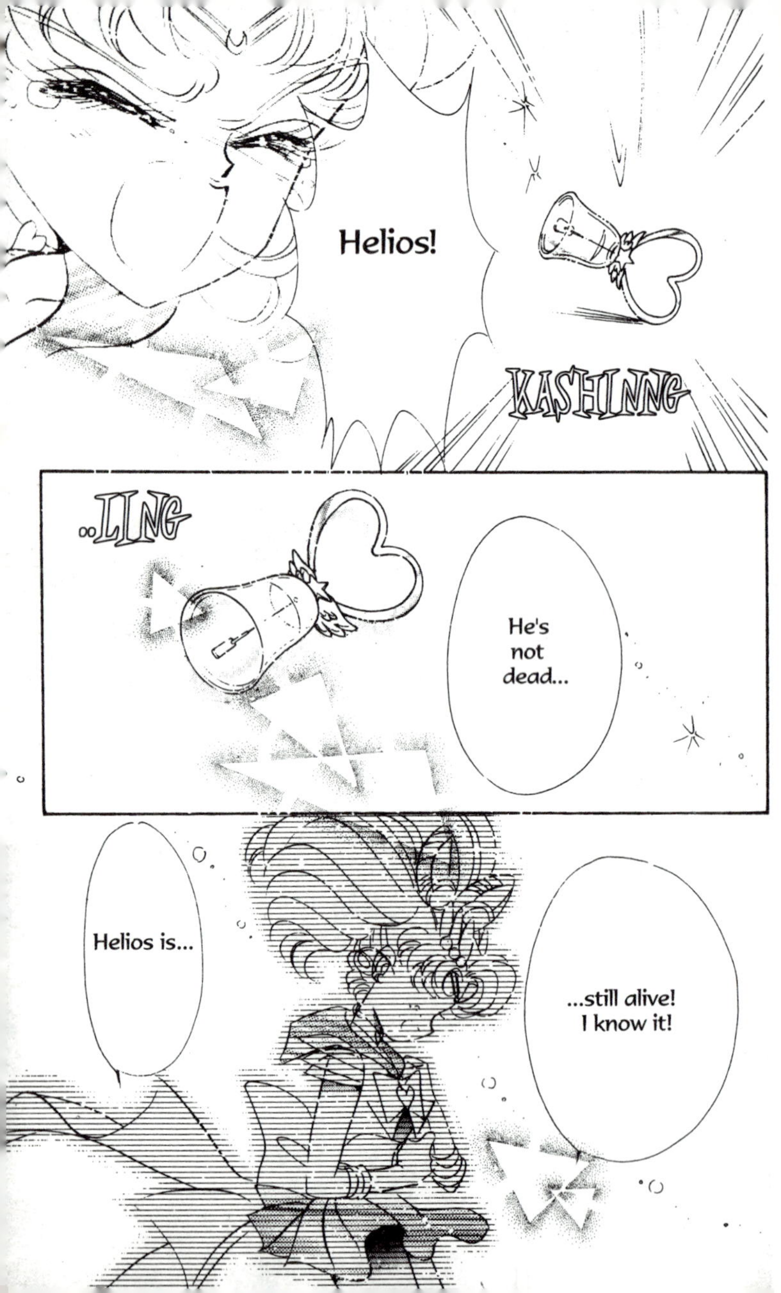

Helios!
KASHINNG
..LING
He's not dead...
Helios is...
...still alive! I know it!

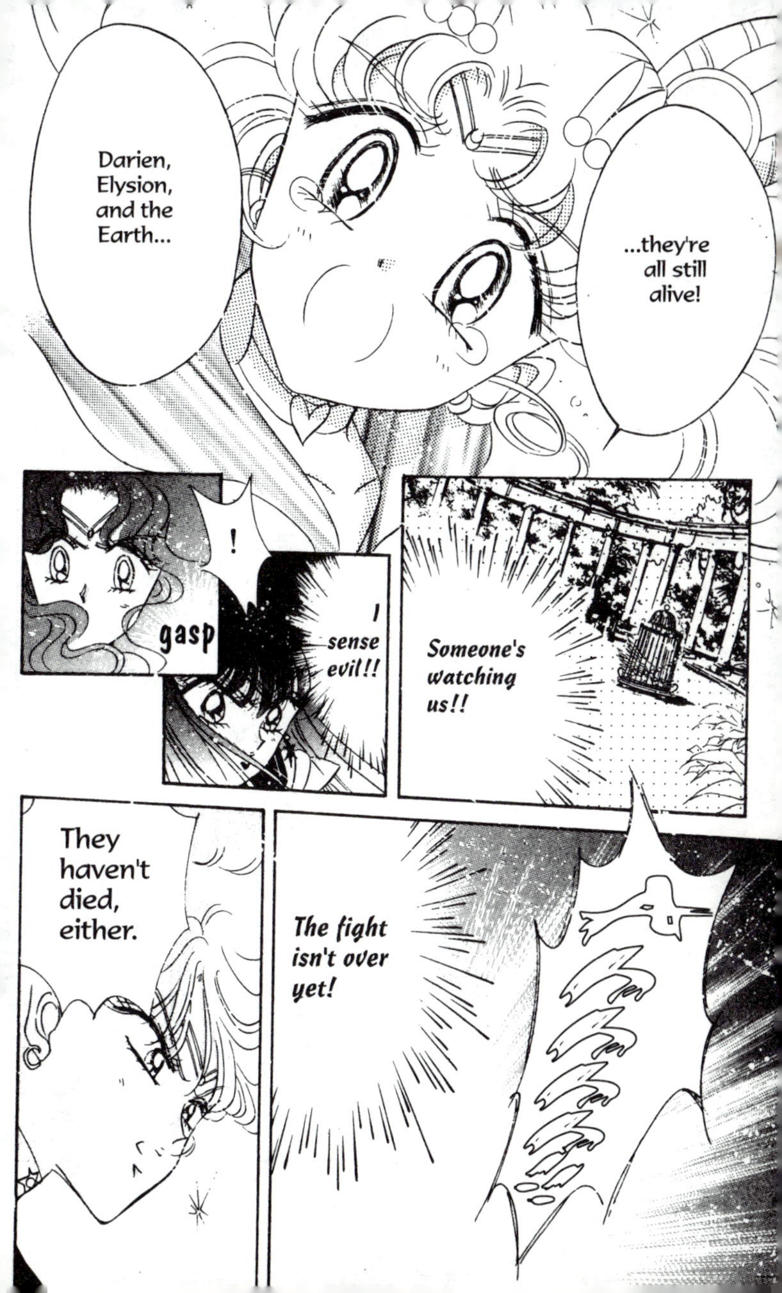
Darien, Elysion, and the Earth...
...they're all still alive!
!
gasp
I sense evil!!
Someone's watching us!!
They haven't died, either.
The fight isn't over yet!

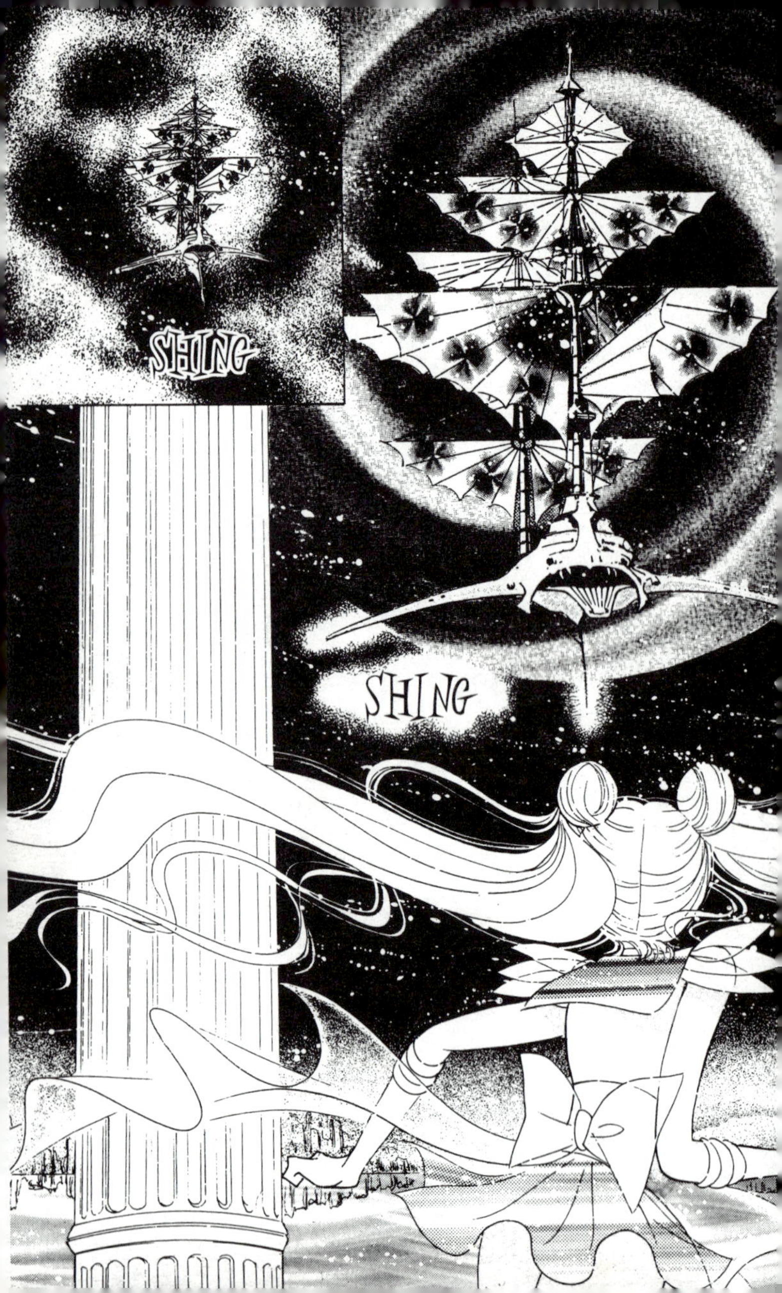
SHING
SHING

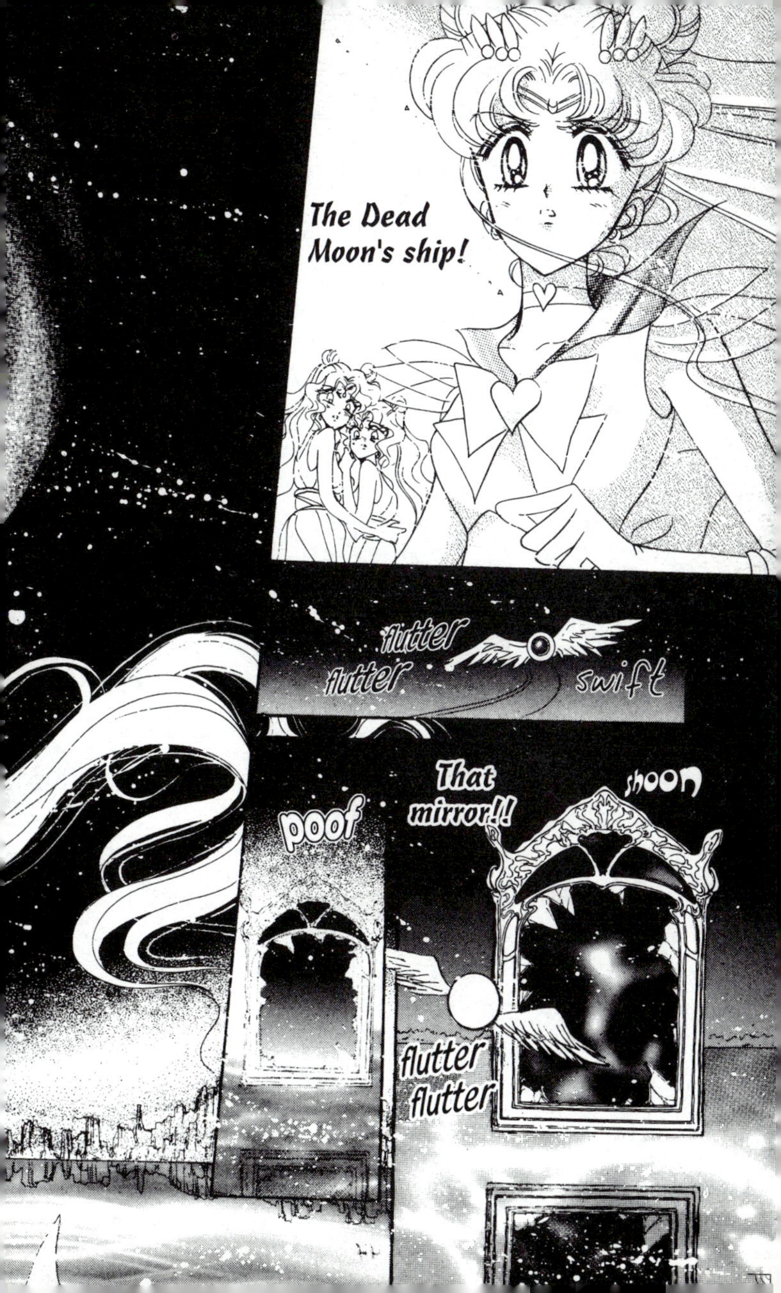
The Dead Moon's ship!
flutter flutter
swift
poof
That mirror!!
shoon
flutter flutter

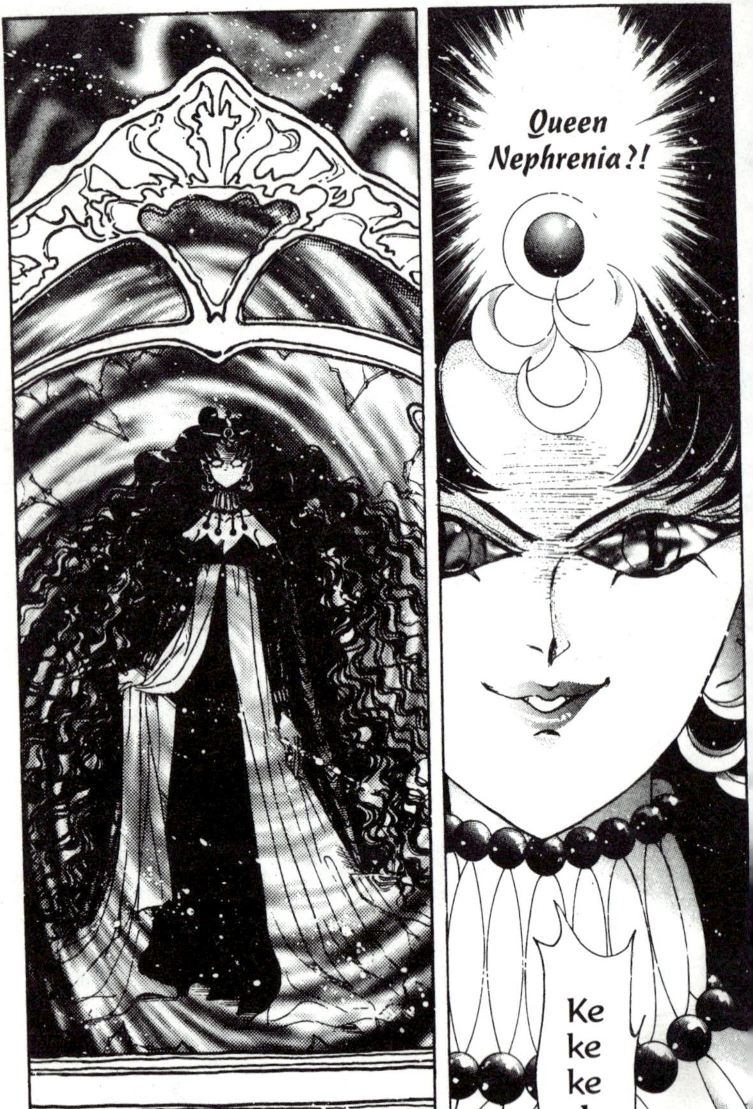
Queen Nephrenia?!
Ke ke ke!

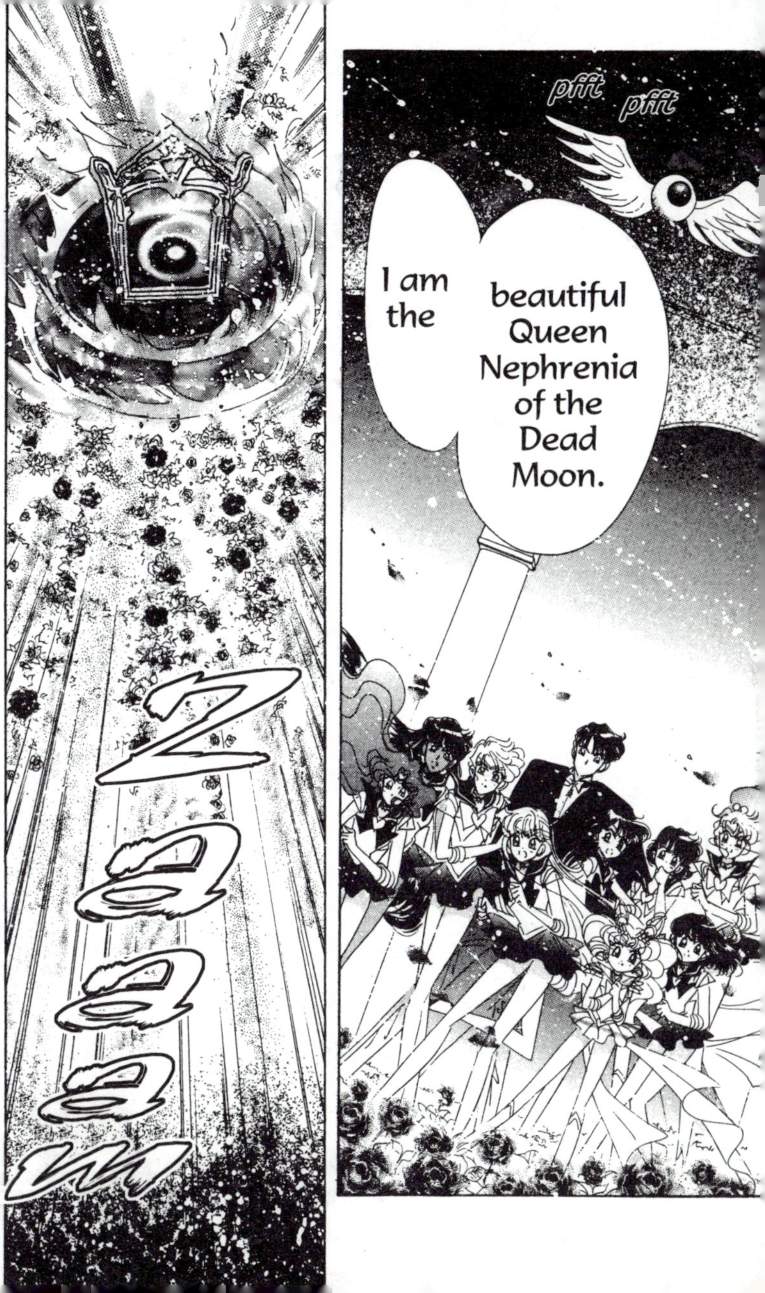
pfft pfft
I am the beautiful Queen Nephrenia of the Dead Moon.

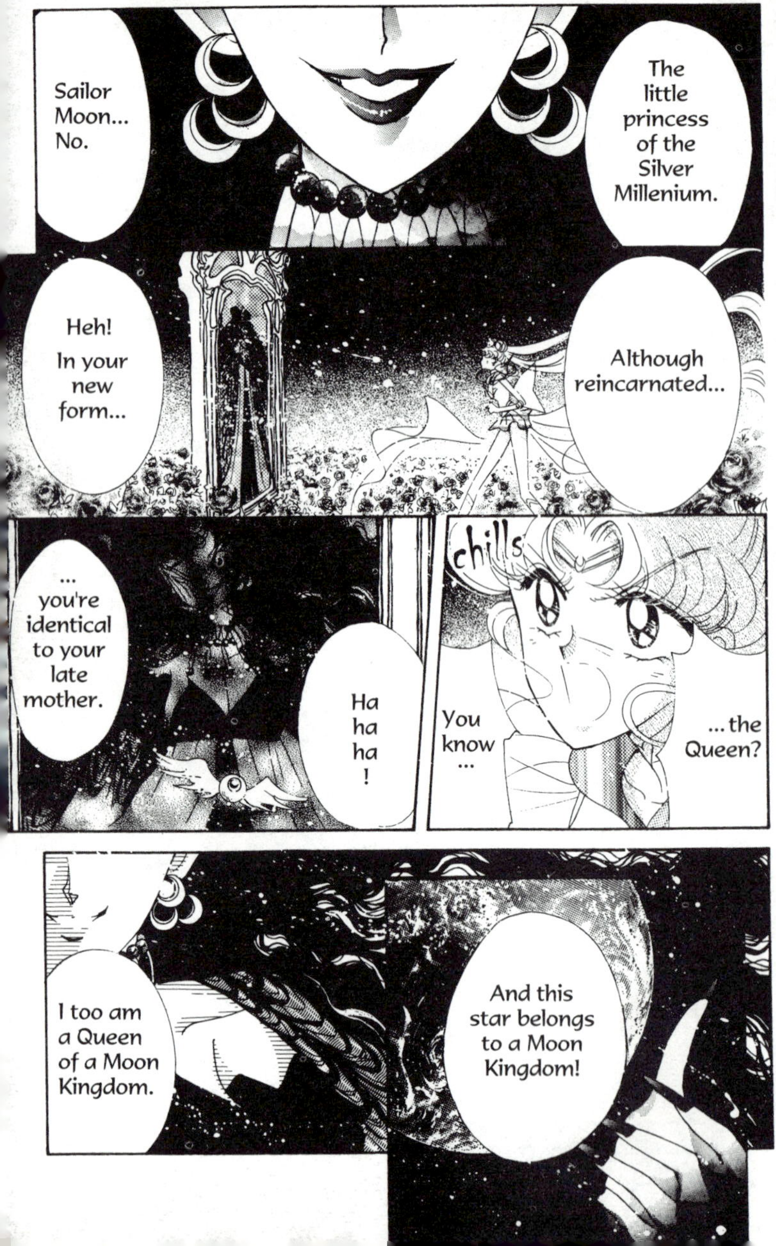
Sailor Moon... No.
The little princess of the Silver Millenium.
Heh! In your new form...
Although reincarnated...
... you're identical to your late mother.
Ha ha ha!
chills
You know ...
...the Queen?
I too am a Queen of a Moon Kingdom.
And this star belongs to a Moon Kingdom!

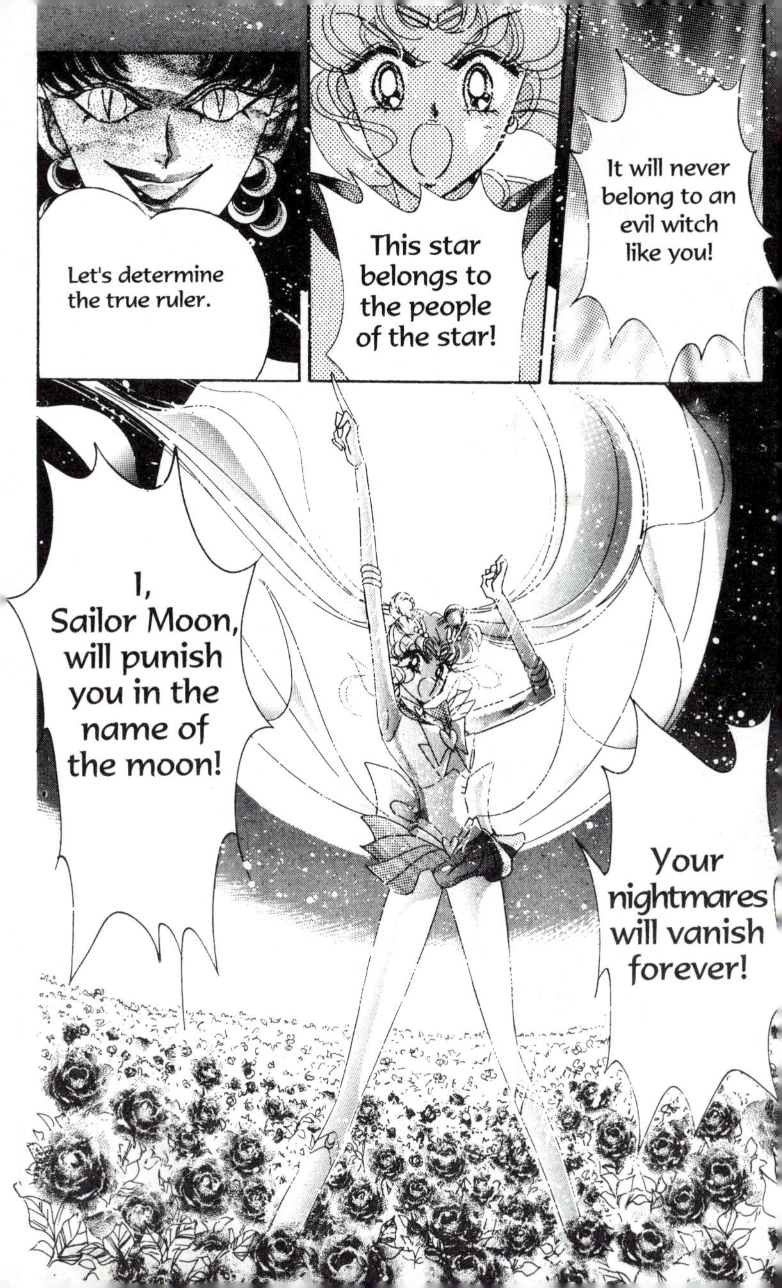
Let's determine the true ruler.
This star belongs to the people of the star!
It will never belong to an evil witch like you!
I, Sailor Moon, will punish you in the name of the moon!
Your nightmares will vanish forever!

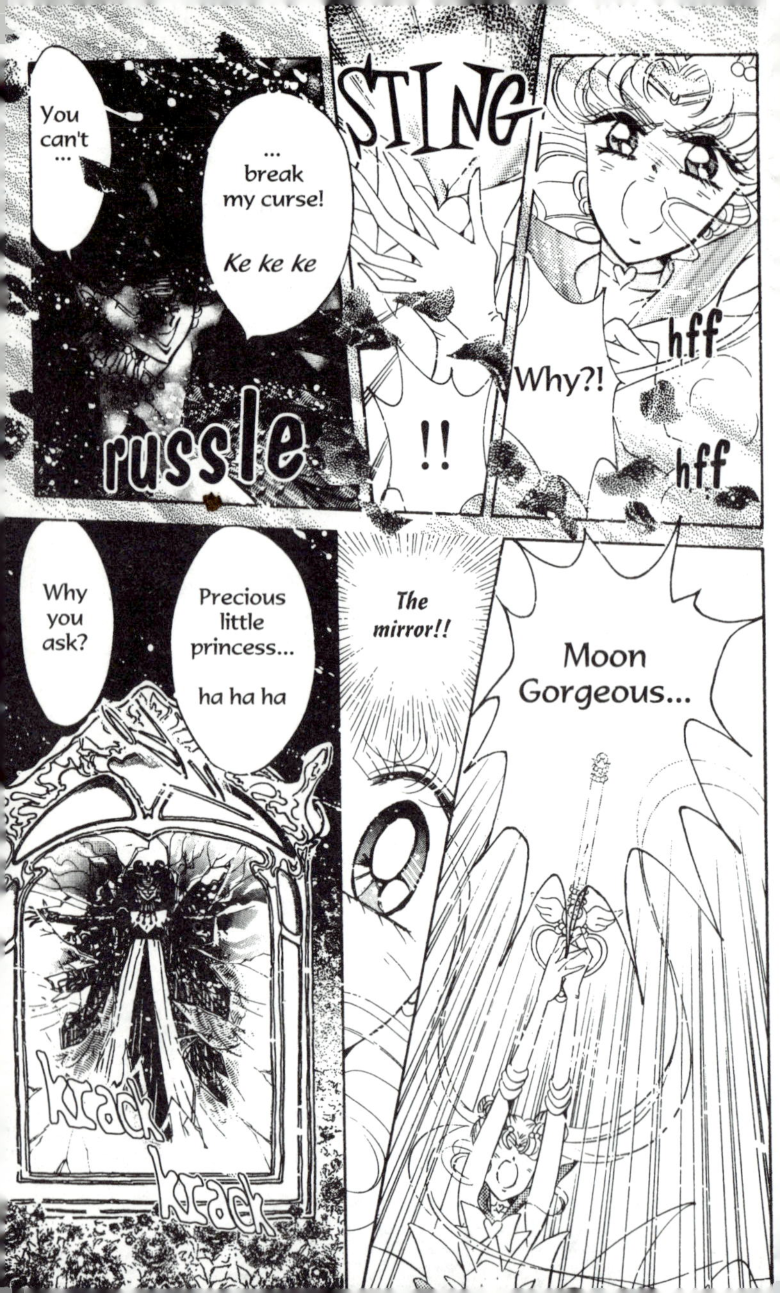
You can't ...
... break my curse!
Ke ke ke
russle
STING
!!
Why?!
hff
hff
Why you ask?
Precious little princess...
ha ha ha
krack
krack
The mirror!!
Moon Gorgeous...

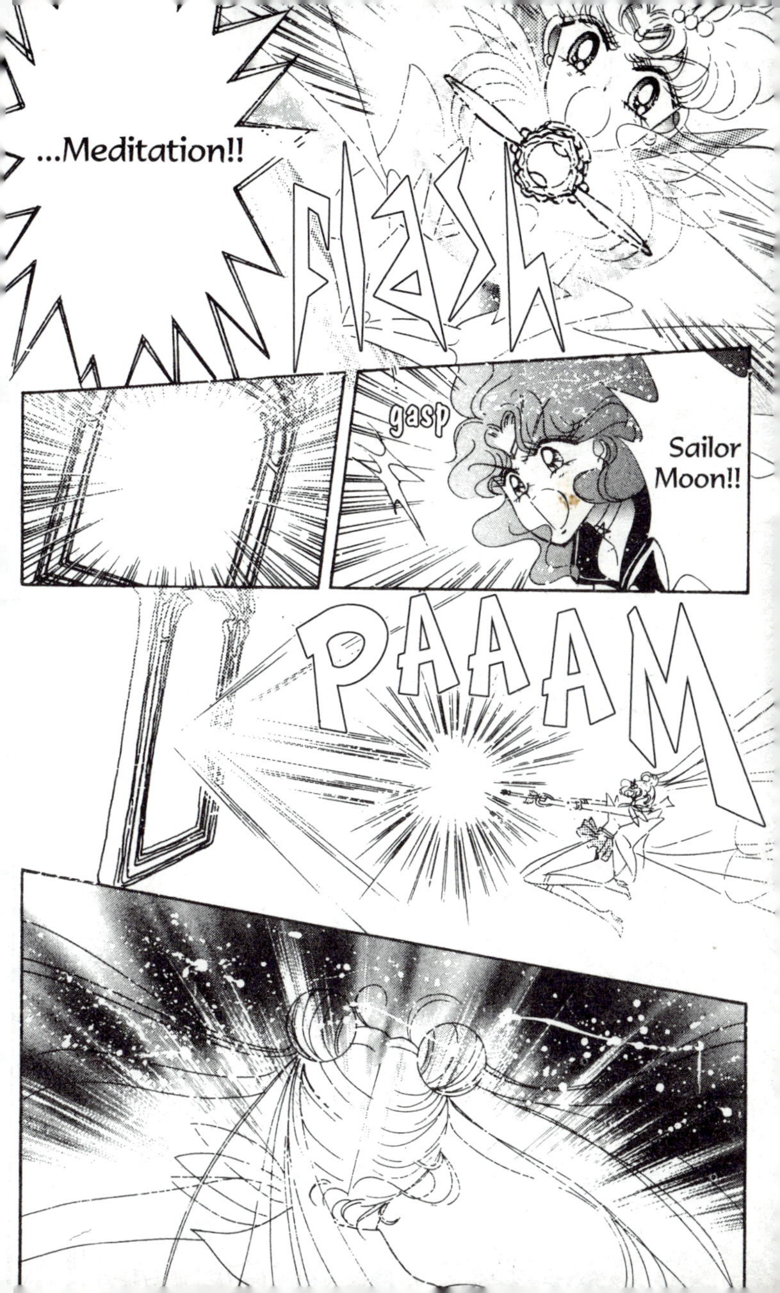

...Meditation!!
FLASH
Sailor Moon!!
gasp
PAAAM

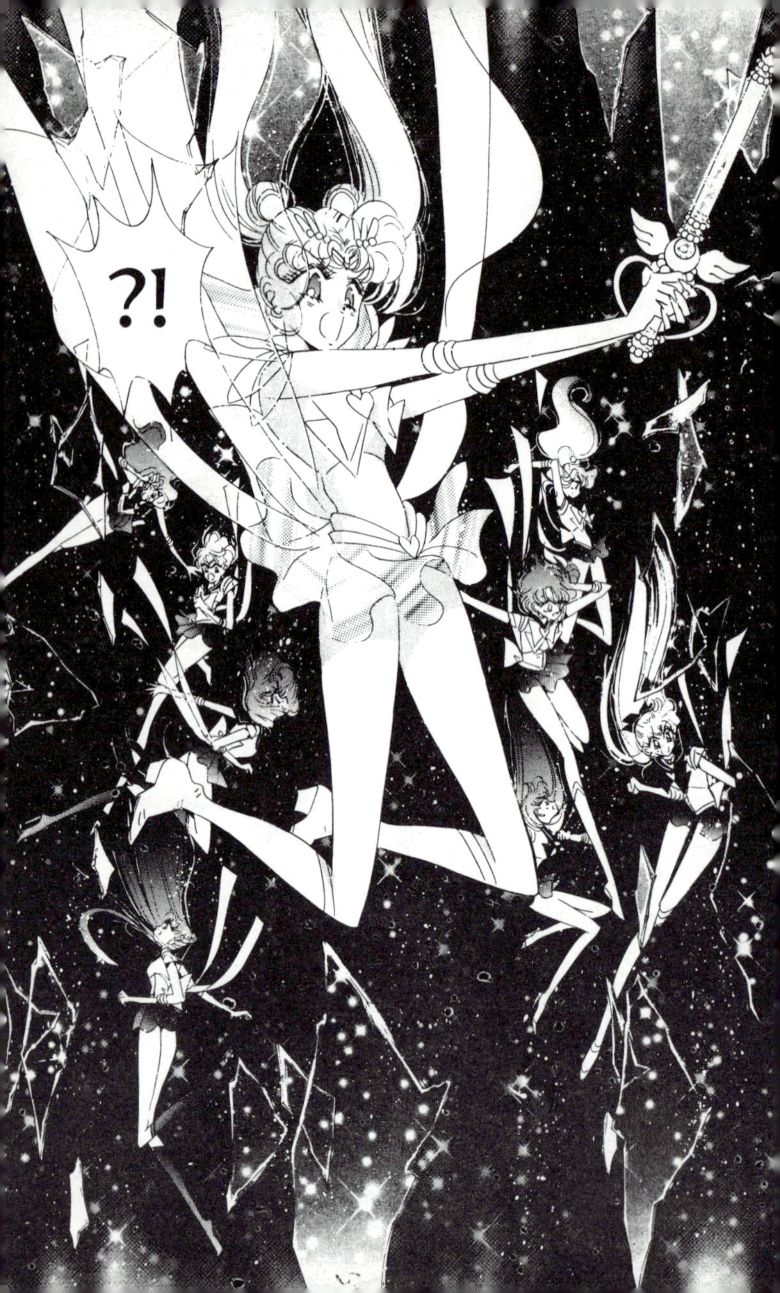
?!

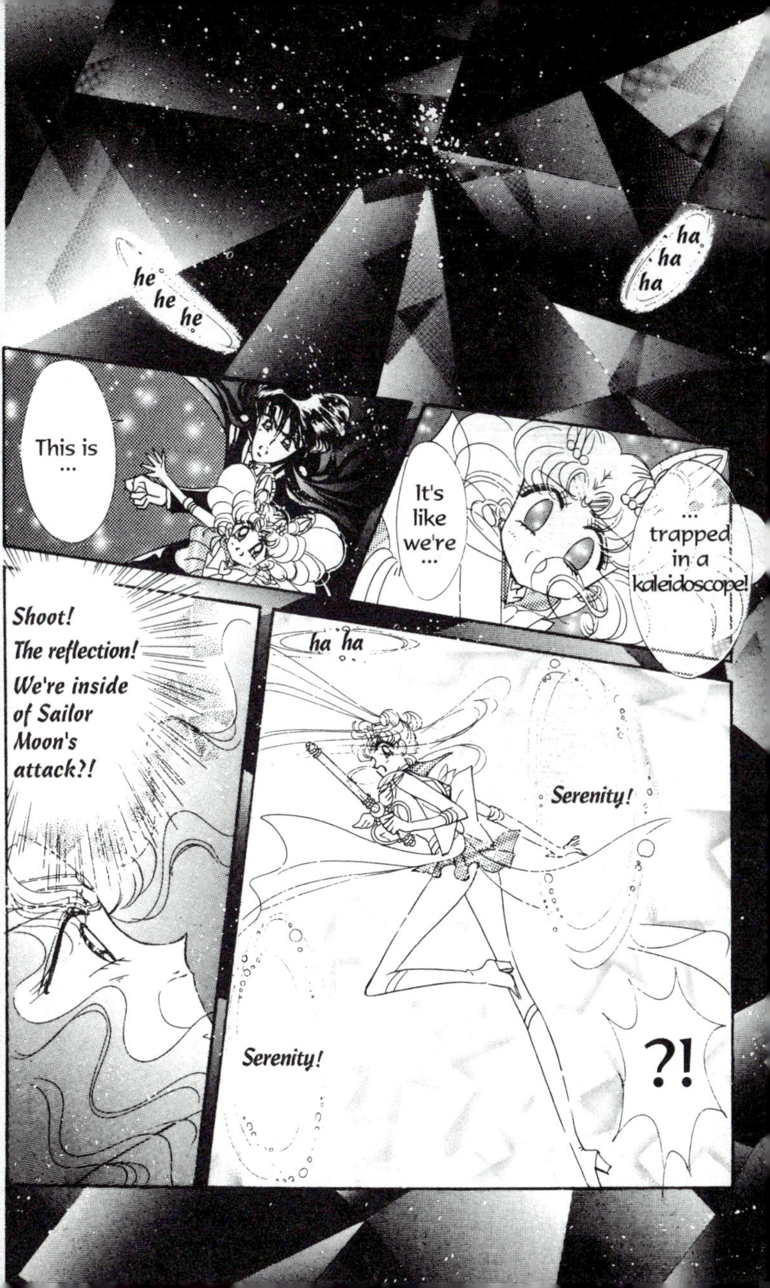
he he he
ha ha ha
This is ...
It's like we're ...
... trapped in a kaleidoscope!
Shoot! The reflection! We're inside of Sailor Moon's attack?!
ha ha
Serenity!
Serenity!
?!

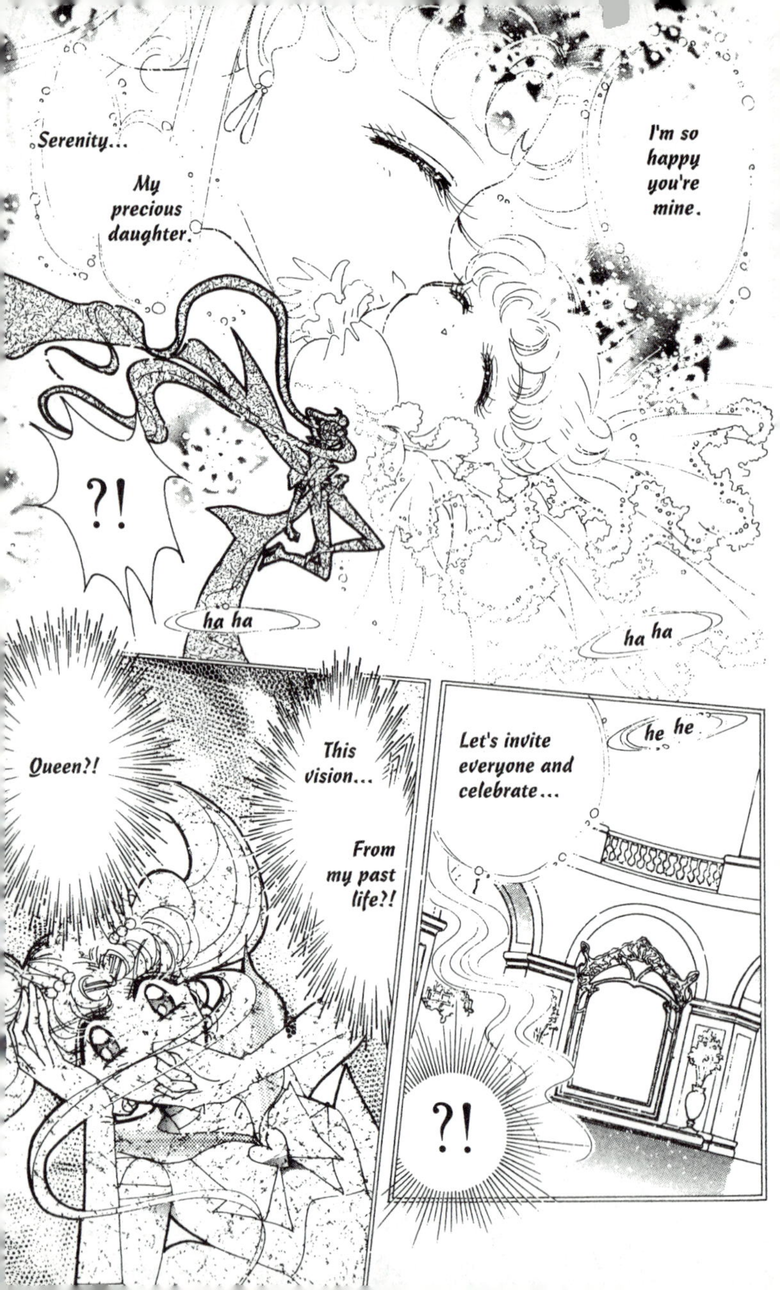
Serenity...
My precious daughter.
I'm so happy you're mine.
?!
ha ha
ha ha
Queen?!
This vision...
From my past life?!
Let's invite everyone and celebrate...
he he
?!

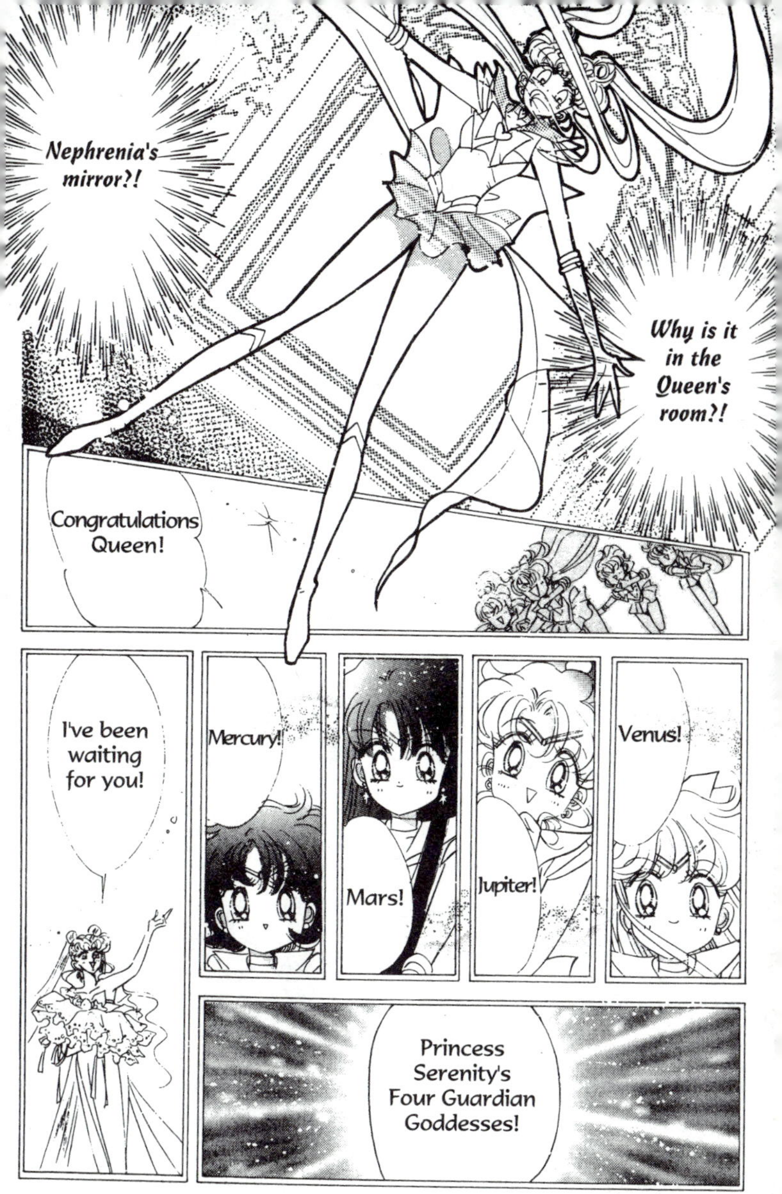
Nephrenia's mirror?!
Why is it in the Queen's room?!
Congratulations Queen!
I've been waiting for you!
Mercury!
Mars!
Jupiter!
Venus!
Princess Serenity's Four Guardian Goddesses!

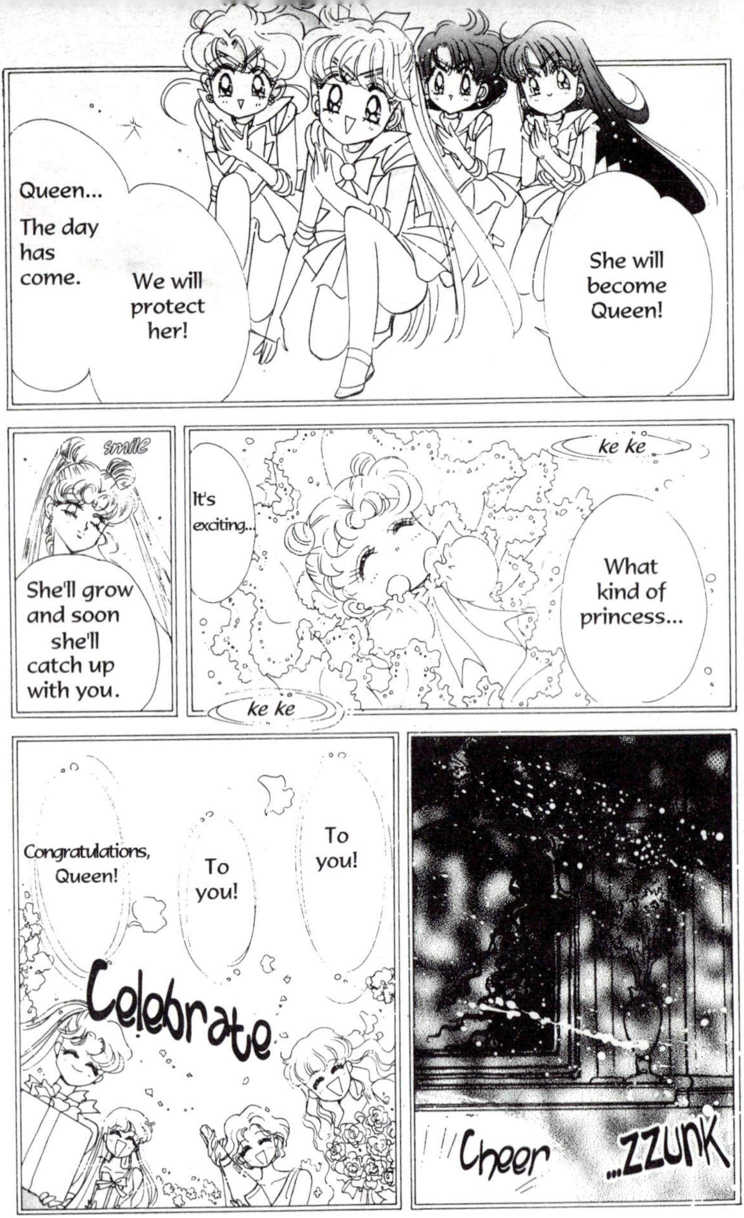
Queen... The day has come.
We will protect her!
She will become Queen!
smile
She'll grow and soon she'll catch up with you.
It's exciting...
ke ke
What kind of princess...
ke ke
Congratulations, Queen!
To you!
To you!
Celebrate
Cheer
...ZZUNK

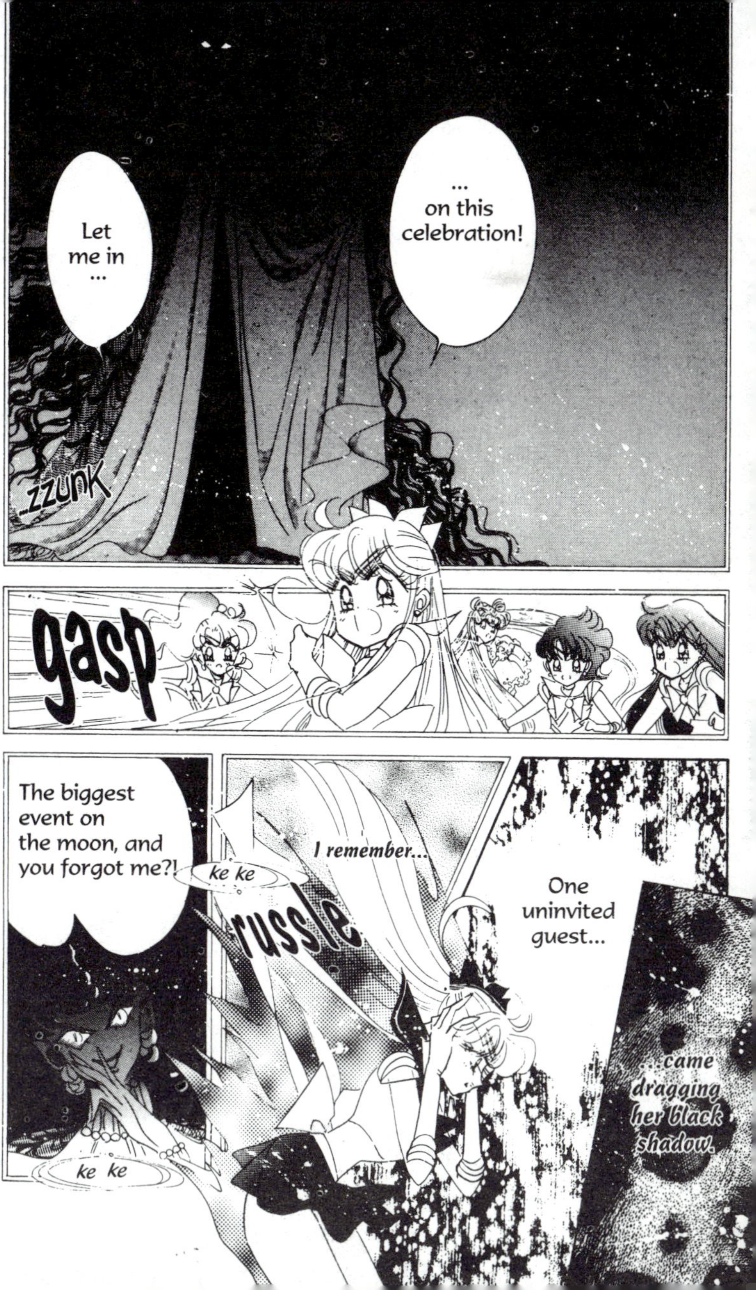
Let me in ...
... on this celebration!
...zzunk
gasp
The biggest event on the moon, and you forgot me?!
ke ke
ke ke
I remember...
russle
One uninvited guest...
...came dragging her black shadow.

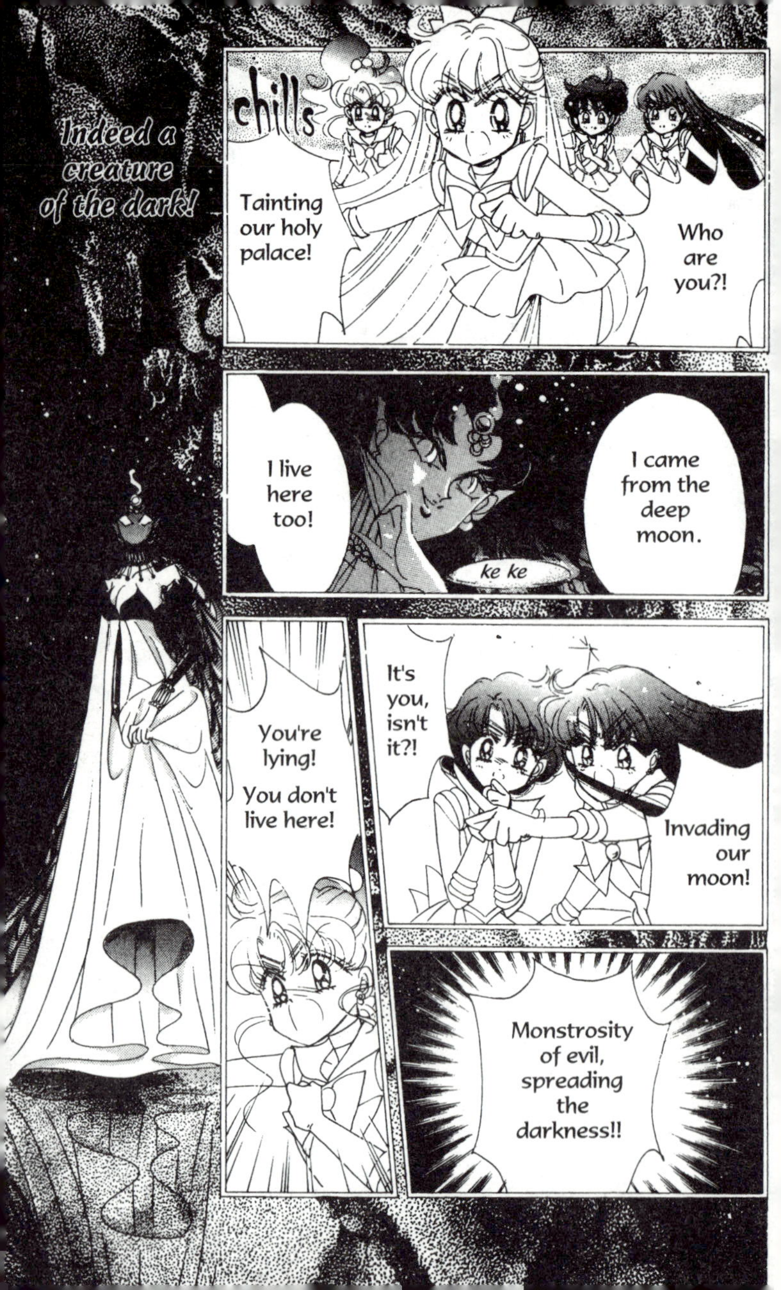
Who are you?!
chills
Tainting our holy palace!
I came from the deep moon.
ke ke
I live here too!
It's you, isn't it?!
Invading our moon!
Monstrosity of evil, spreading the darkness!!
You're lying!
You don't live here!
Indeed a creature of the dark!

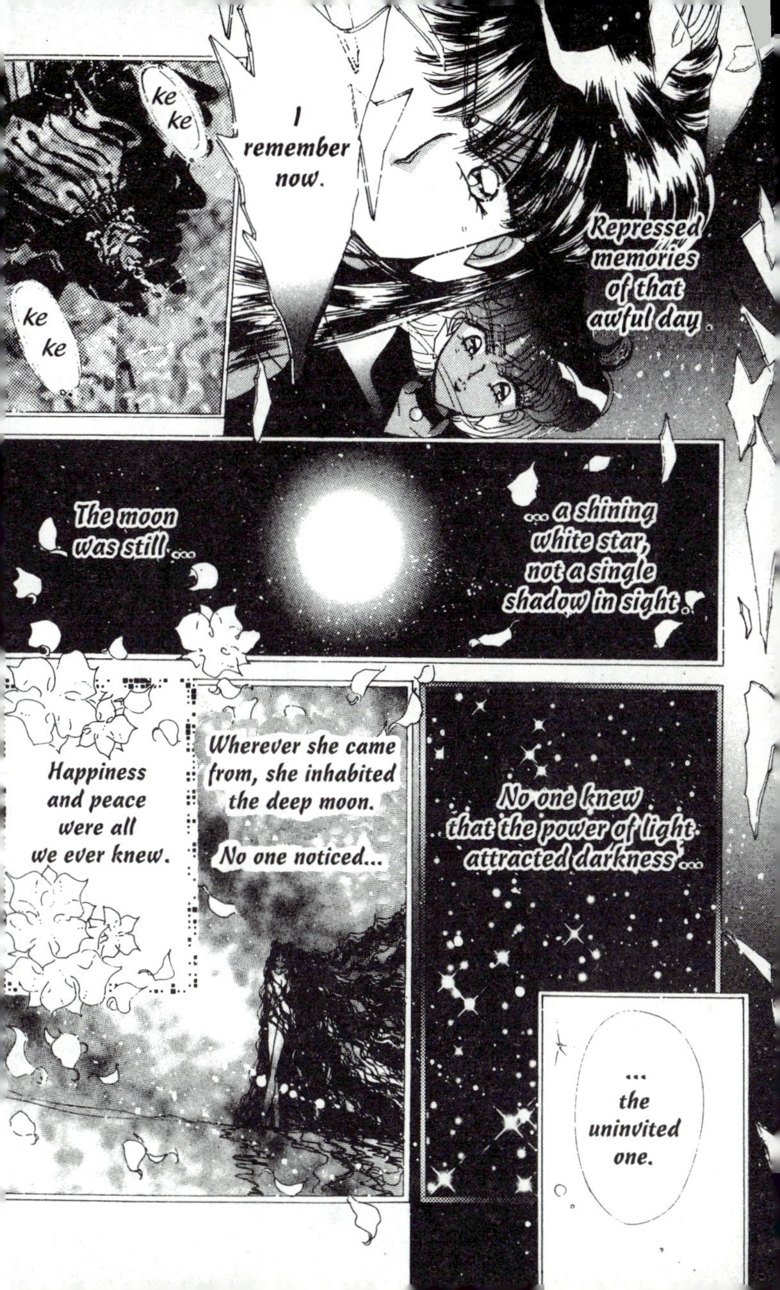

ke ke
ke ke
I remember now.
Repressed memories of that awful day.
The moon was still...
...a shining white star, not a single shadow in sight.
Happiness and peace were all we ever knew.
Wherever she came from, she inhabited the deep moon.
No one noticed...
No one knew that the power of light attracted darkness...
... the uninvited one.

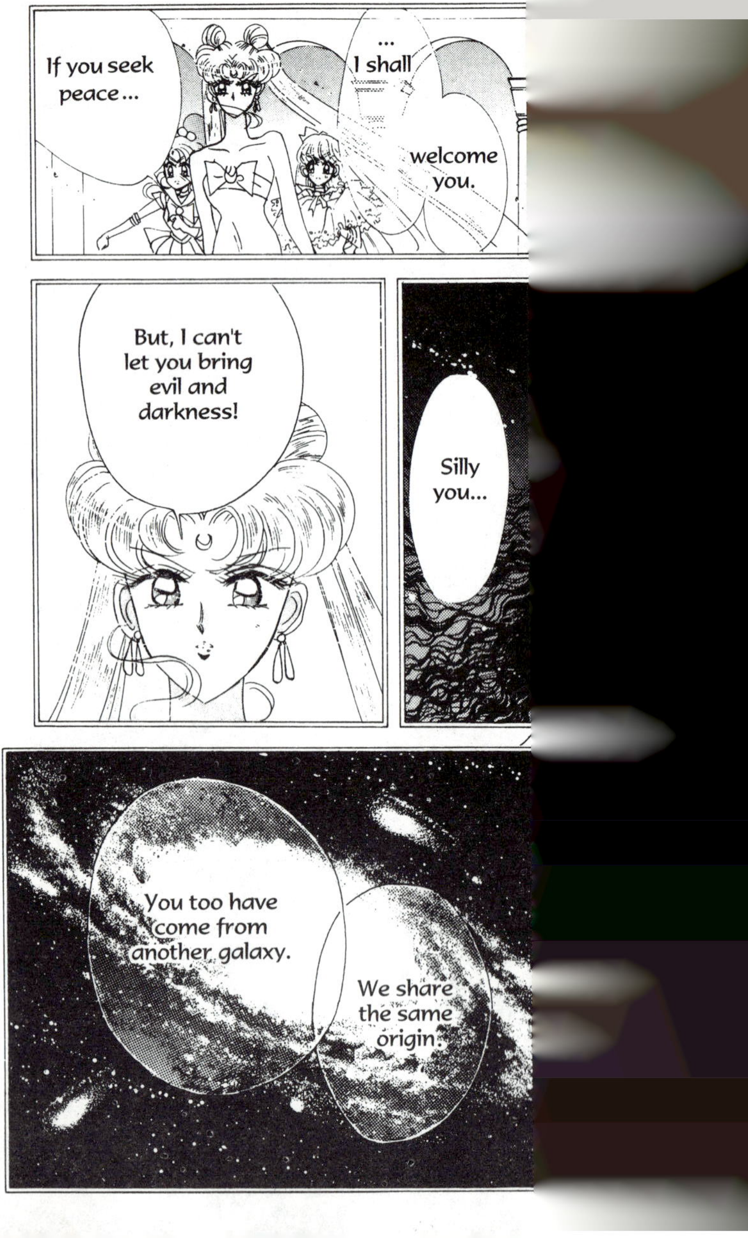
If you seek peace...
... I shall
welcome you.
But, I can't let you bring evil and darkness!
Silly you...
You too have come from another galaxy.
We share the same origin.

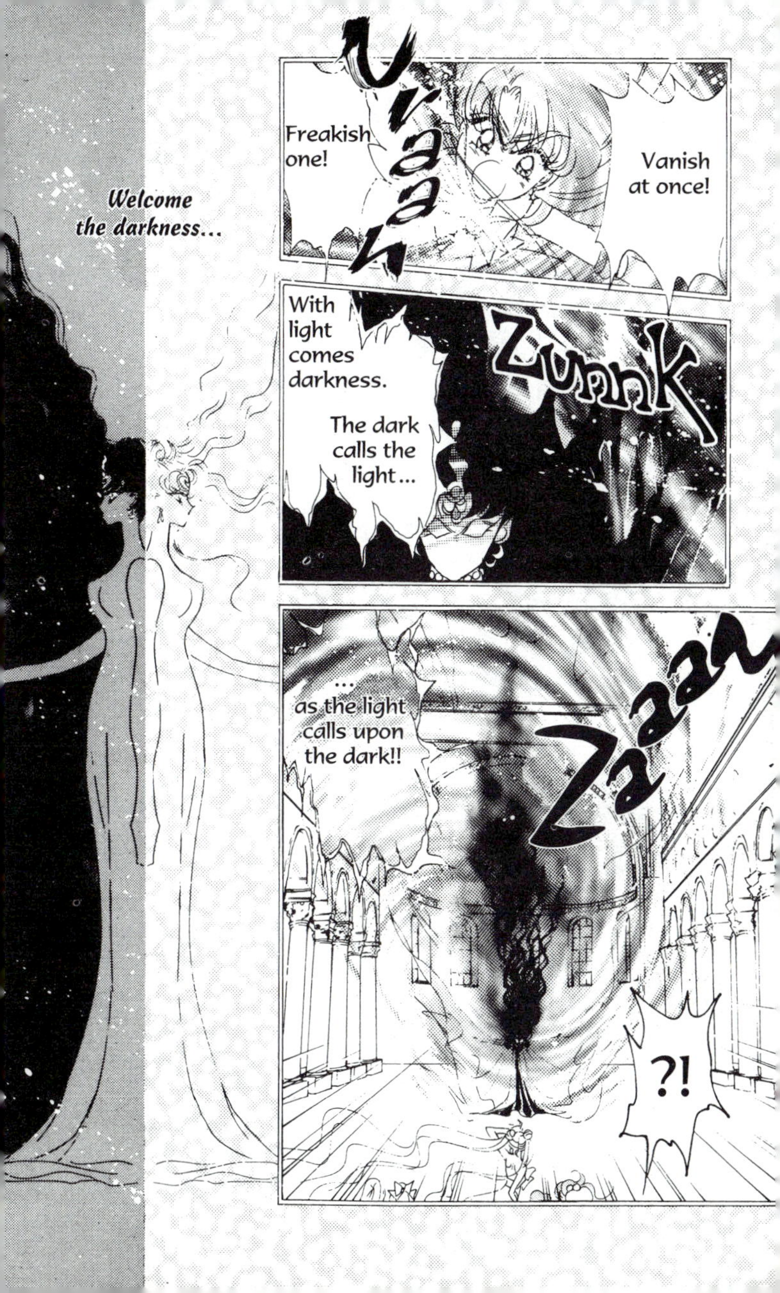
Vanish at once!
Freakish one!
Zunnk
With light comes darkness.
The dark calls the light...
... as the light calls upon the dark!!
?!
Welcome the darkness...

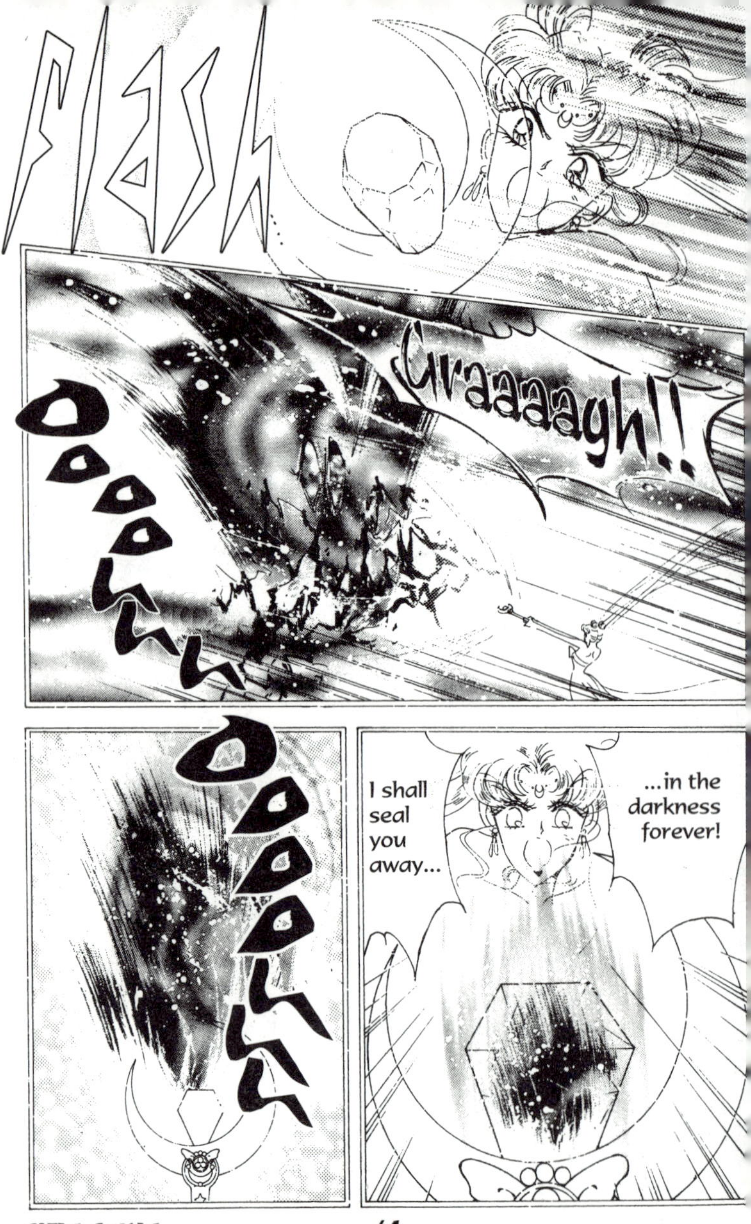
FLASH
Graaaagh!!
DOOOOMMM
DOOOOMMM
I shall seal you away...
...in the darkness forever!

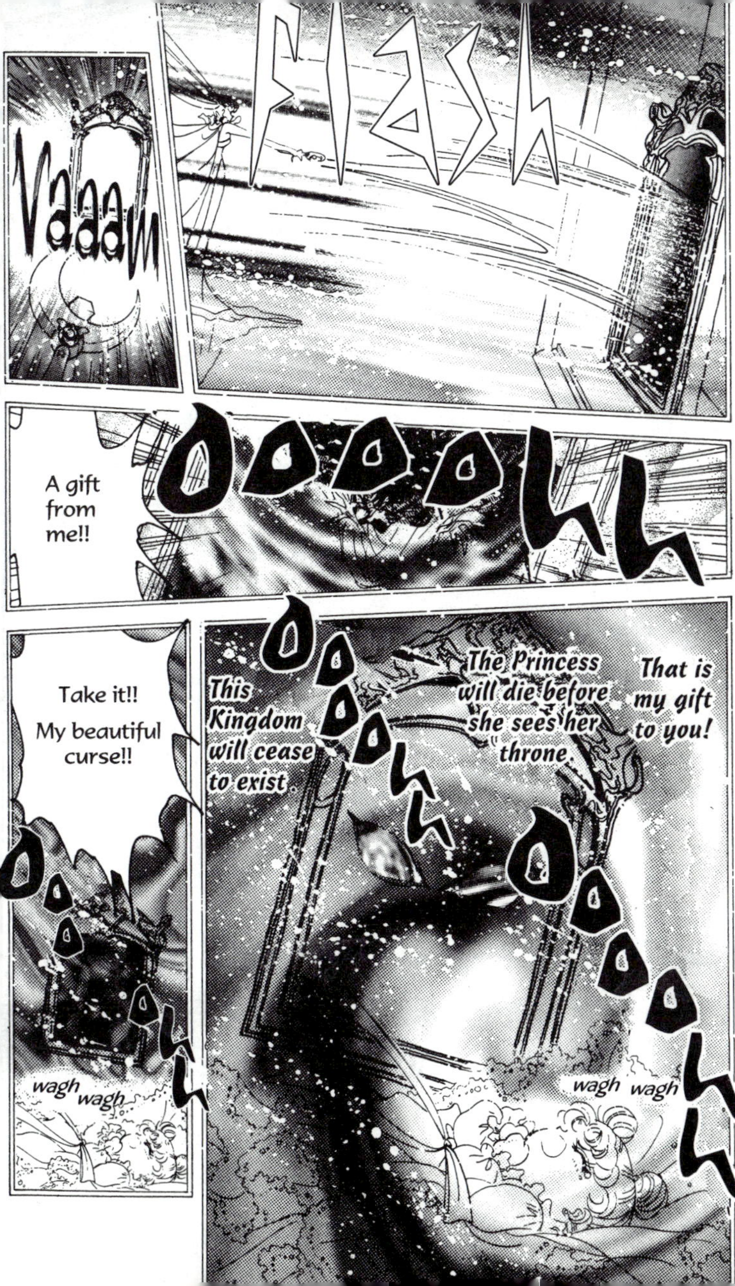
Vaaam
Flash
A gift from me!!
Oooohh
Take it!! My beautiful curse!!
Oooohh
wagh wagh
Oooohh
This Kingdom will cease to exist.
The Princess will die before she sees her throne.
That is my gift to you!
Ooooohh
wagh wagh

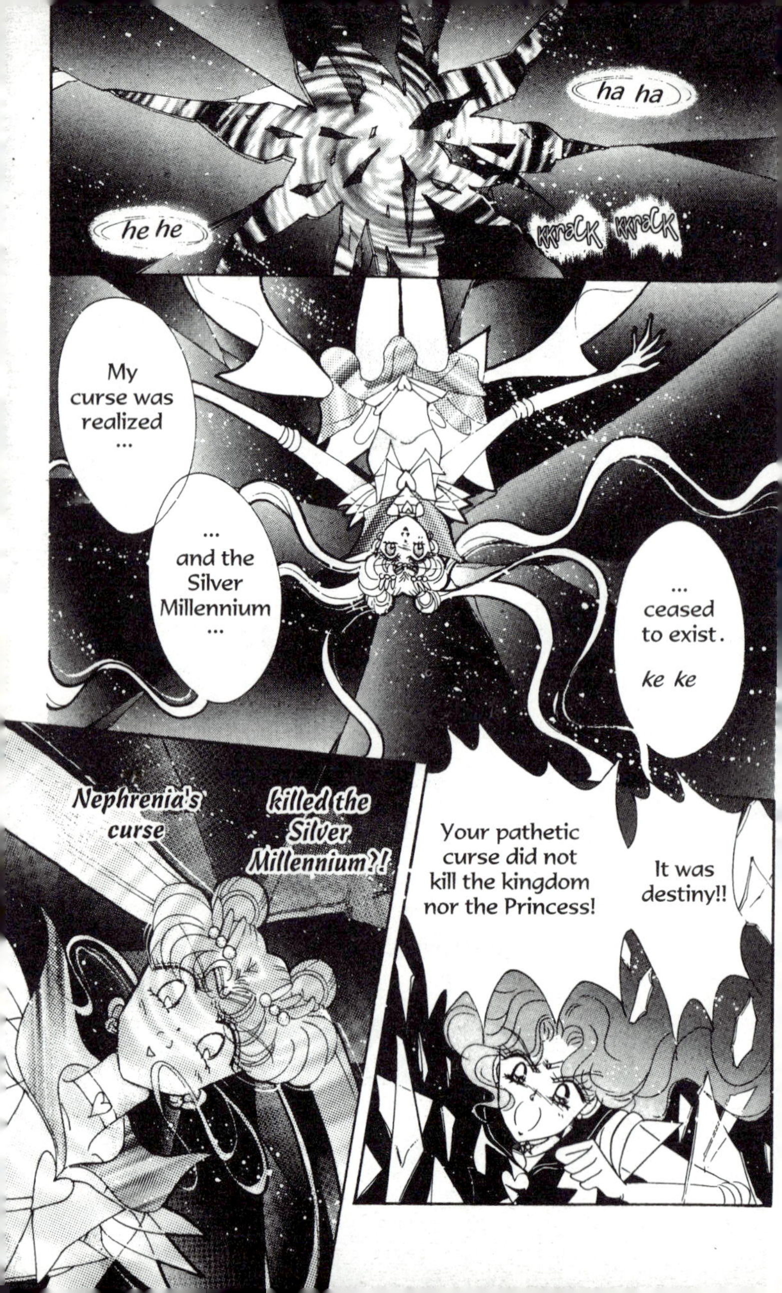

ha ha
he he
KKRACK KKRACK
My curse was realized ...
... and the Silver Millennium ...
... ceased to exist.
ke ke
Nephrenia's curse
killed the Silver Millennium?!
Your pathetic curse did not kill the kingdom nor the Princess!
It was destiny!!

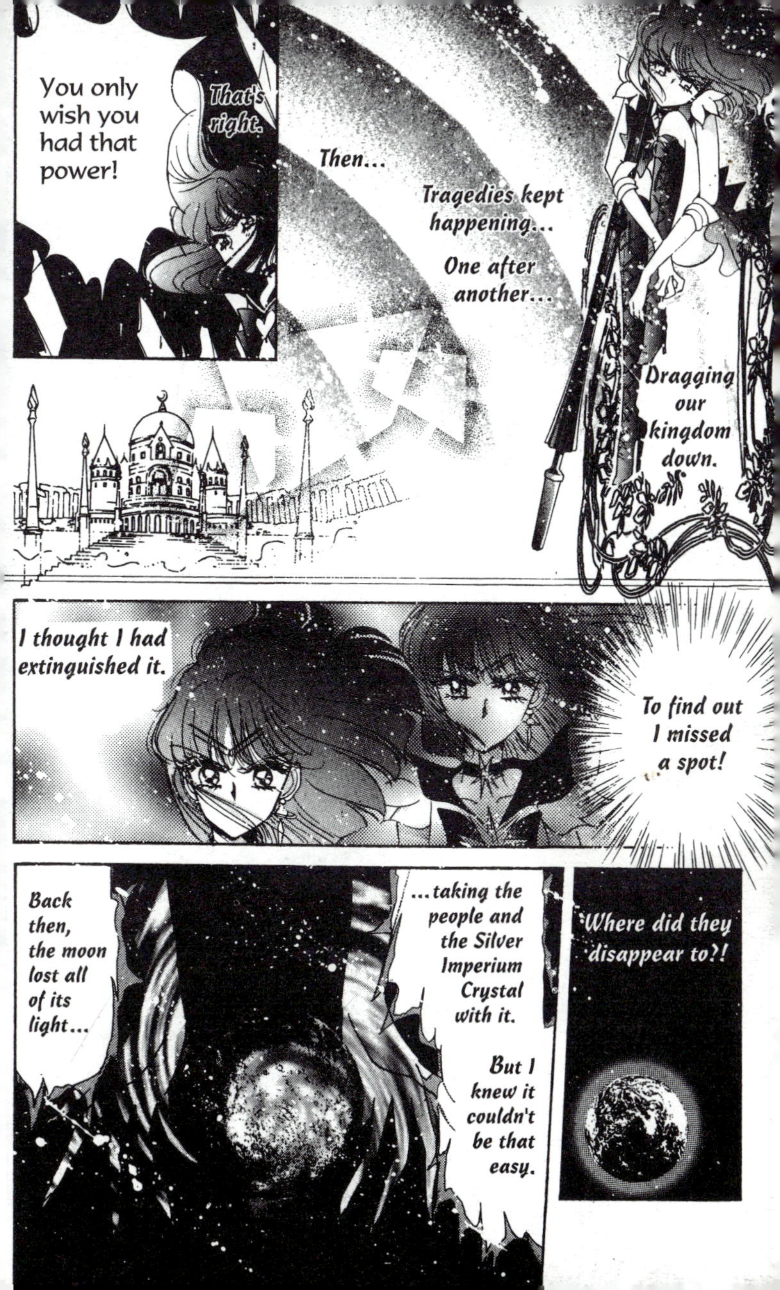

You only wish you had that power!
That's right.
Then...
Tragedies kept happening...
One after another...
Dragging our kingdom down.
I thought I had extinguished it.
To find out I missed a spot!
Back then, the moon lost all of its light...
...taking the people and the Silver Imperium Crystal with it.
But I knew it couldn't be that easy.
Where did they disappear to?!

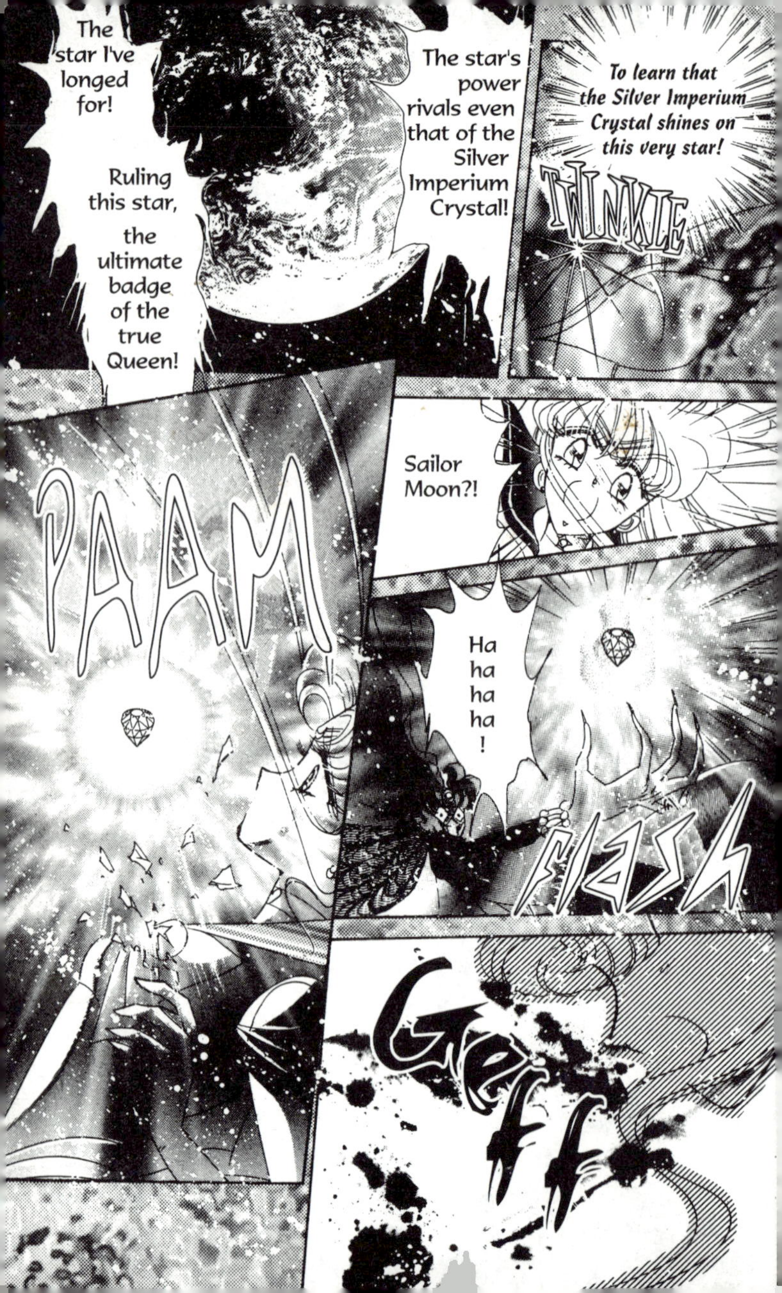
The star I've longed for!
Ruling this star, the ultimate badge of the true Queen!
The star's power rivals even that of the Silver Imperium Crystal!
To learn that the Silver Imperium Crystal shines on this very star!
TWINKLE
PAAM
Sailor Moon?!
Ha ha ha ha!
FLASH
Geff

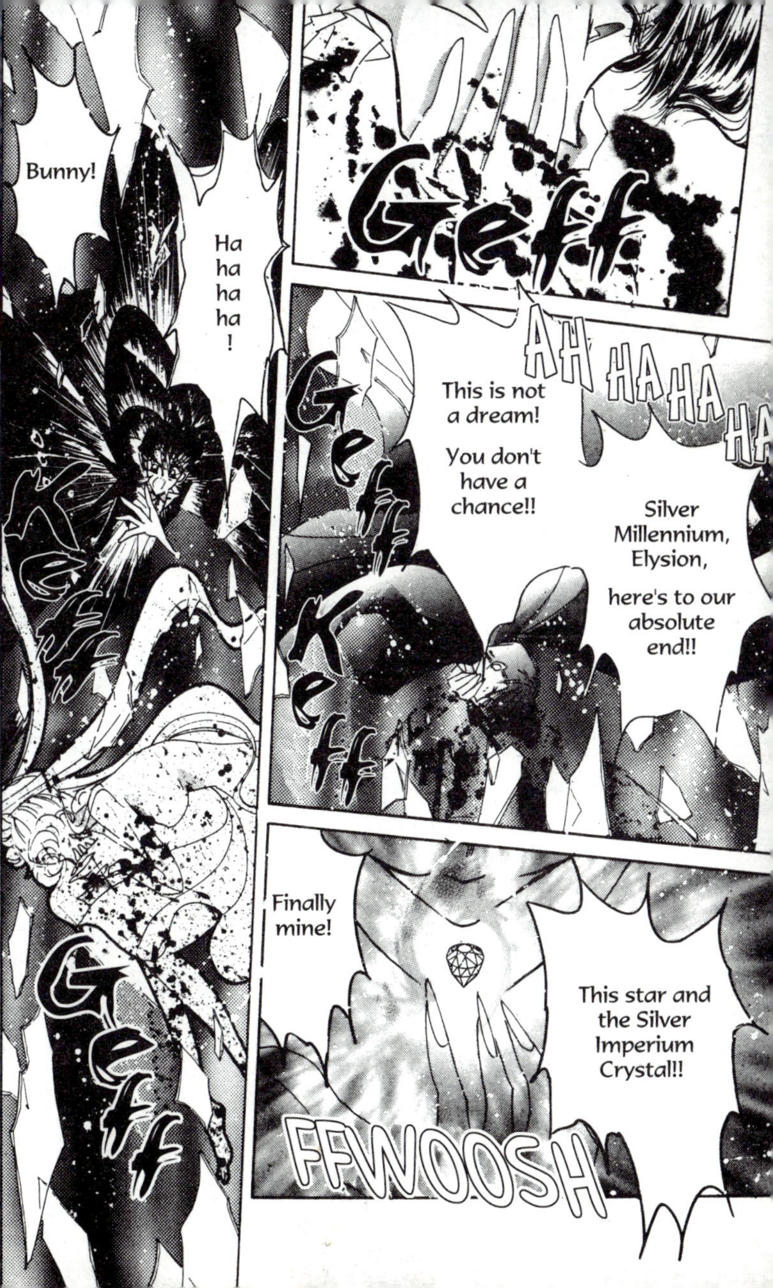
Bunny!
Ha ha ha ha!
Geff
Geff
AH HA HA HA
Geff
Keff
This is not a dream!
You don't have a chance!!
Silver Millennium, Elysion,
here's to our absolute end!!
Finally mine!
This star and the Silver Imperium Crystal!!
FFWOOSH

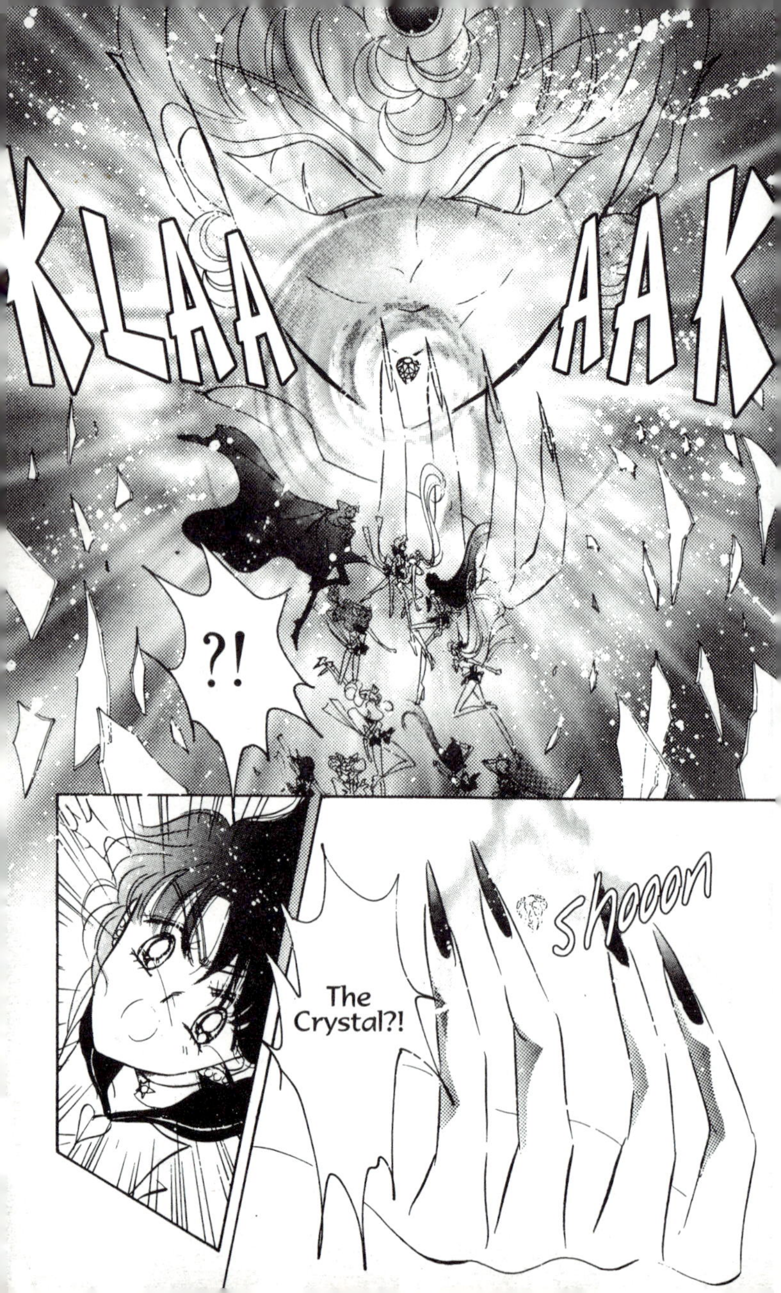
KLAAAAK
?!
Shooon
The Crystal?!

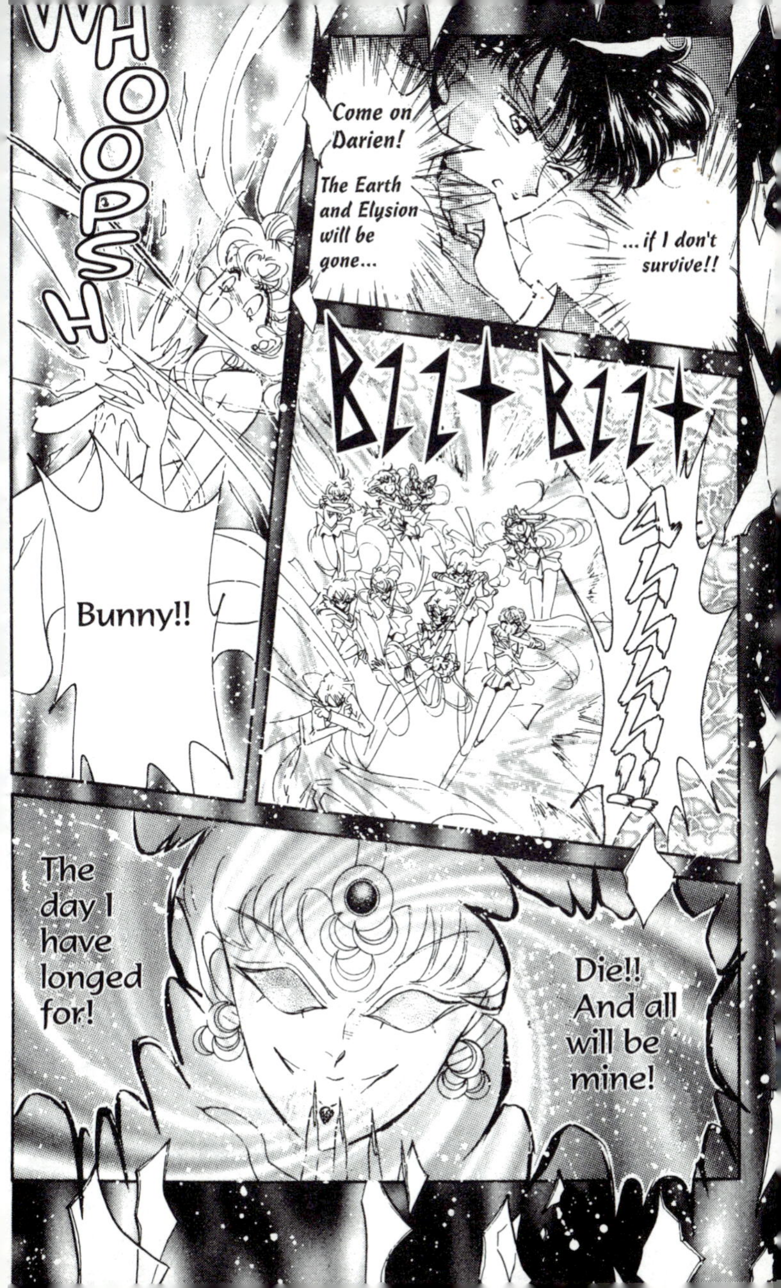
WHOOSH
Bunny!!
Come on Darien!
The Earth and Elysion will be gone...
...if I don't survive!!
BZZT BZZT
The day I have longed for!
Die!! And all will be mine!

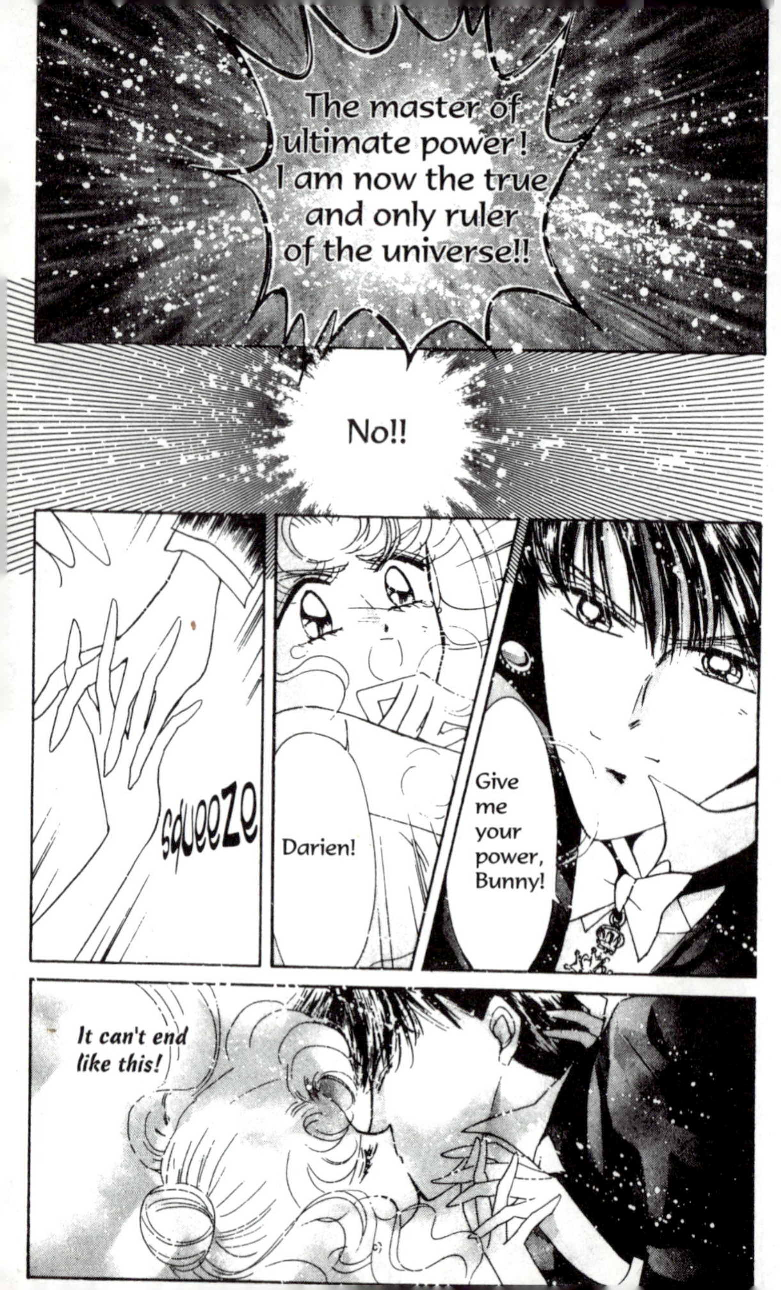
The master of ultimate power! I am now the true and only ruler of the universe!!
No!!
squeeze
Darien!
Give me your power, Bunny!
It can't end like this!

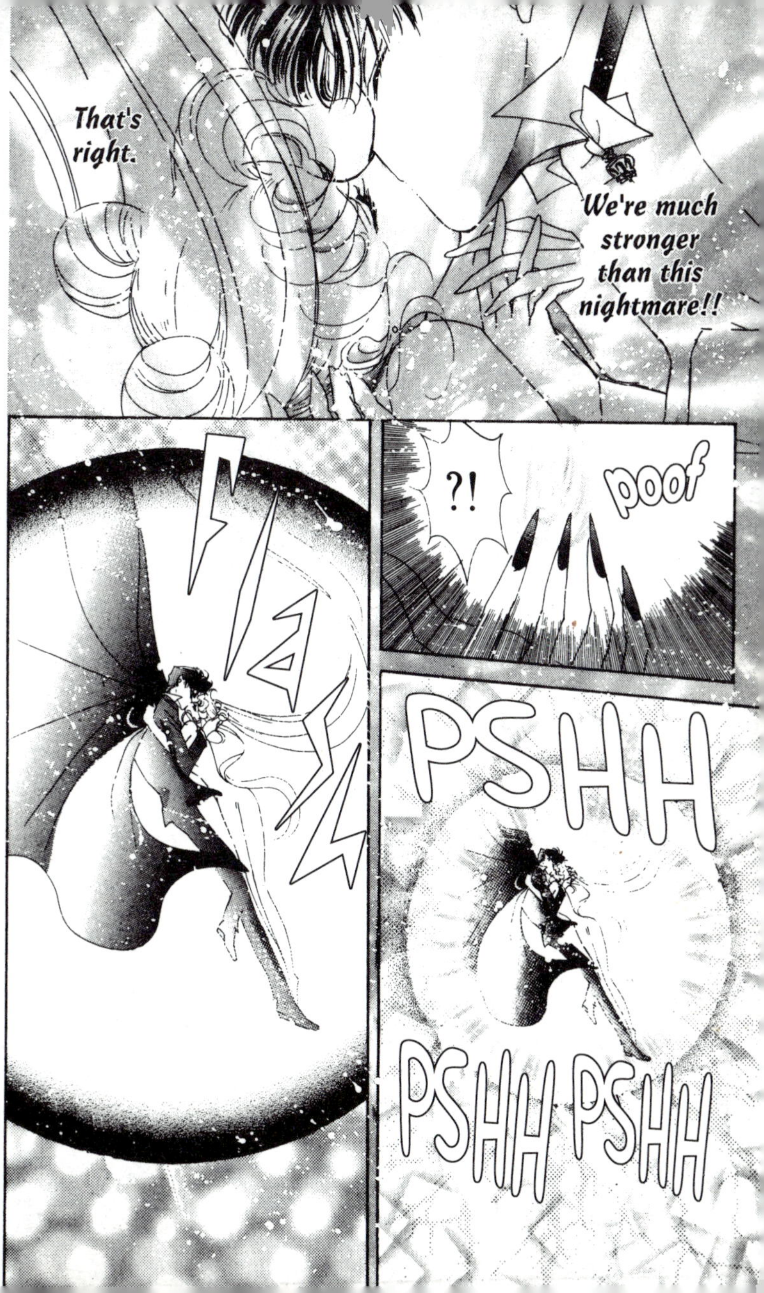
That's right.
We're much stronger than this nightmare!!
?!
poof
PSHH
PSHH PSHH

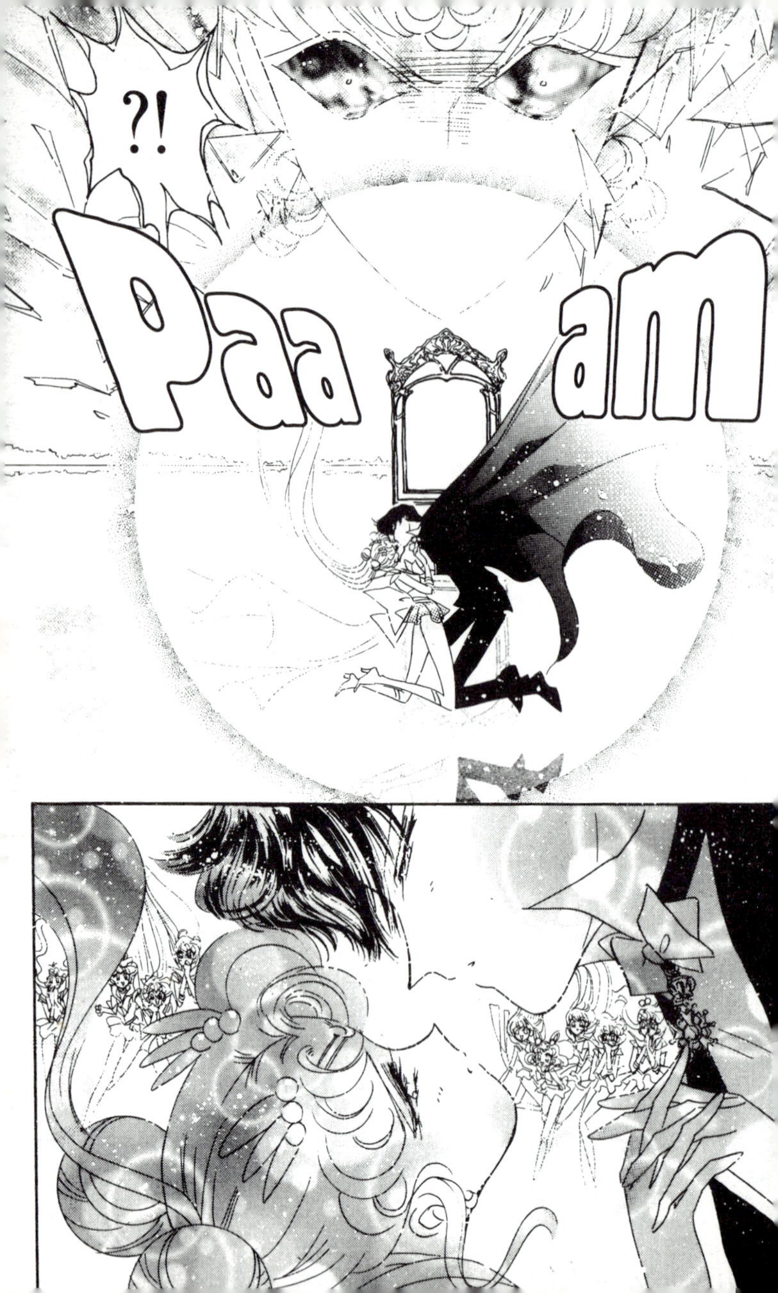
?!
Paa am

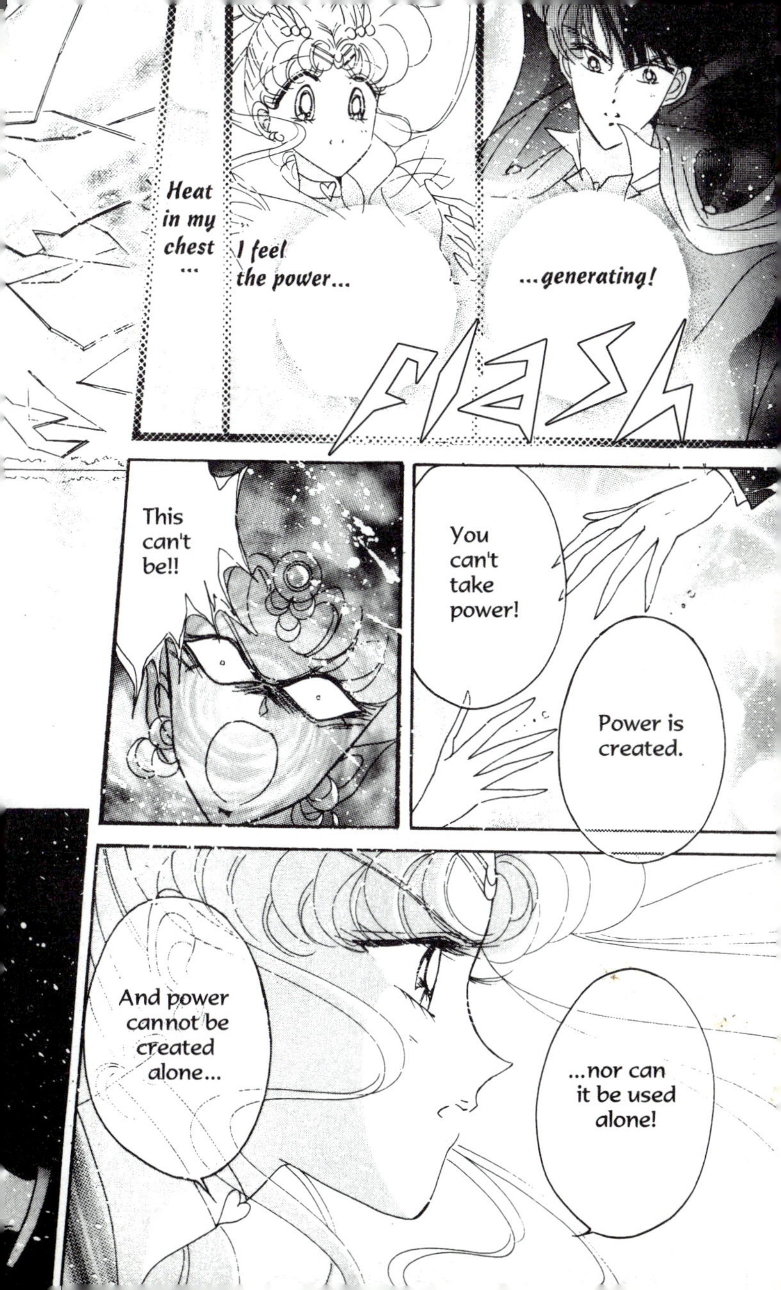
Heat in my chest ...
I feel the power...
...generating!
FLASH
This can't be!!
You can't take power!
Power is created.
And power cannot be created alone...
...nor can it be used alone!

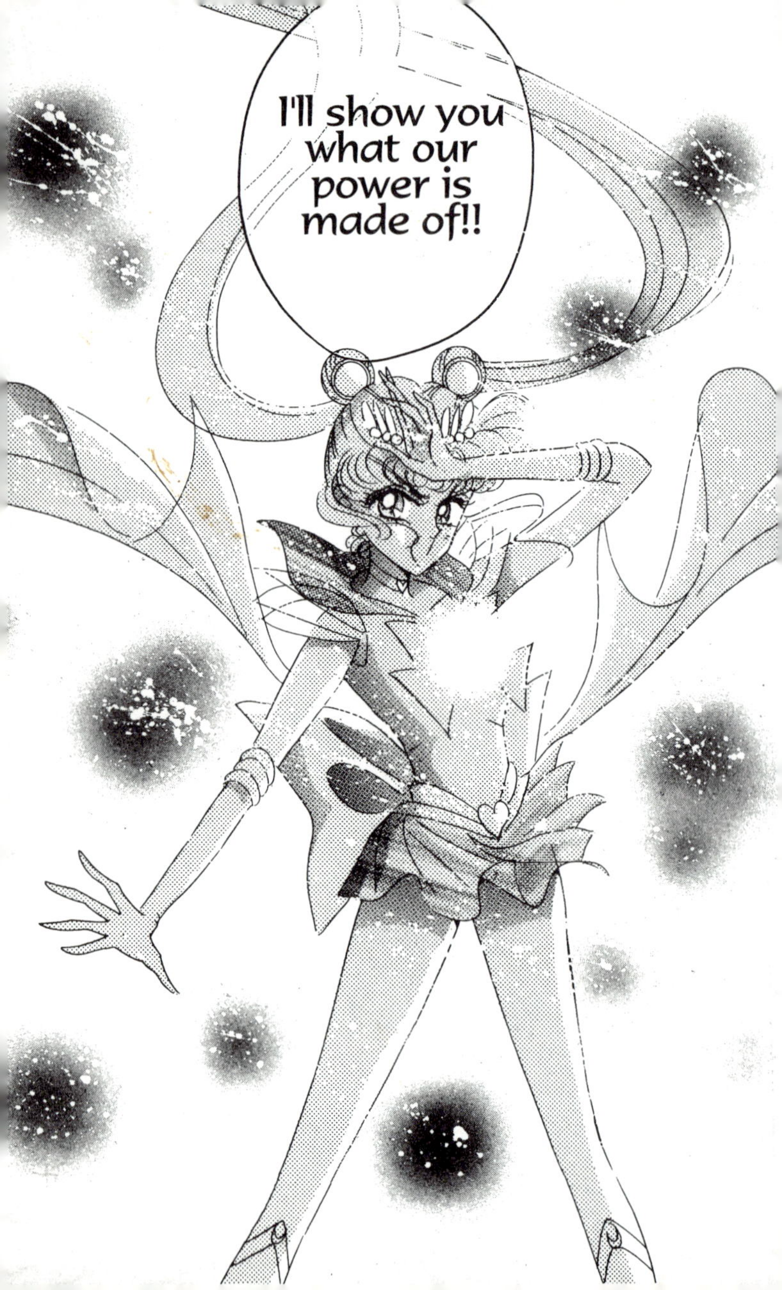
I'll show you what our power is made of!!

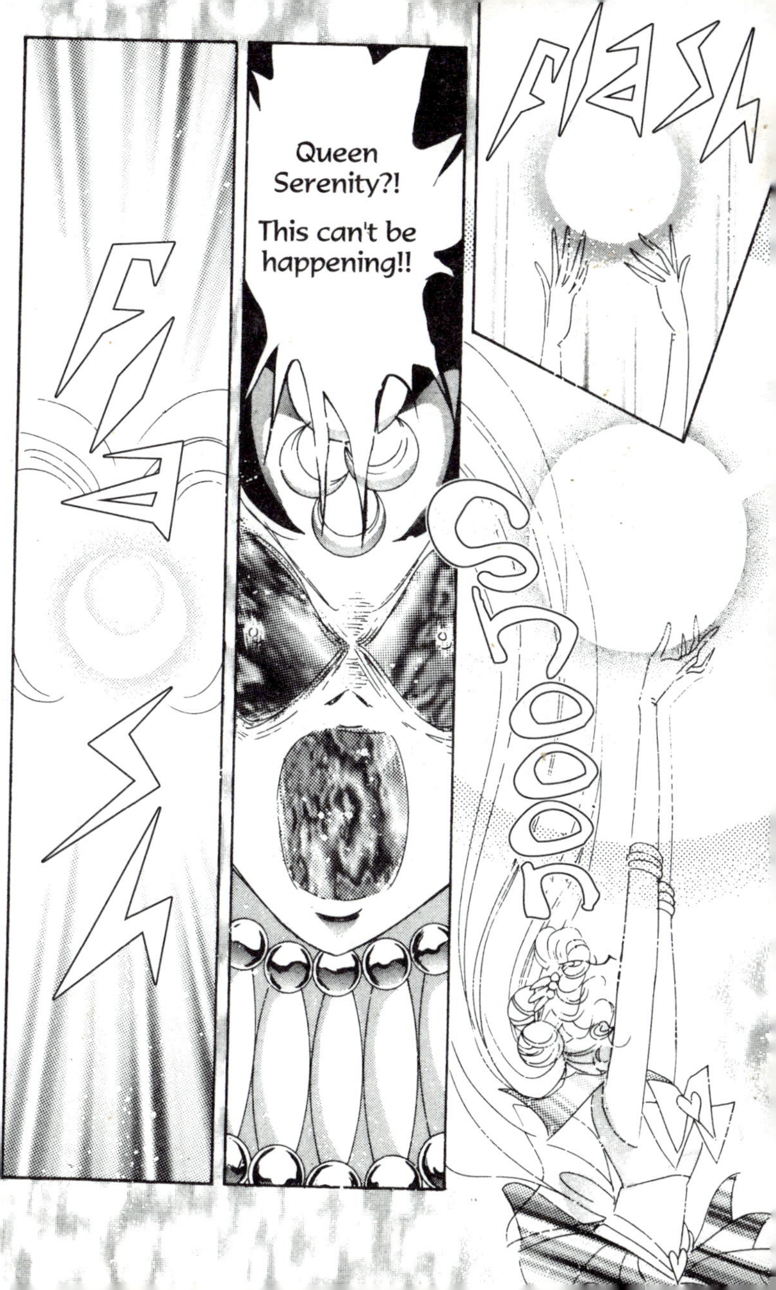
FLASH
Queen Serenity?!
This can't be happening!!
FLASH
SHOOOOM

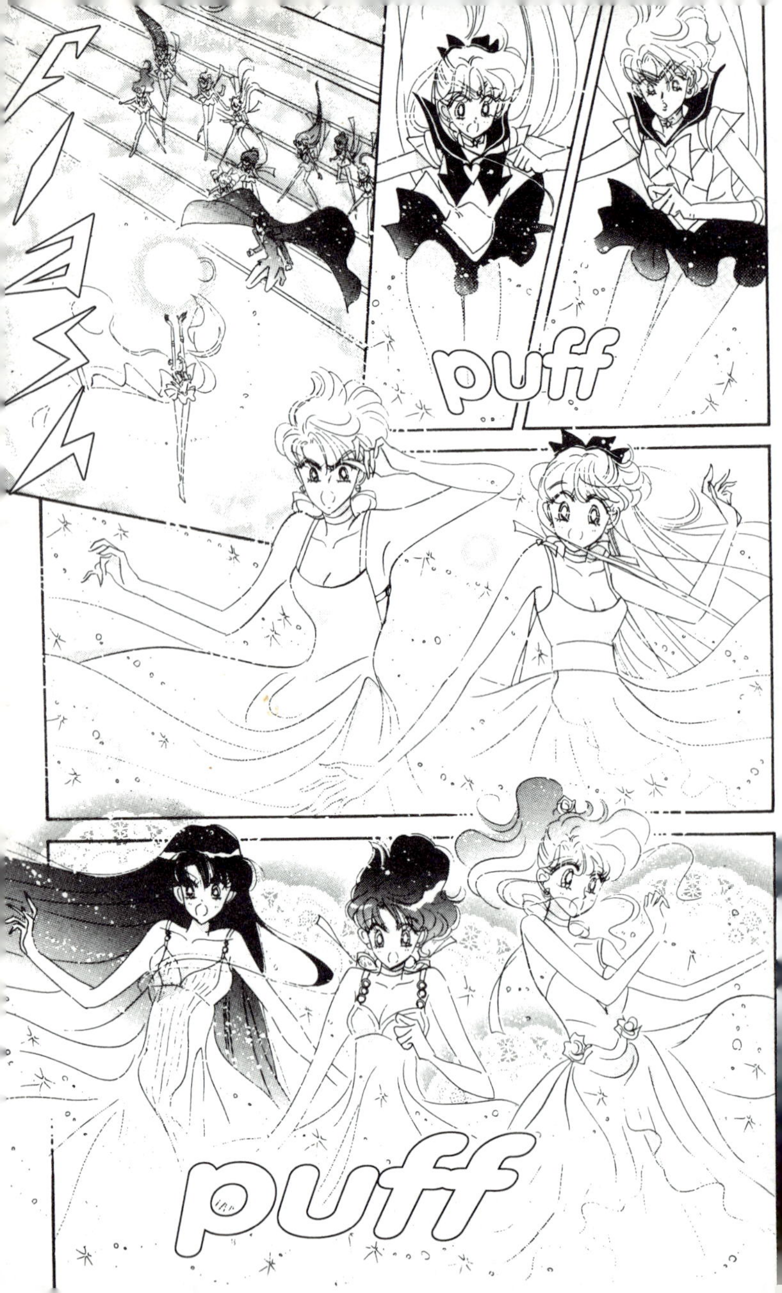
puff
puff

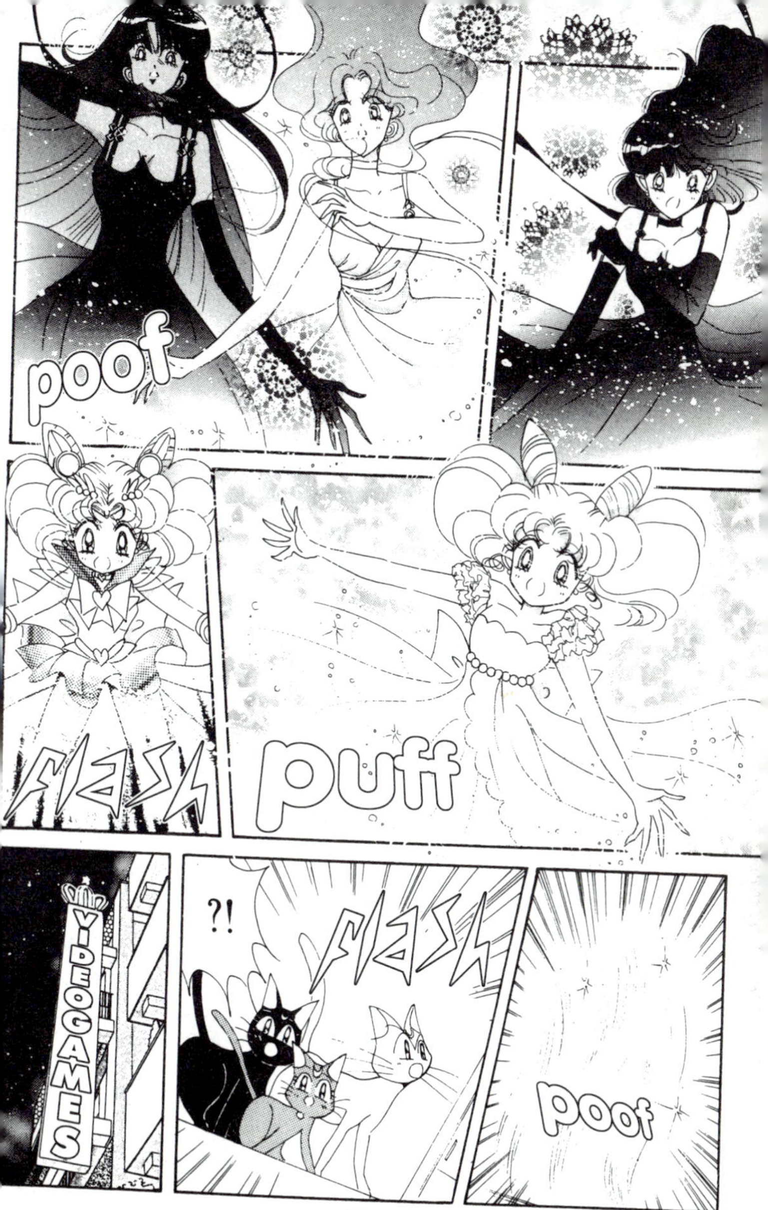
poof
FLASH
puff
VIDEOGAMES
?!
FLASH
poof

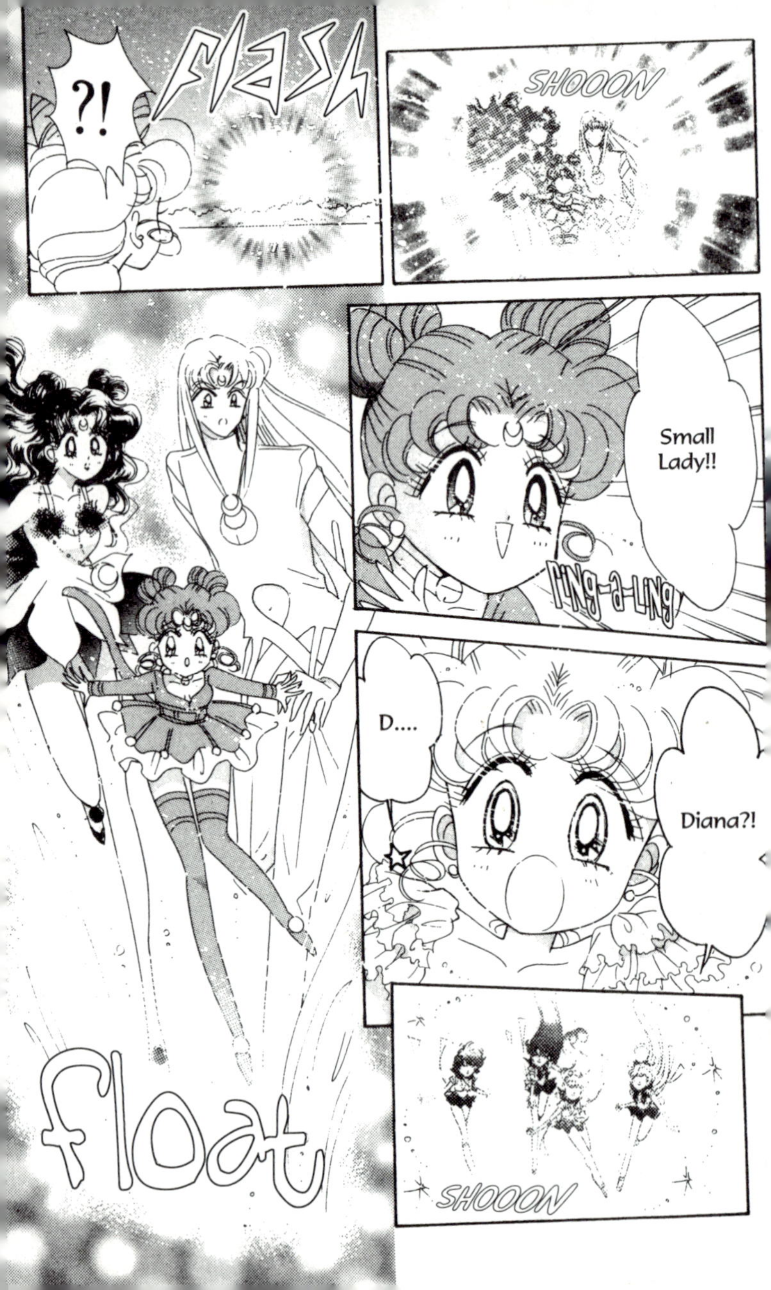
?!
FLASH
SHOOON
float
Small Lady!!
ring-a-ling
D....
Diana?!
SHOOON

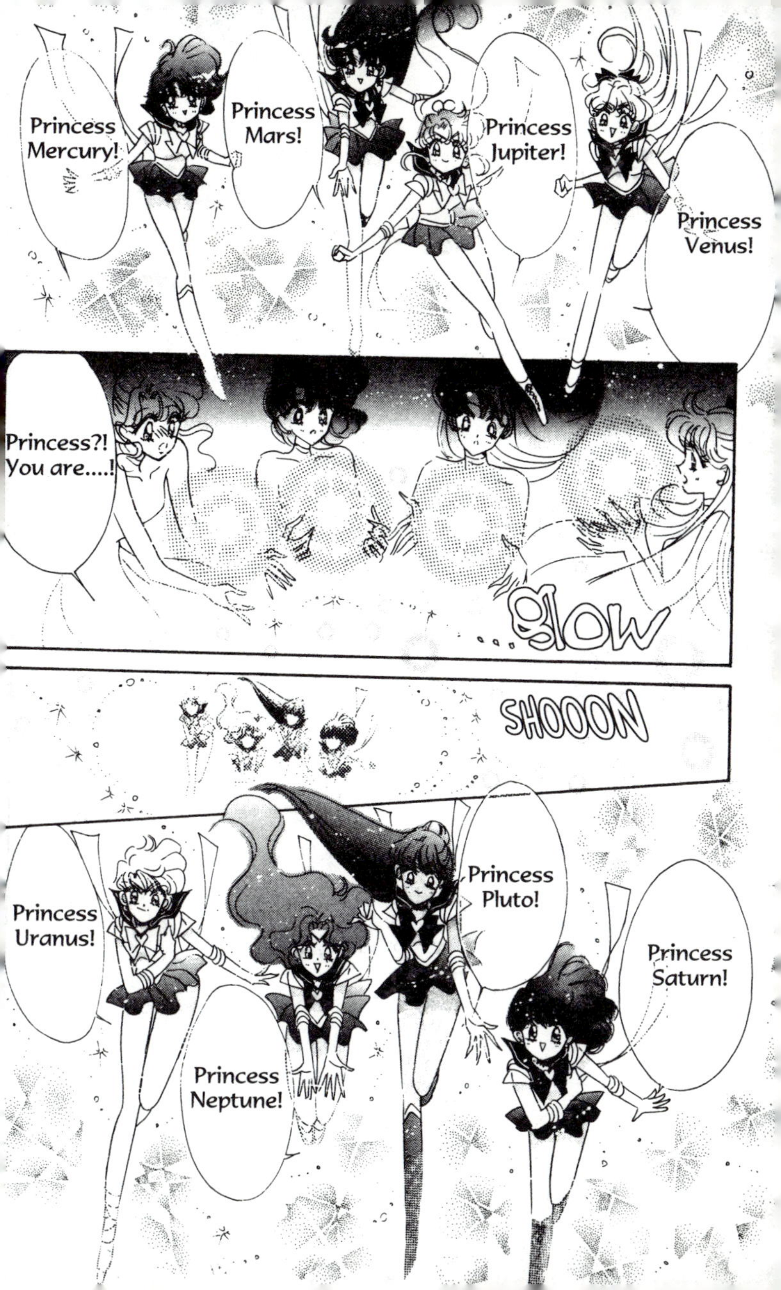
Princess Mercury!
Princess Mars!
Princess Jupiter!
Princess Venus!
Princess?! You are....!
...glow
SHOOON
Princess Uranus!
Princess Neptune!
Princess Pluto!
Princess Saturn!

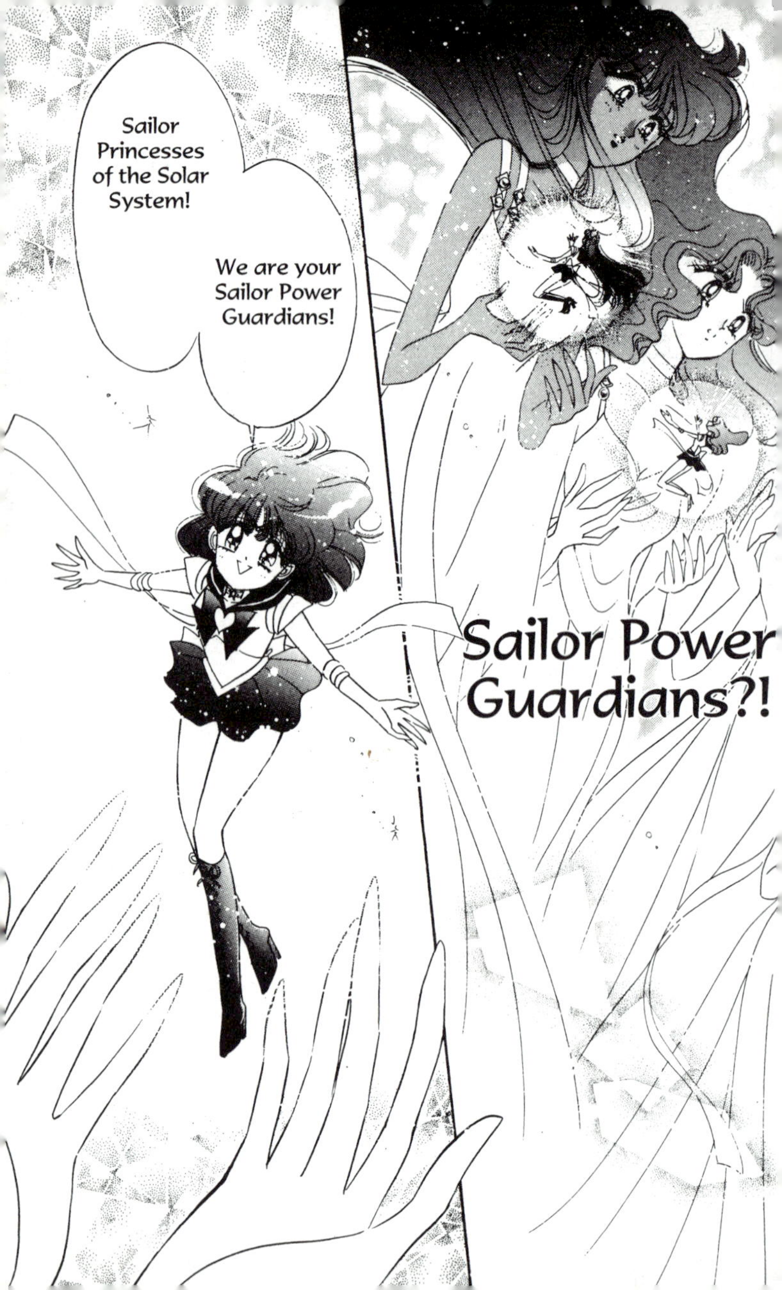

Sailor Princesses of the Solar System!
We are your Sailor Power Guardians!
Sailor Power Guardians?!

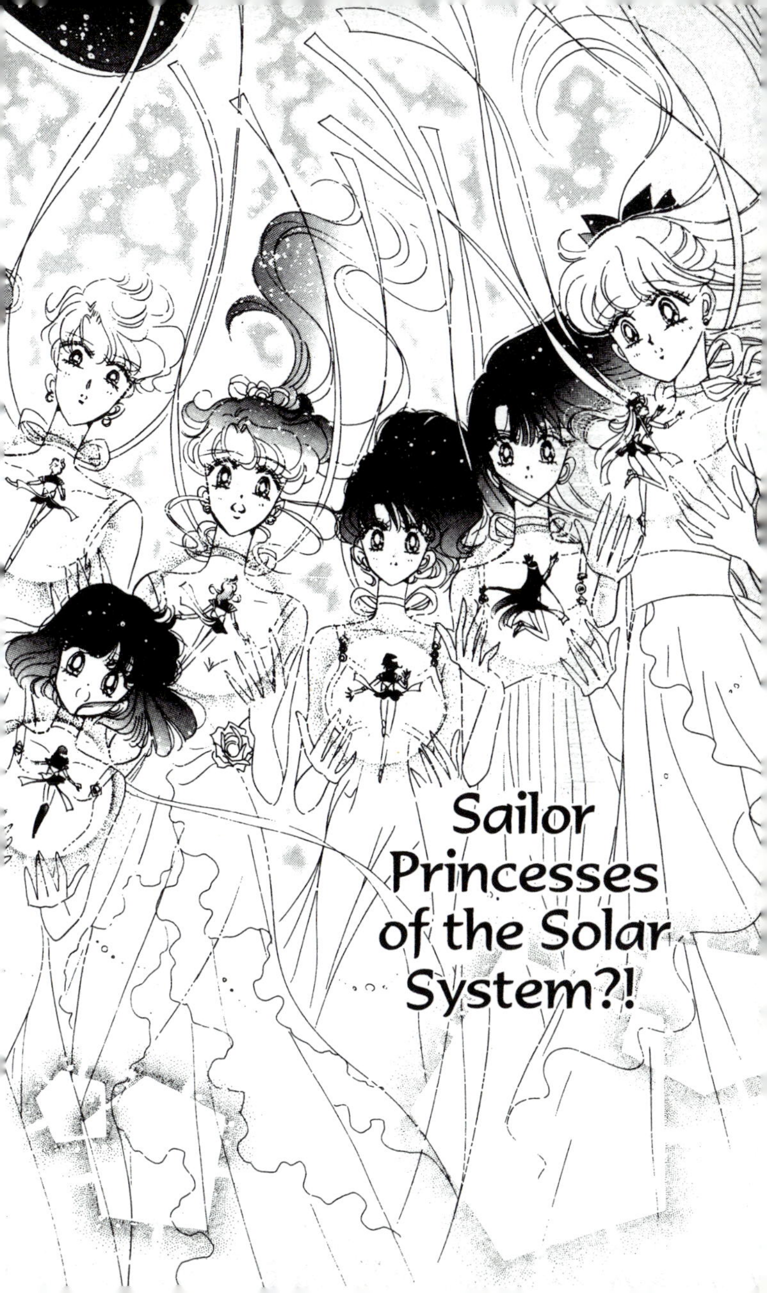
Sailor Princesses of the Solar System?!

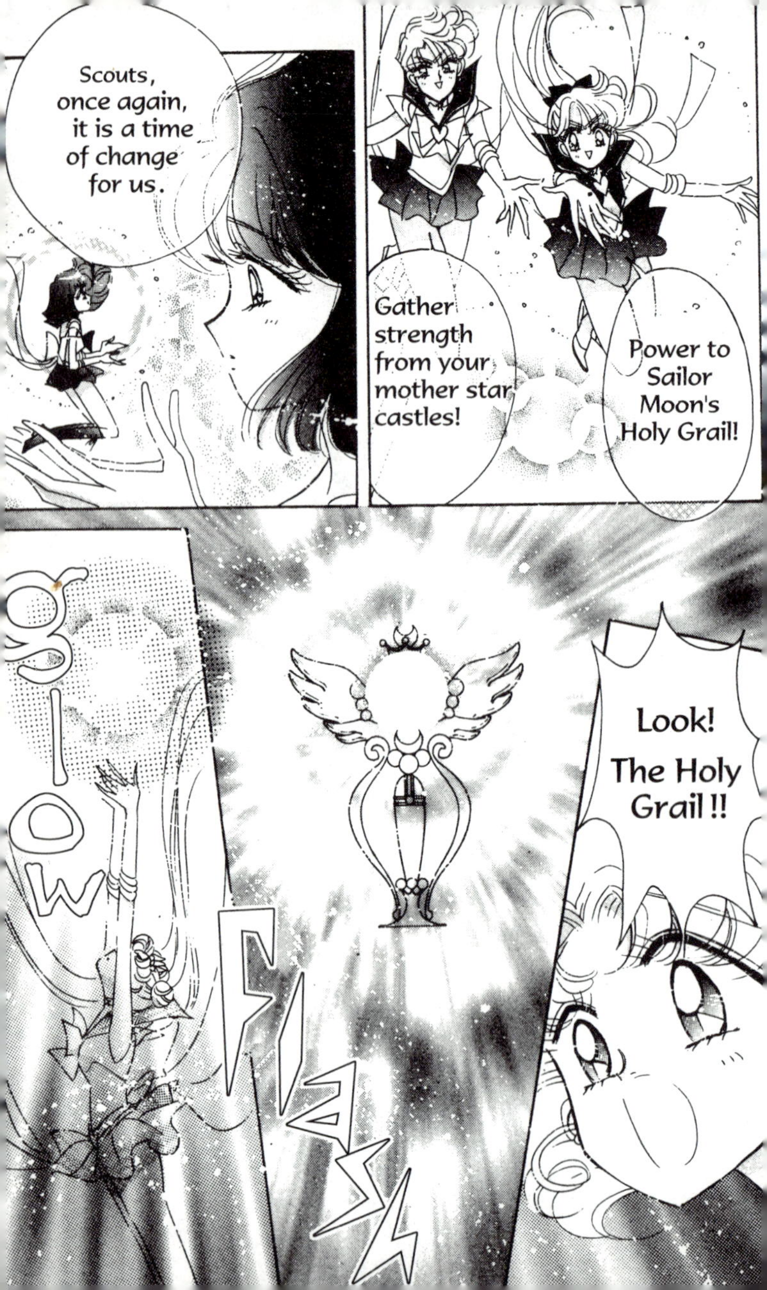
Scouts, once again, it is a time of change for us.
Gather strength from your mother star castles!
Power to Sailor Moon's Holy Grail!
glow
FLASH
Look! The Holy Grail!!

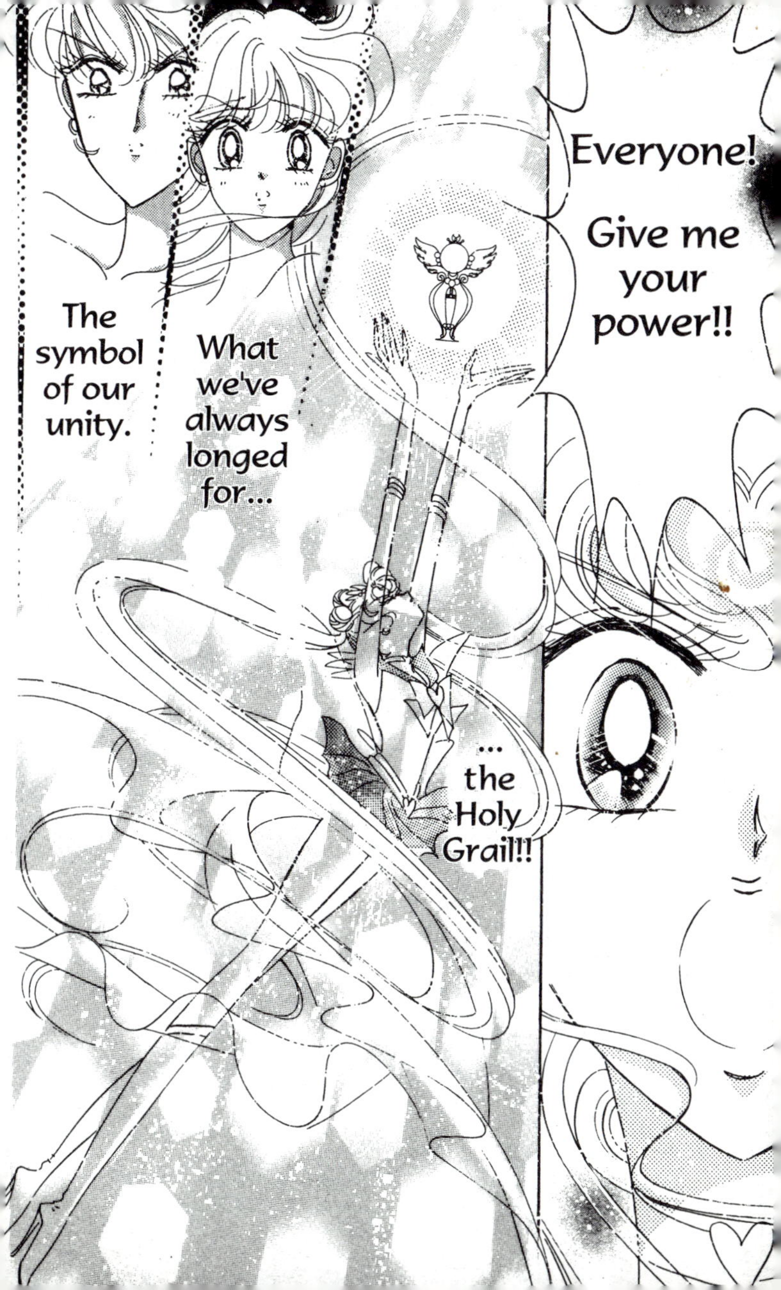
The symbol of our unity.
What we've always longed for...
... the Holy Grail!!
Everyone!
Give me your power!!

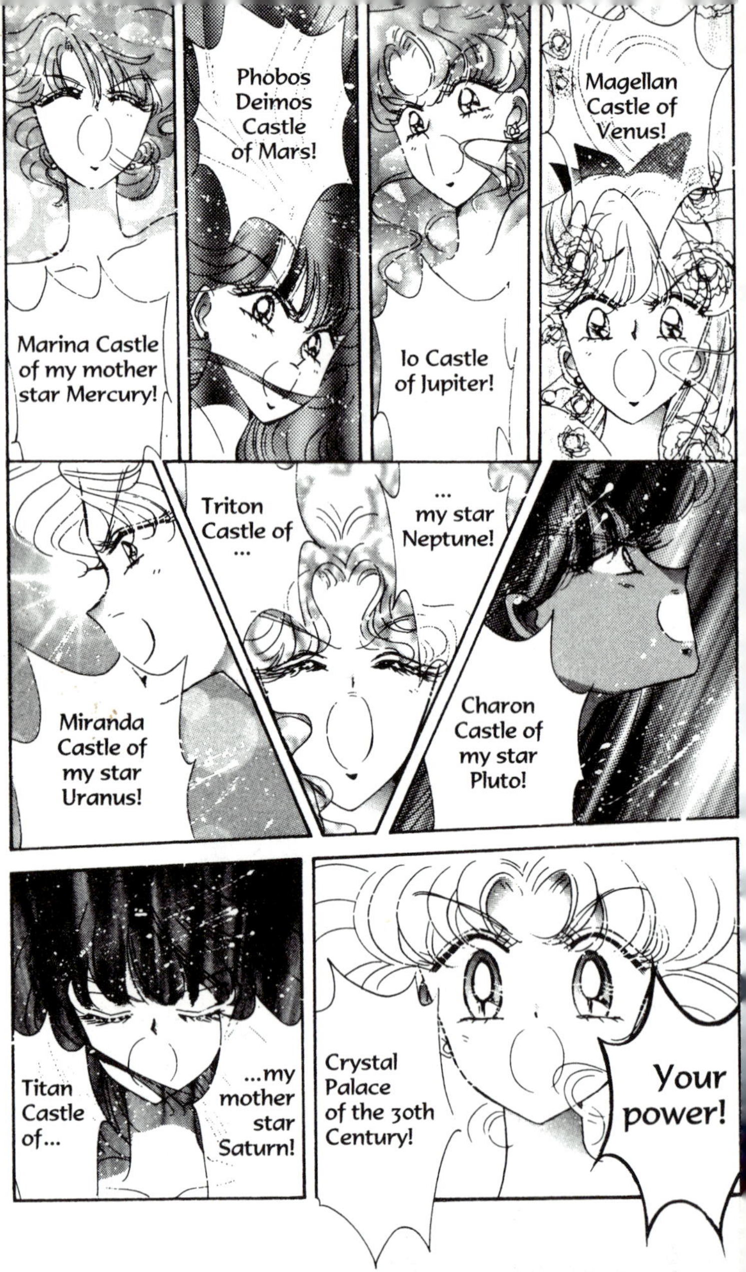
Marina Castle of my mother star Mercury!
Phobos Deimos Castle of Mars!
Io Castle of Jupiter!
Magellan Castle of Venus!
Miranda Castle of my star Uranus!
Triton Castle of ...
... my star Neptune!
Charon Castle of my star Pluto!
Titan Castle of...
...my mother star Saturn!
Crystal Palace of the 30th Century!
Your power!

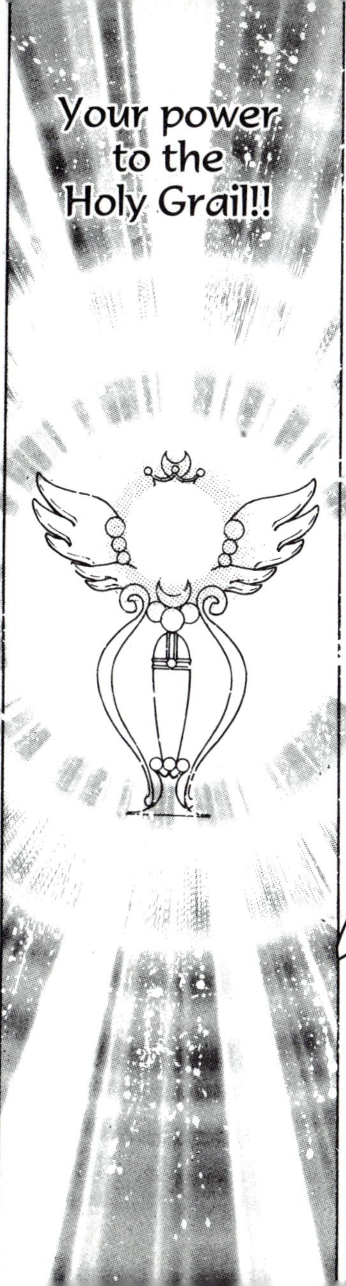
Your power to the Holy Grail!!

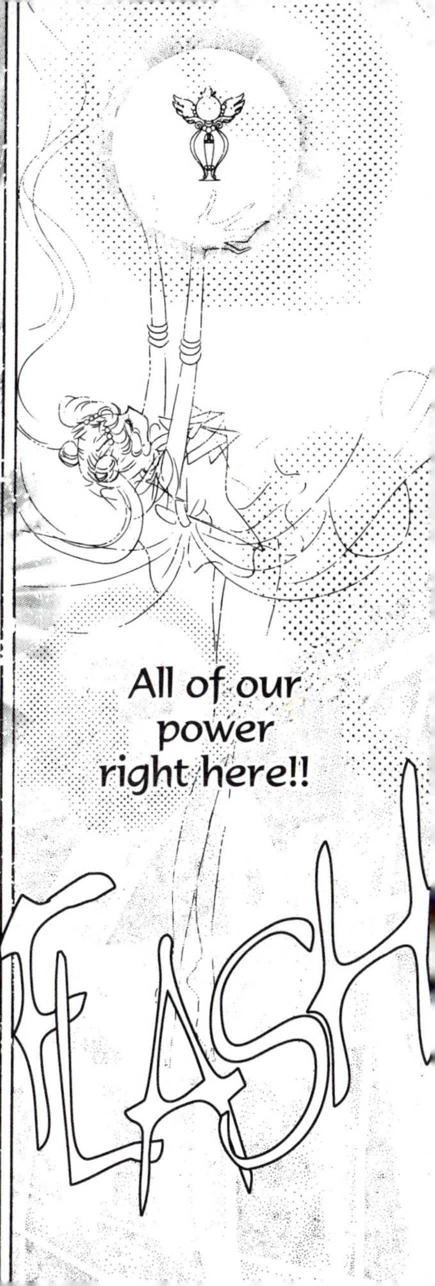
All of our power right here!!
FLASH

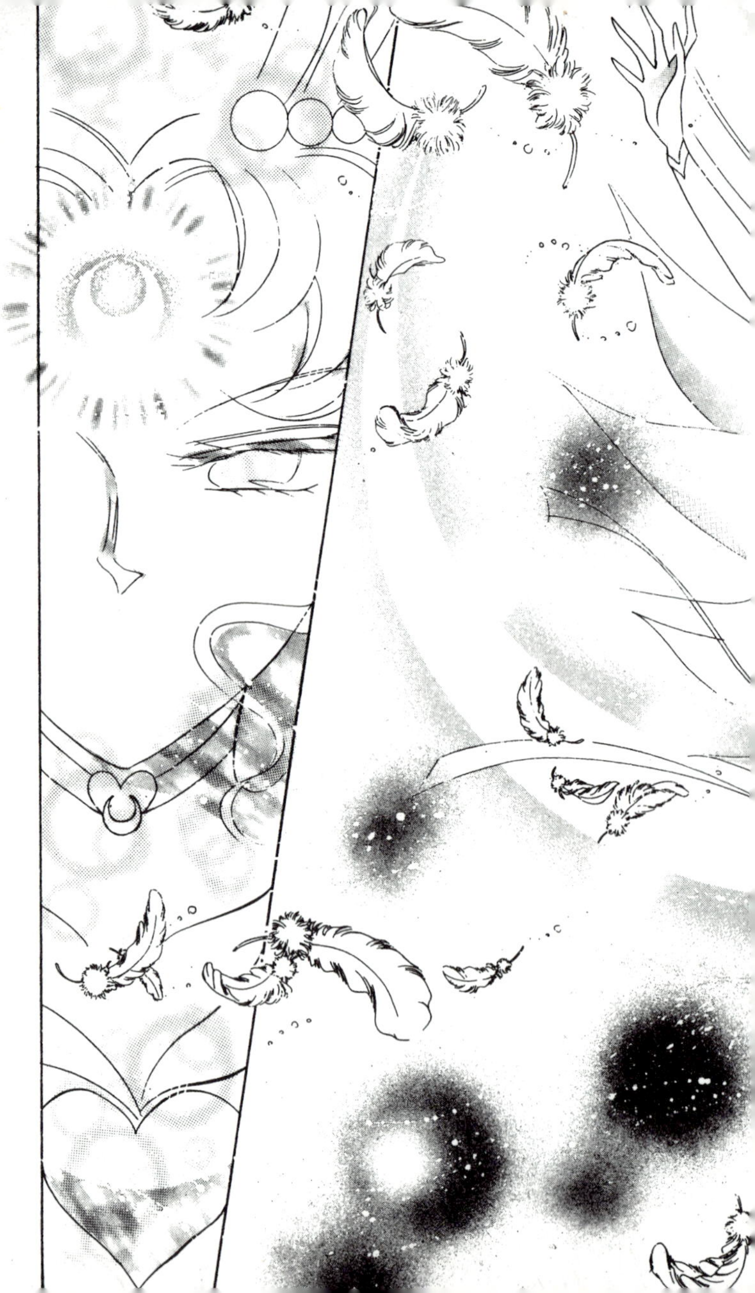

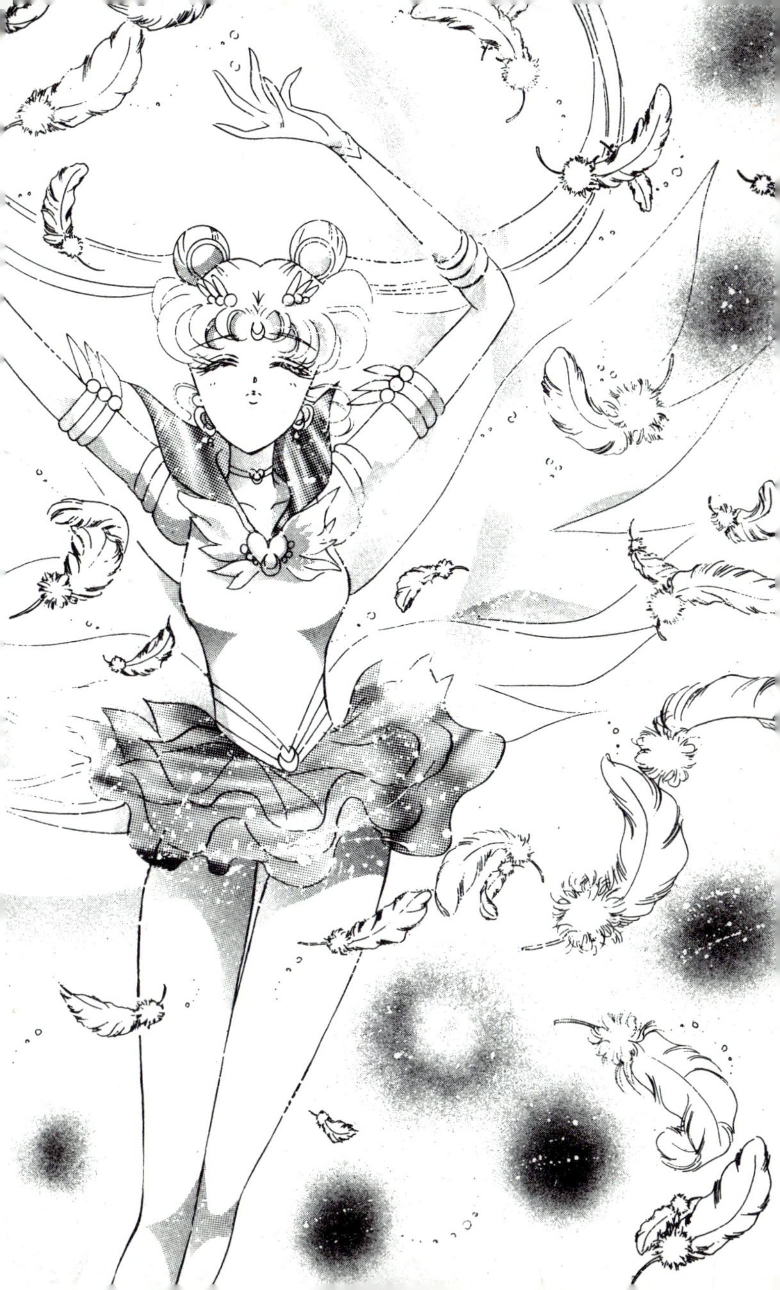

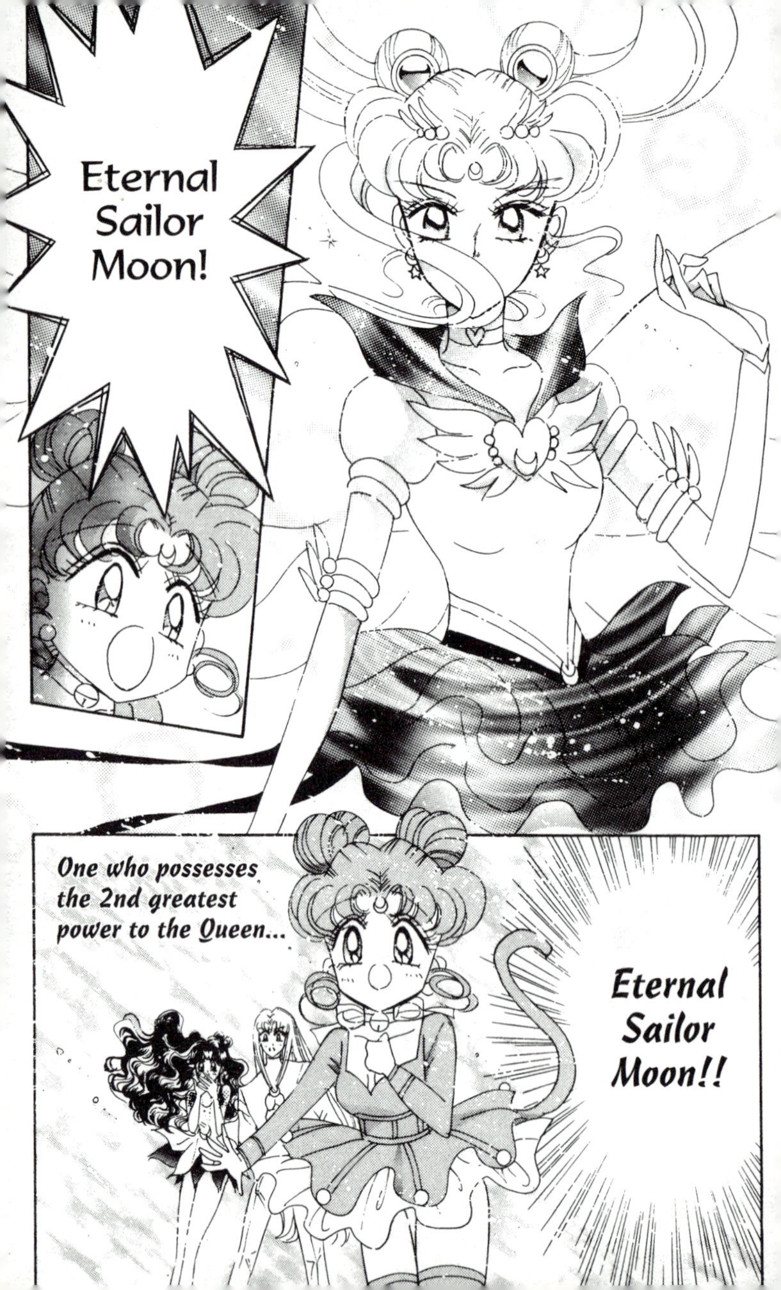
Eternal Sailor Moon!
One who possesses the 2nd greatest power to the Queen...
Eternal Sailor Moon!!

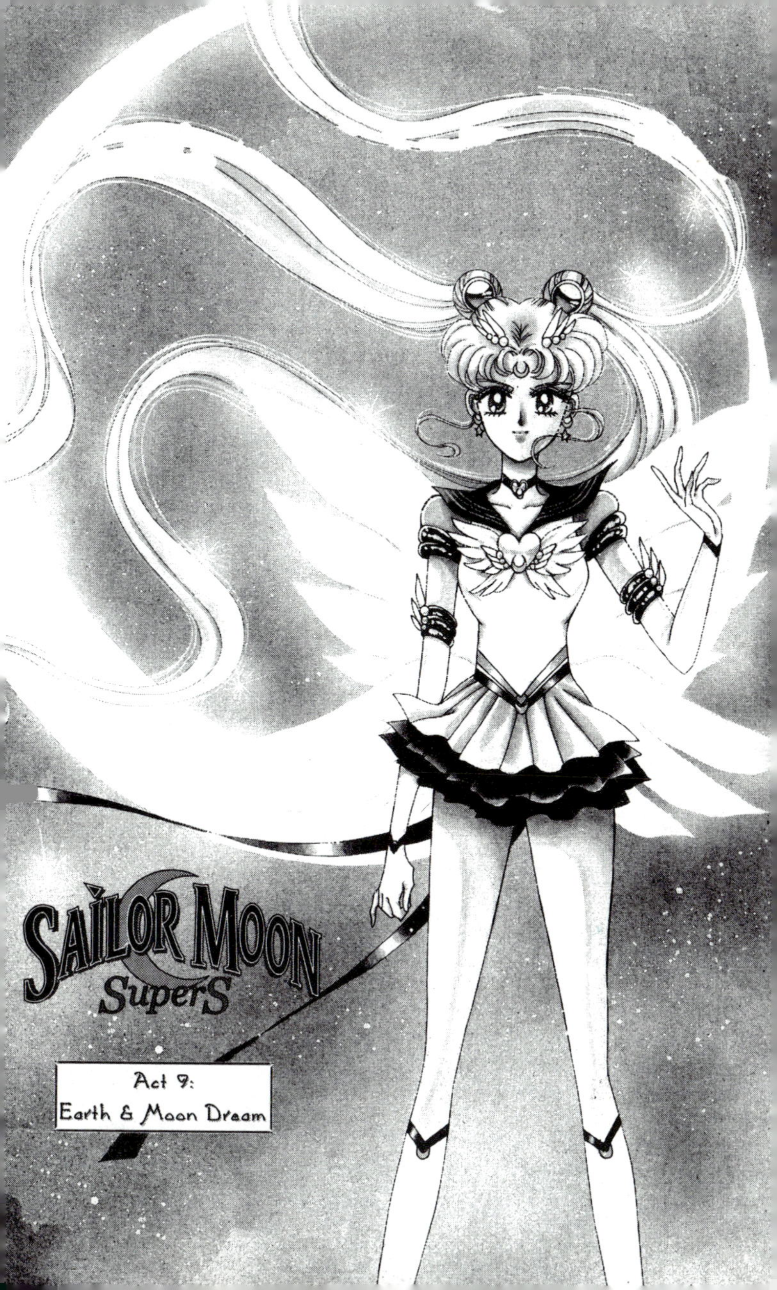

Sailor Moon
SuperS
Act 9:
Earth & Moon Dream

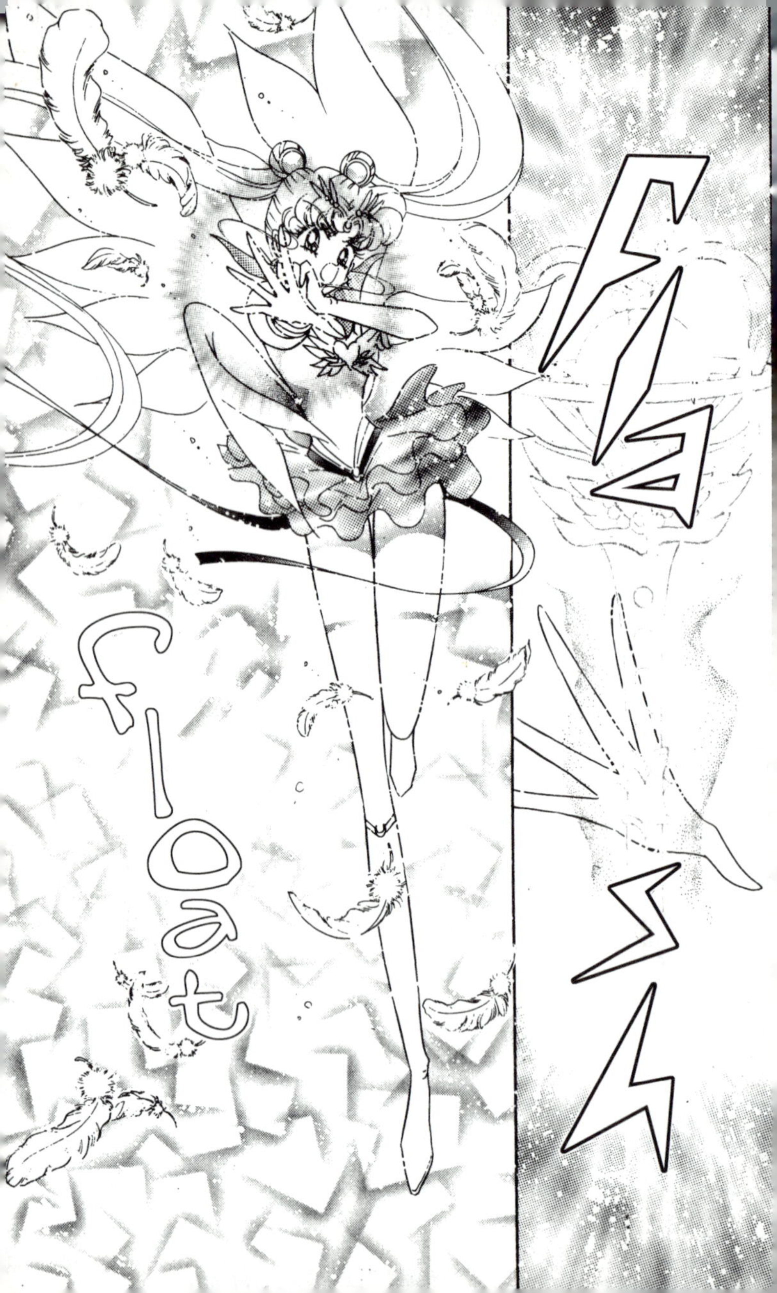
FLASH
float

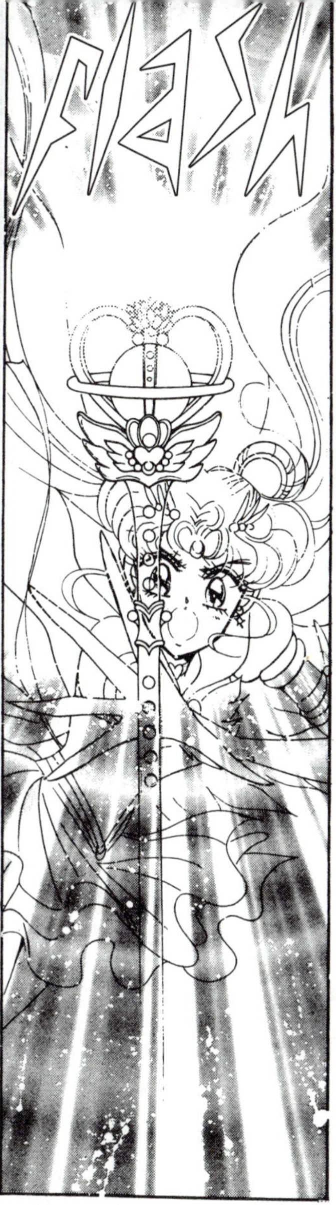
FLASH
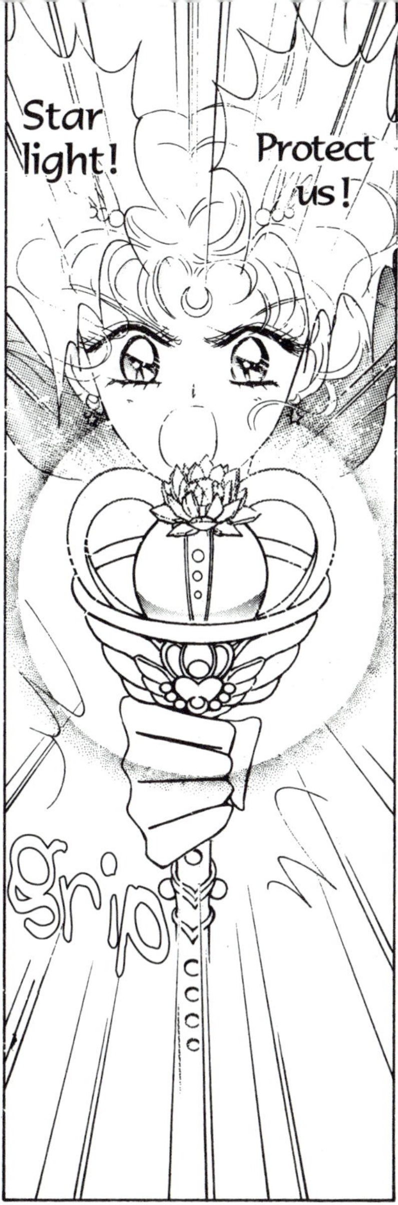
Star light!
Protect us!
grip

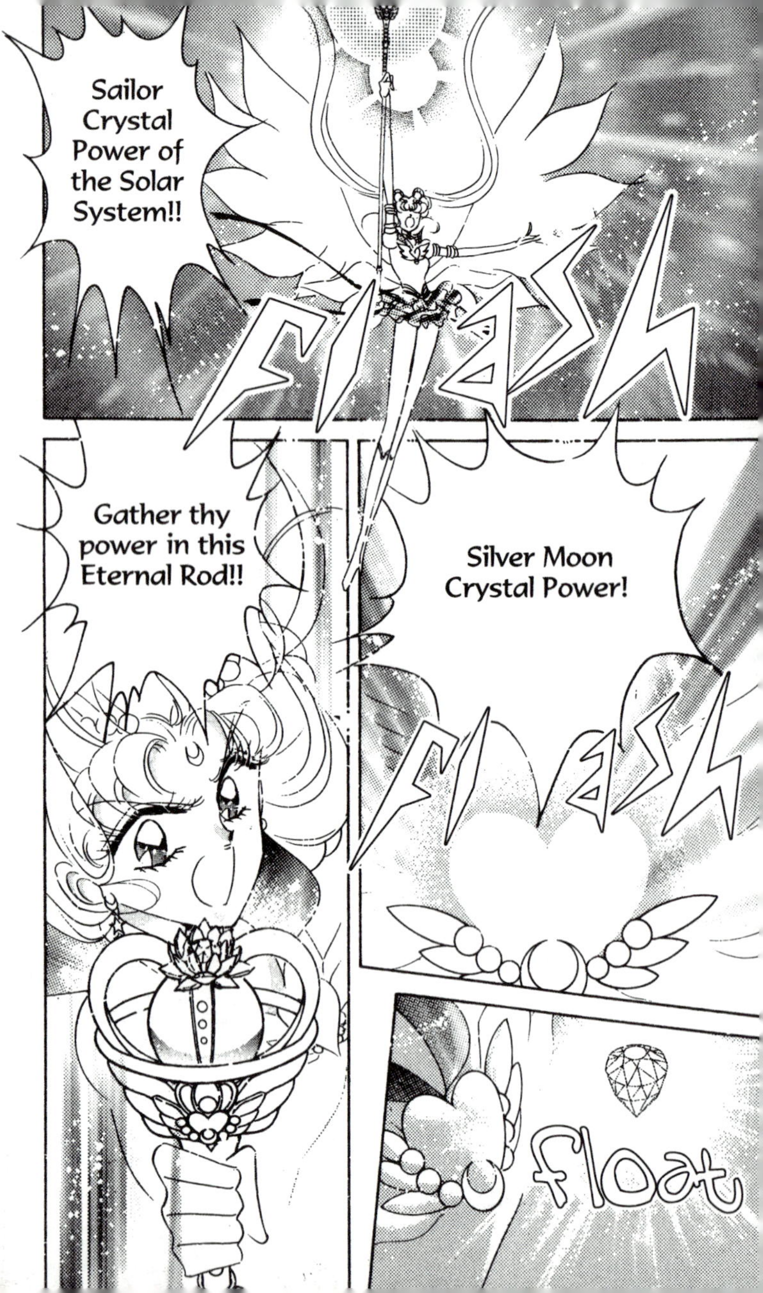
Sailor Crystal Power of the Solar System!!
FLASH
Gather thy power in this Eternal Rod!!
Silver Moon Crystal Power!
FLASH
float

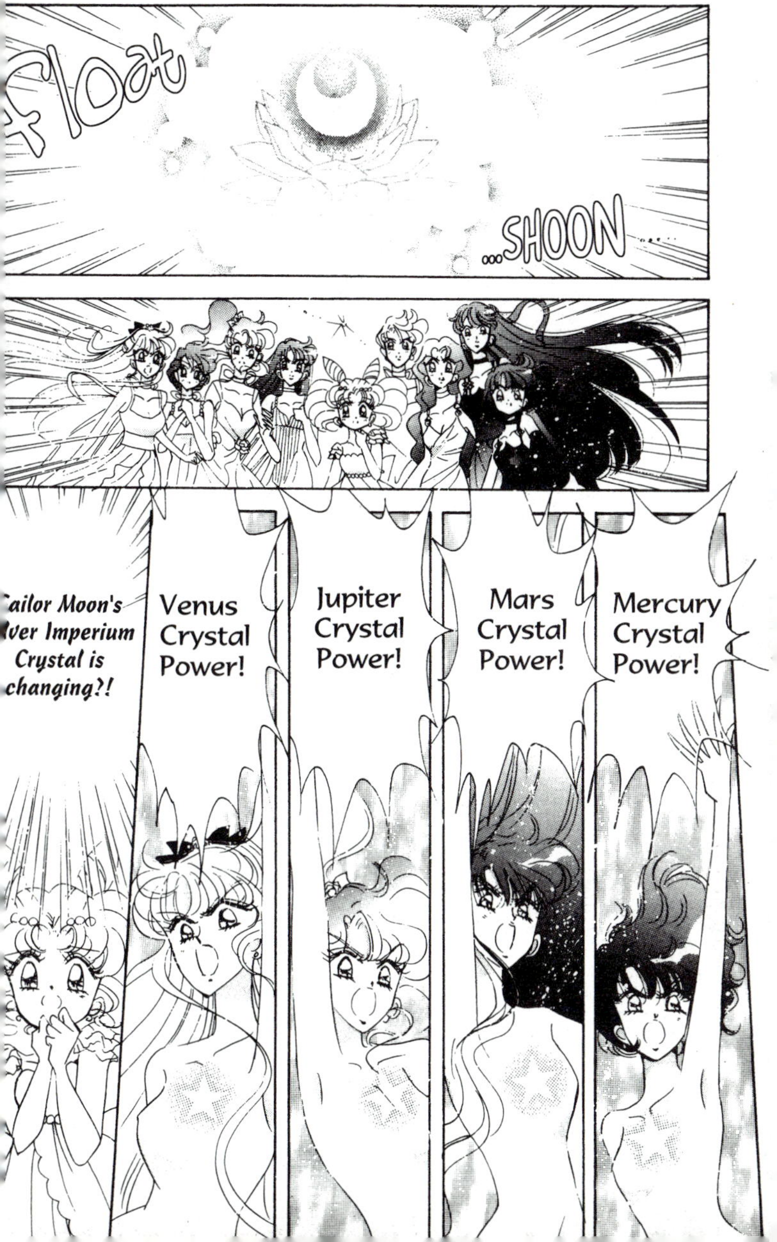
Float
...SHOON...
ailor Moon's
lver Imperium
Crystal is
changing?!
Venus
Crystal
Power!
Jupiter
Crystal
Power!
Mars
Crystal
Power!
Mercury
Crystal
Power!

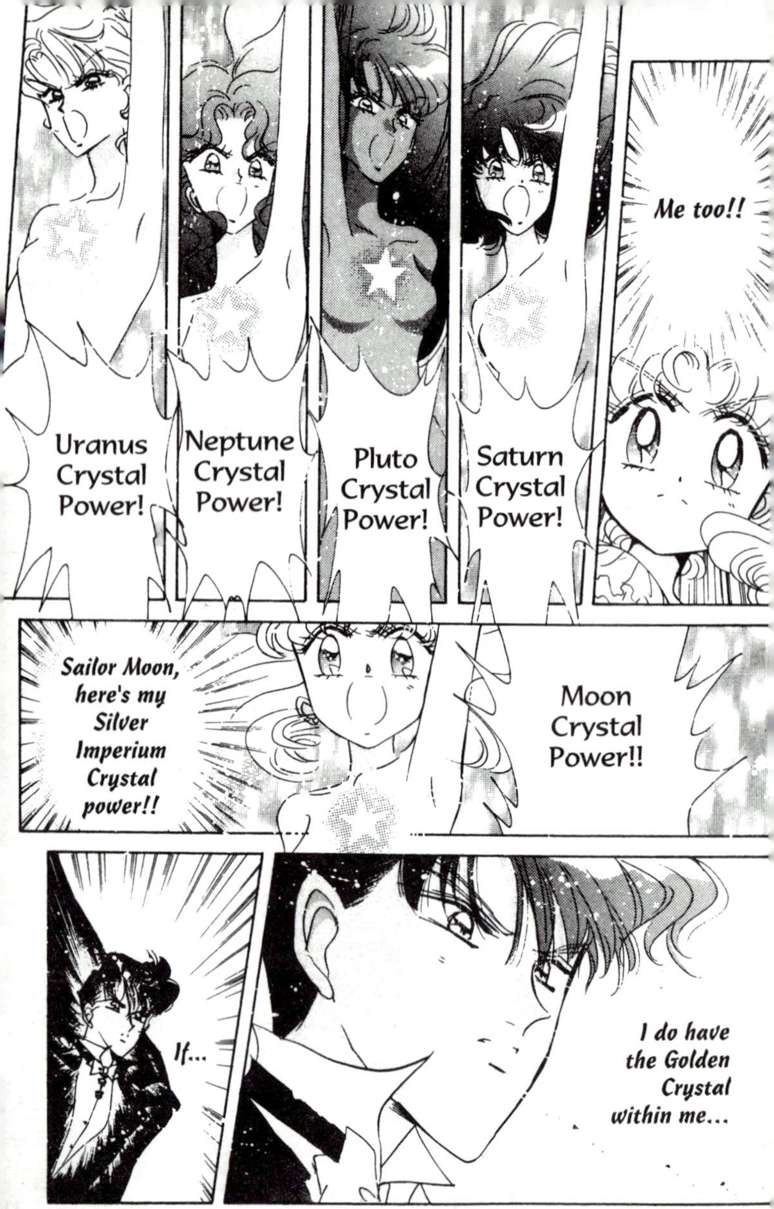
Uranus Crystal Power!
Neptune Crystal Power!
Pluto Crystal Power!
Saturn Crystal Power!
Me too!!
Sailor Moon, here's my Silver Imperium Crystal power!!
Moon Crystal Power!!
If...
I do have the Golden Crystal within me...

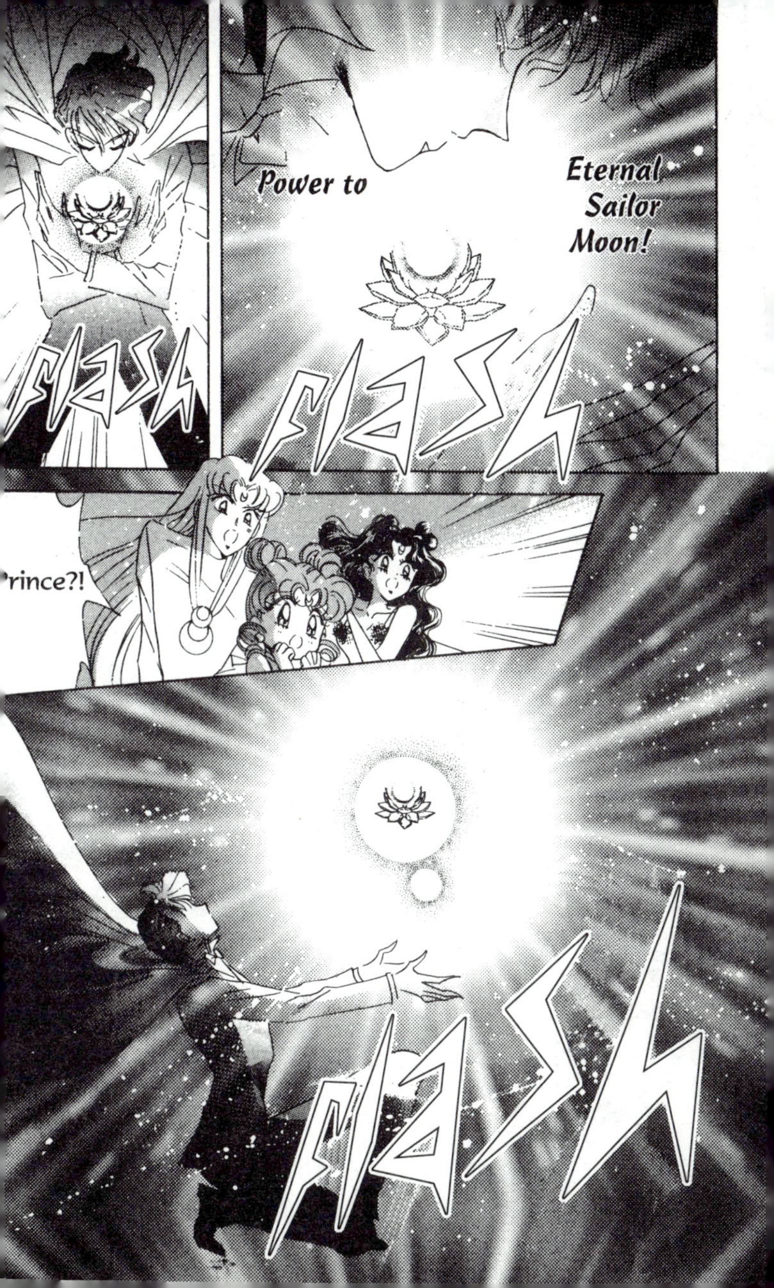
FLASH
Power to
Eternal Sailor Moon!
FLASH
Prince?!
FLASH

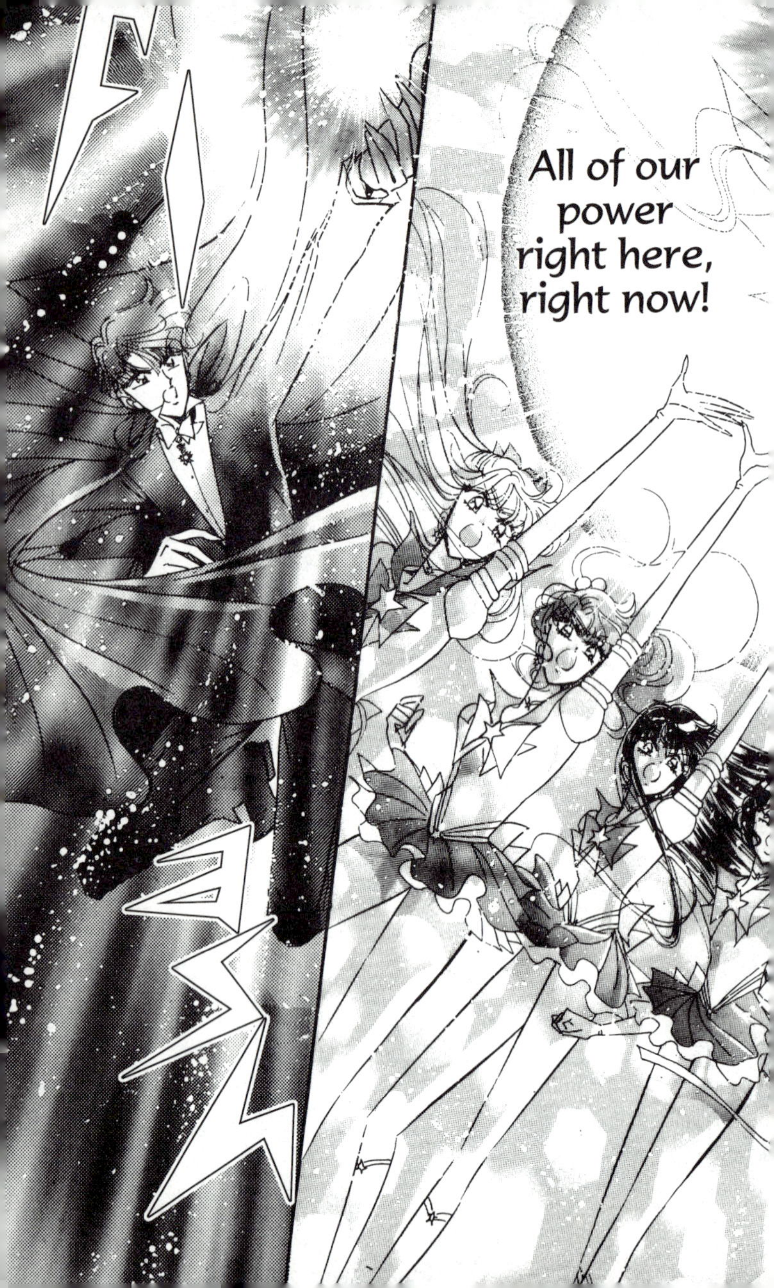
All of our power right here, right now!

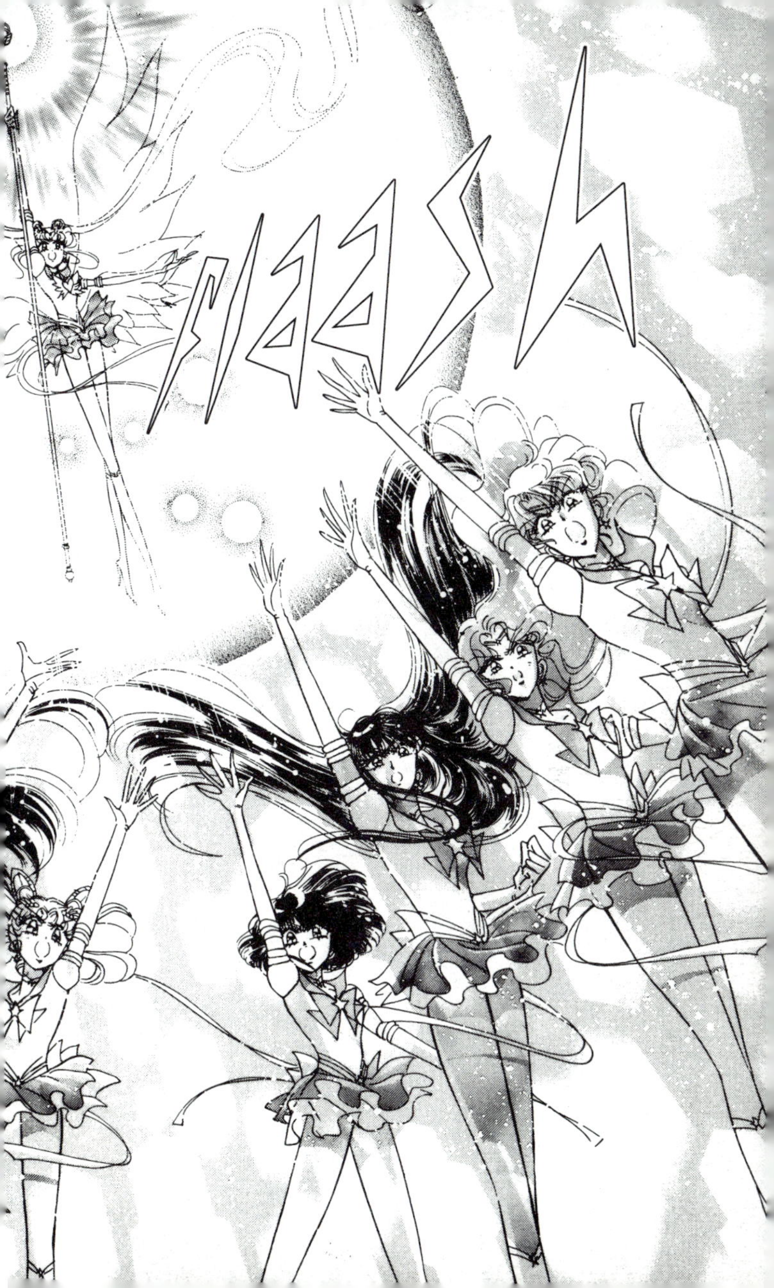
FLAASH

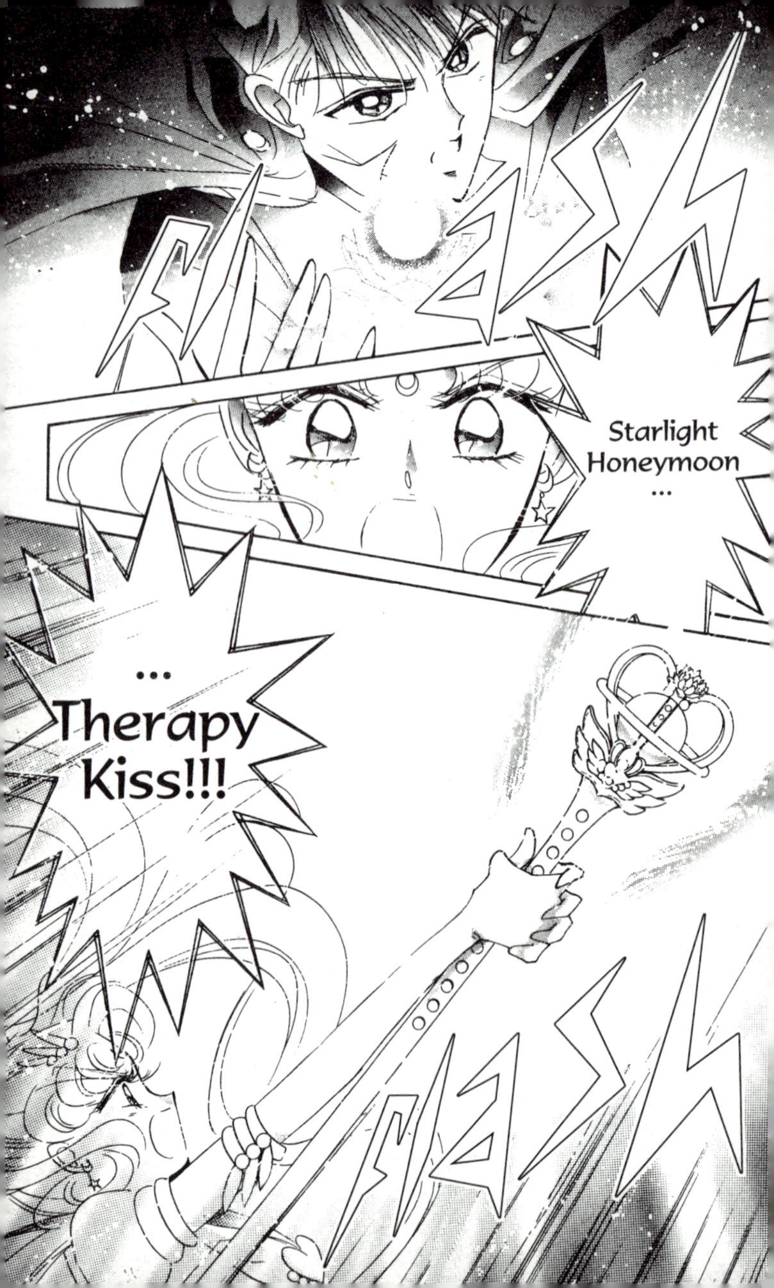
Starlight Honeymoon ...
... Therapy Kiss!!!

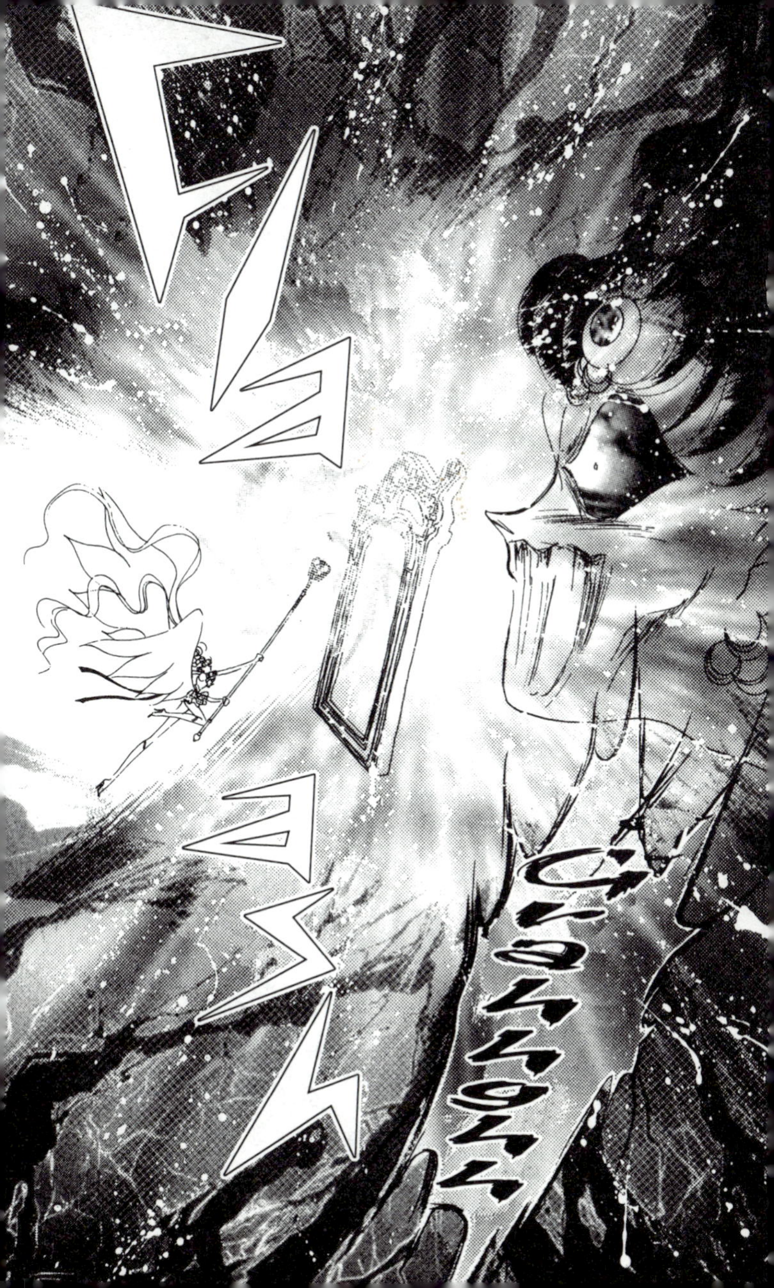

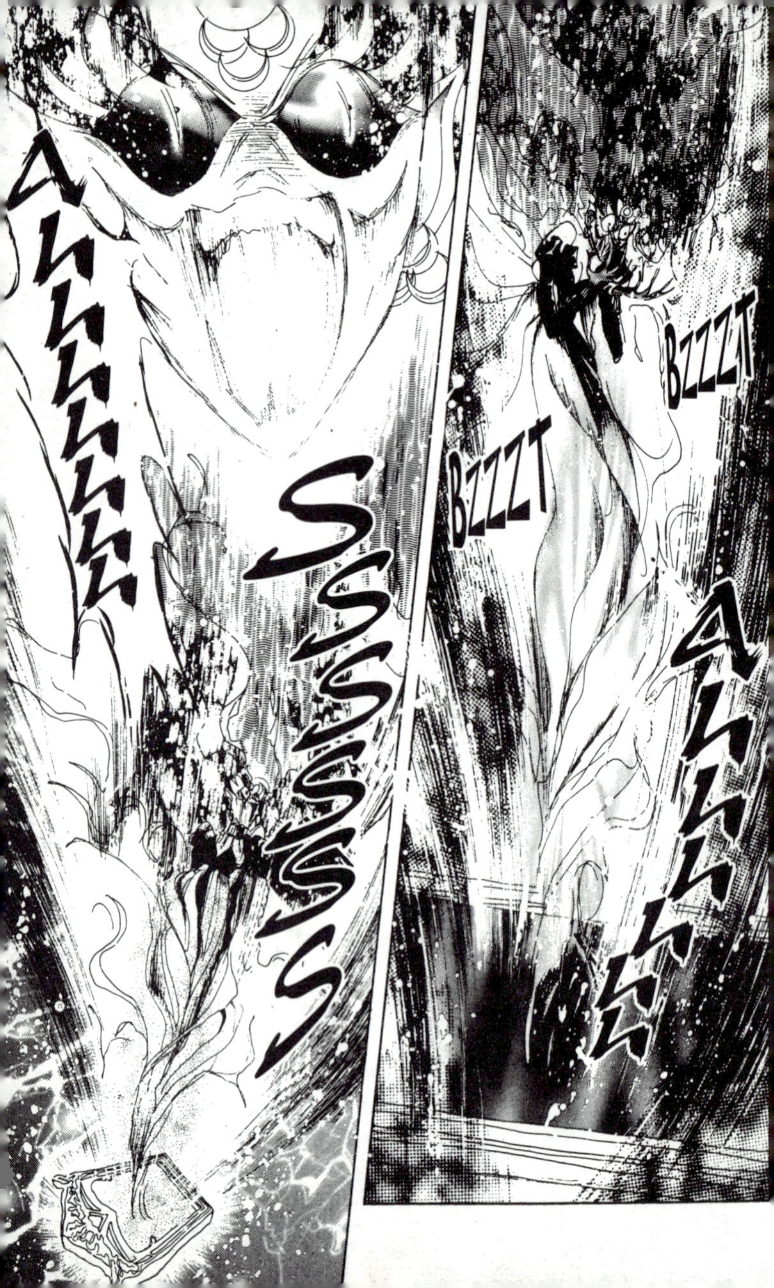
AHHHHHHHH
SSSSSSSSS
BZZZT
BZZZT
AHHHHHH

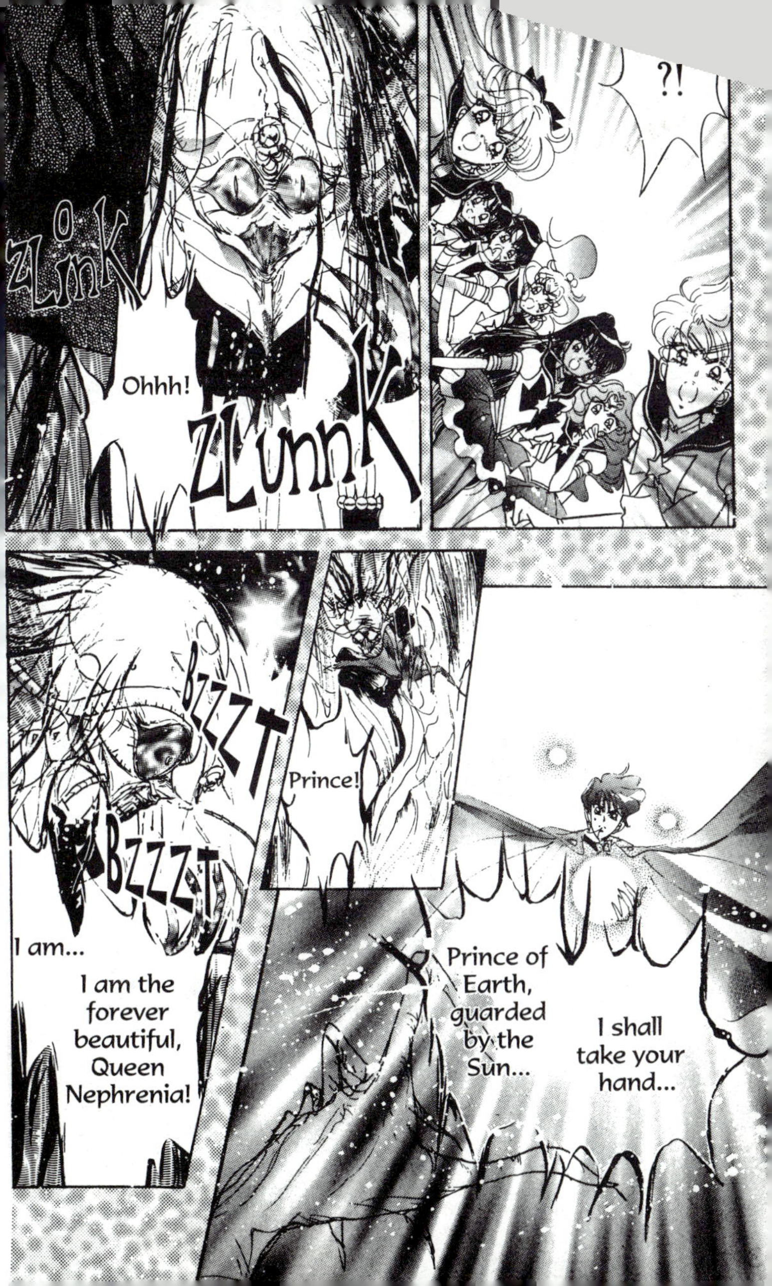
ZLINK
Ohhh!
ZLUNNK
?!
BZZZT
BZZZT
I am...
I am the forever beautiful, Queen Nephrenia!
Prince!
Prince of Earth, guarded by the Sun...
I shall take your hand...

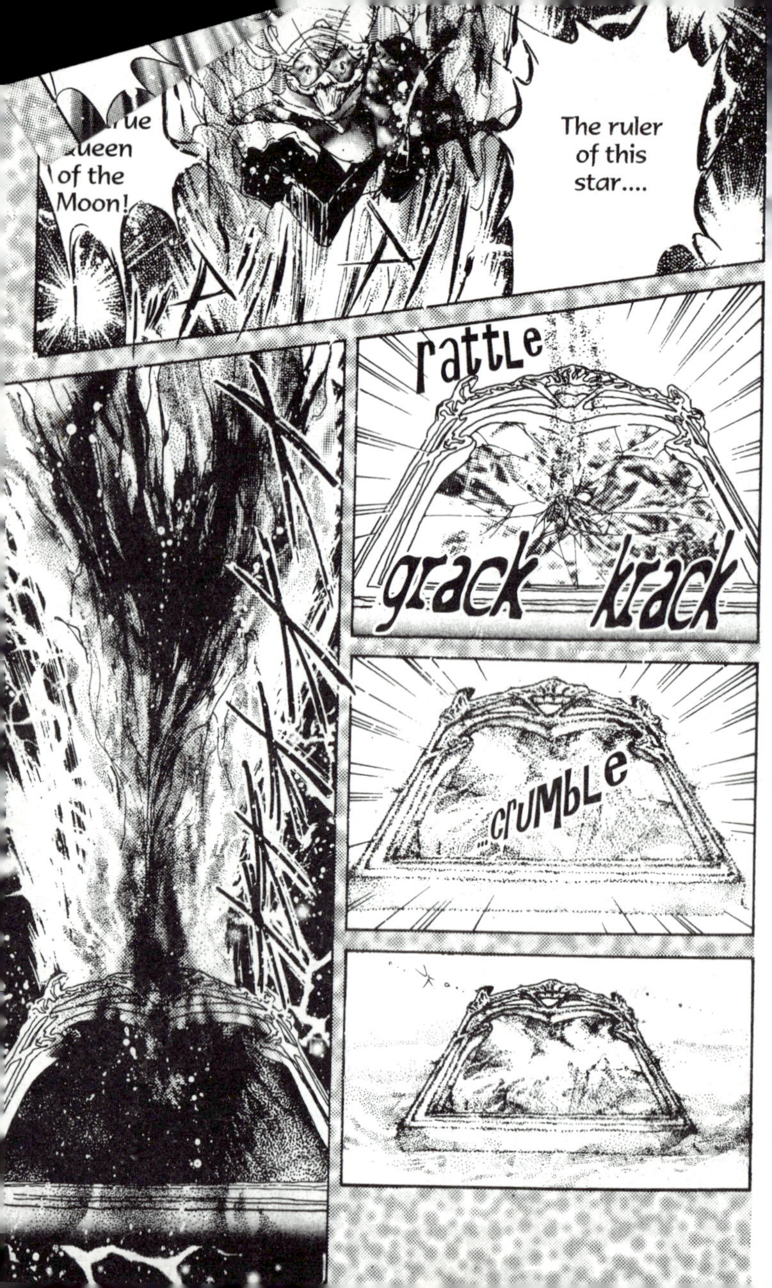
rue ueen of the Moon!
The ruler of this star....
rattle
crack krack
...crumble

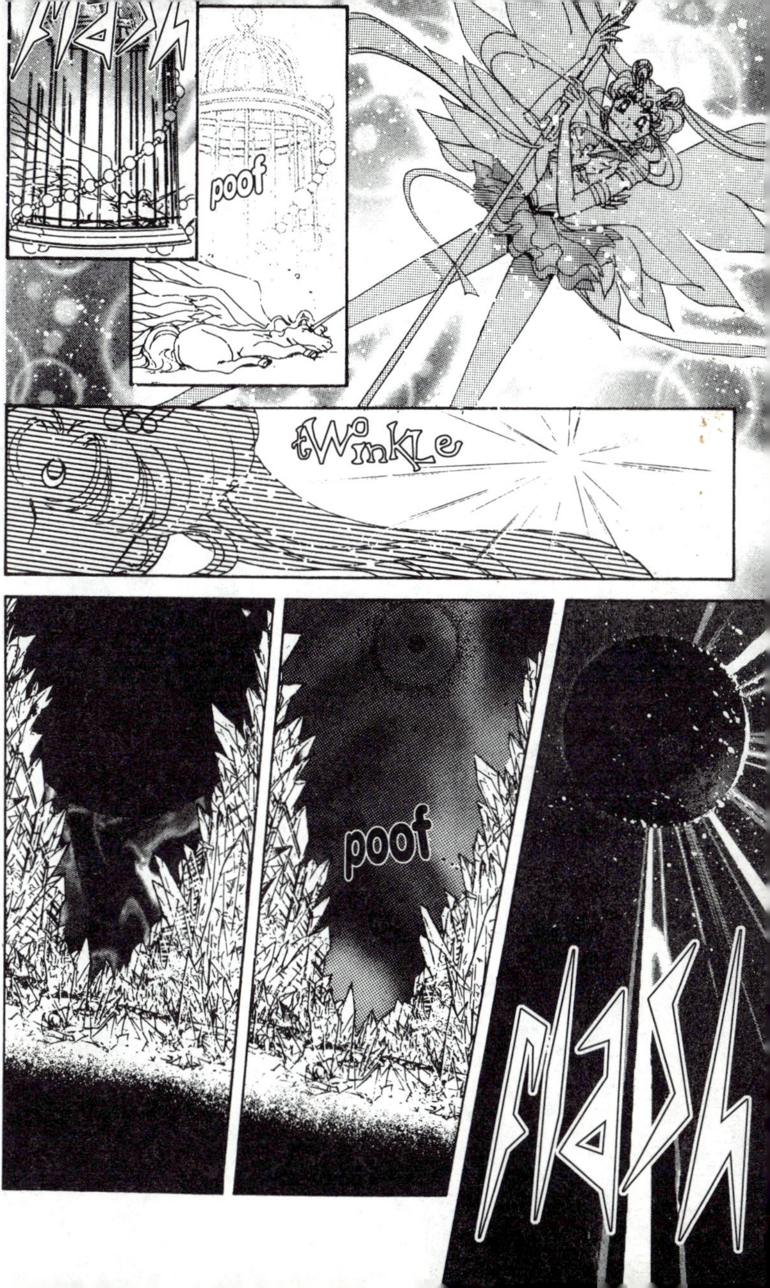
FLASH
poof
twinkle
poof
FLASH

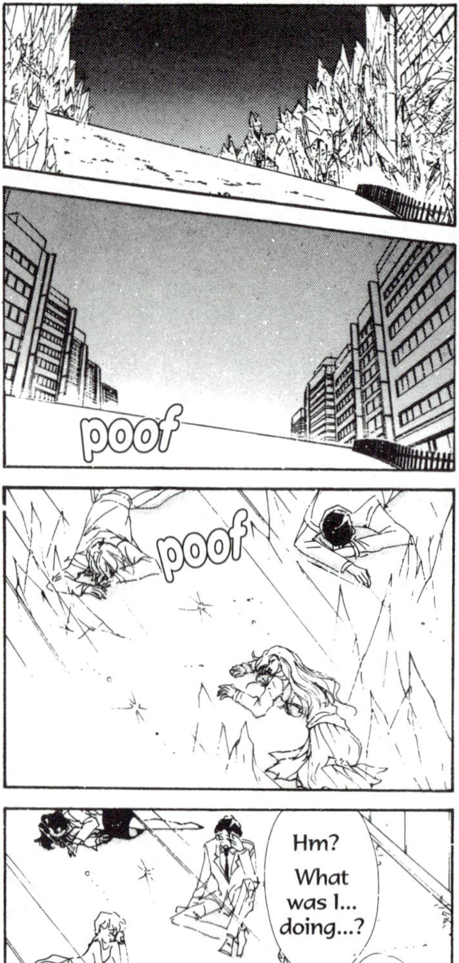
poof
poof
Hm? What was I... doing...?
yawn
Mmm....
How long was I asleep?
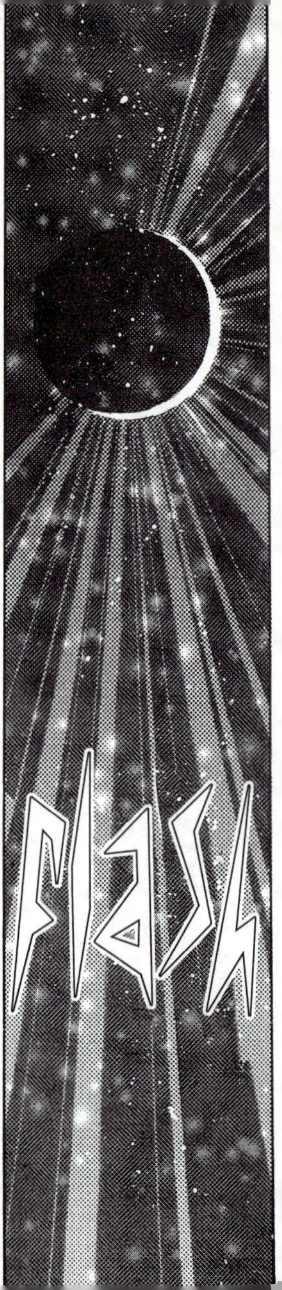
FLASH

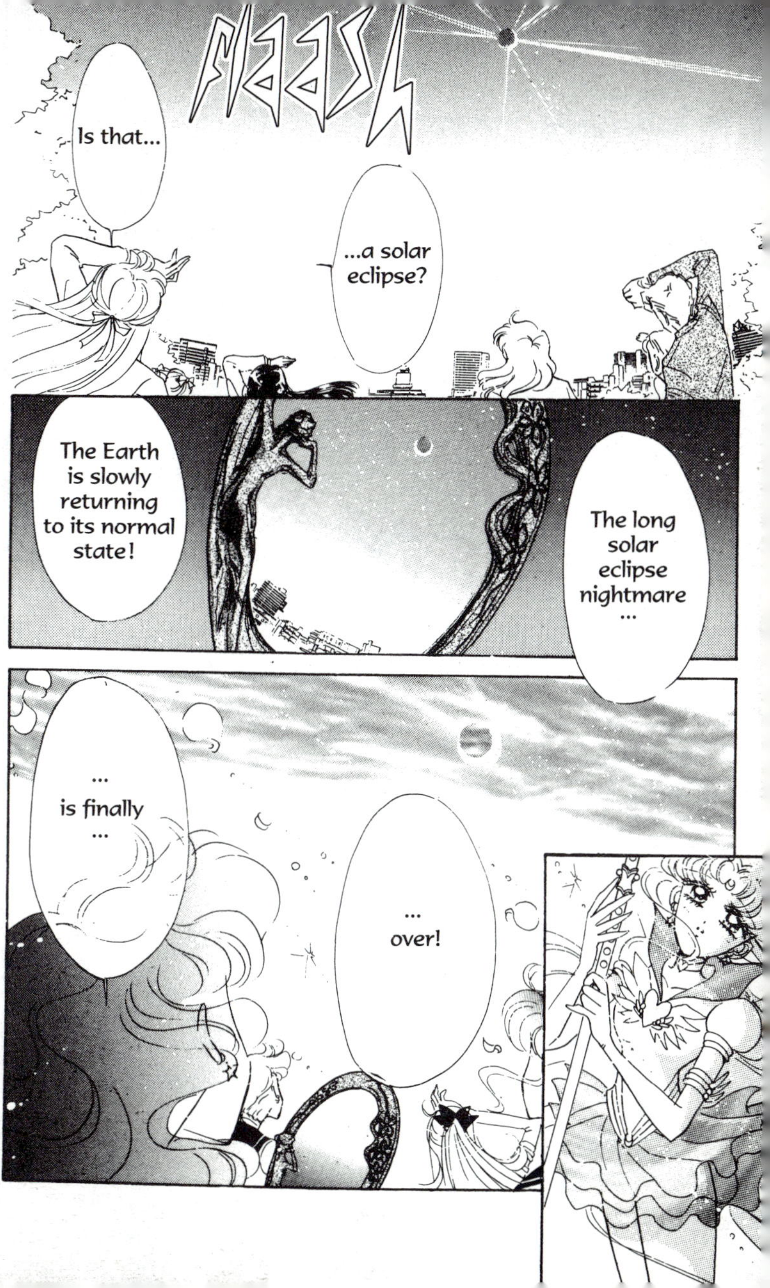
FLAASH
Is that...
...a solar eclipse?
The Earth is slowly returning to its normal state!
The long solar eclipse nightmare ...
... is finally ...
... over!

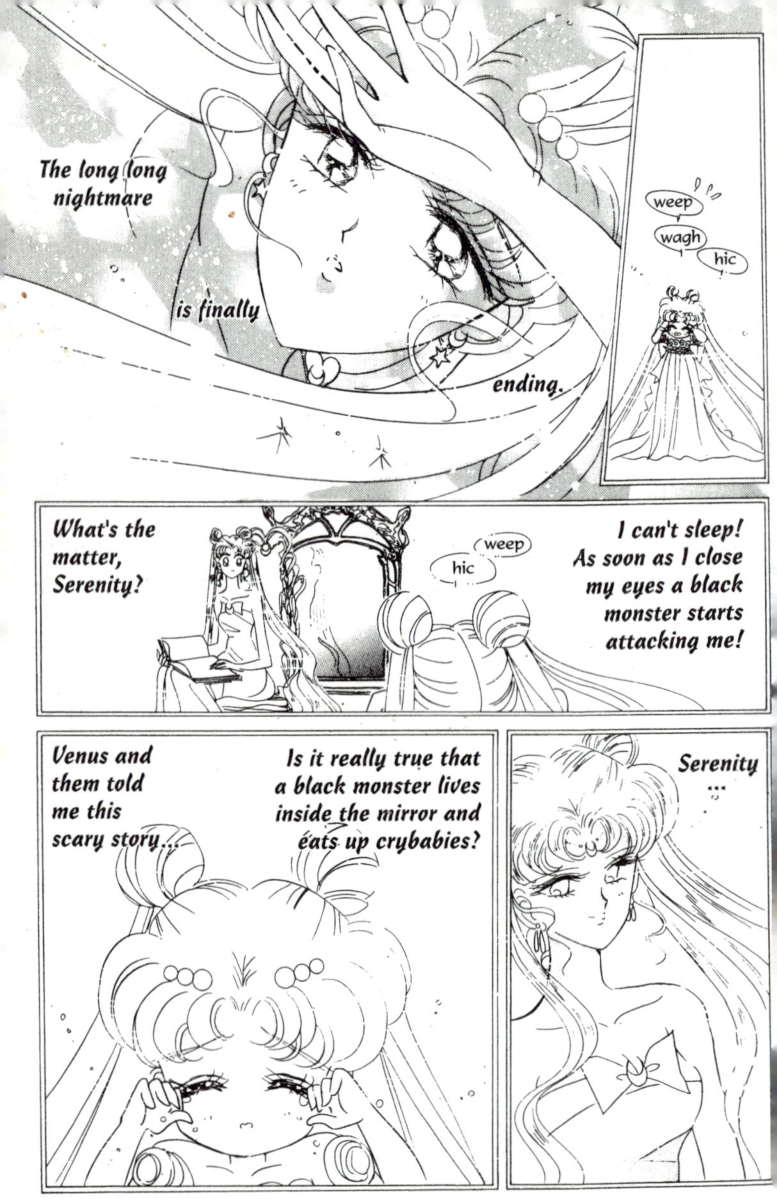
The long long nightmare
is finally
ending.
weep
wagh
hic
What's the matter, Serenity?
hic
weep
I can't sleep! As soon as I close my eyes a black monster starts attacking me!
Venus and them told me this scary story...
Is it really true that a black monster lives inside the mirror and eats up crybabies?
Serenity ...

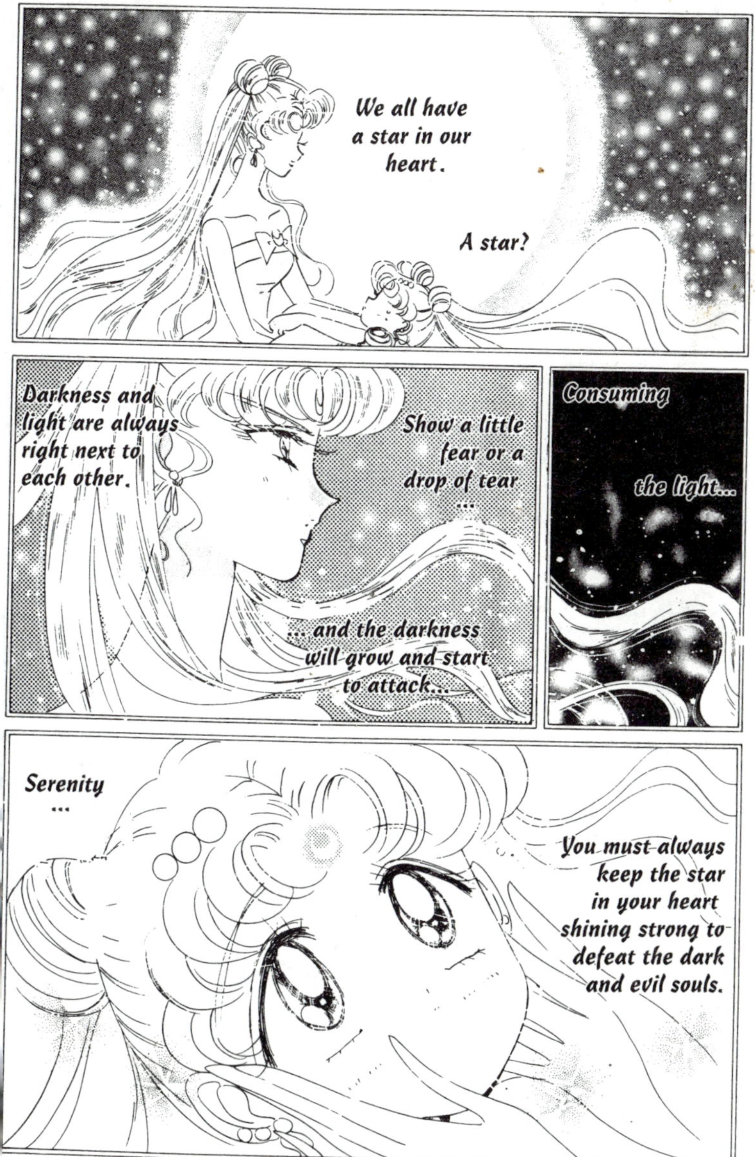
We all have a star in our heart.
A star?
Darkness and light are always right next to each other.
Show a little fear or a drop of tear ...
... and the darkness will grow and start to attack...
Consuming
the light...
Serenity ...
You must always keep the star in your heart shining strong to defeat the dark and evil souls.

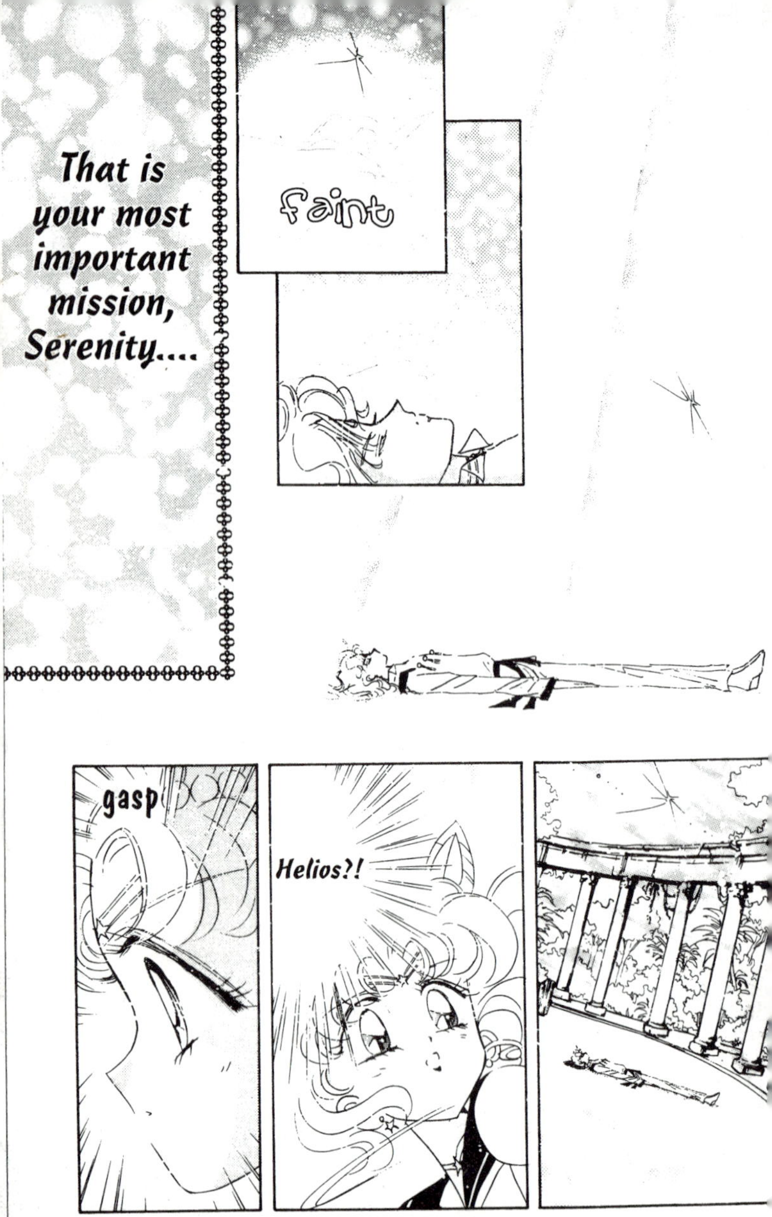
That is your most important mission, Serenity....
faint
gasp
Helios?!

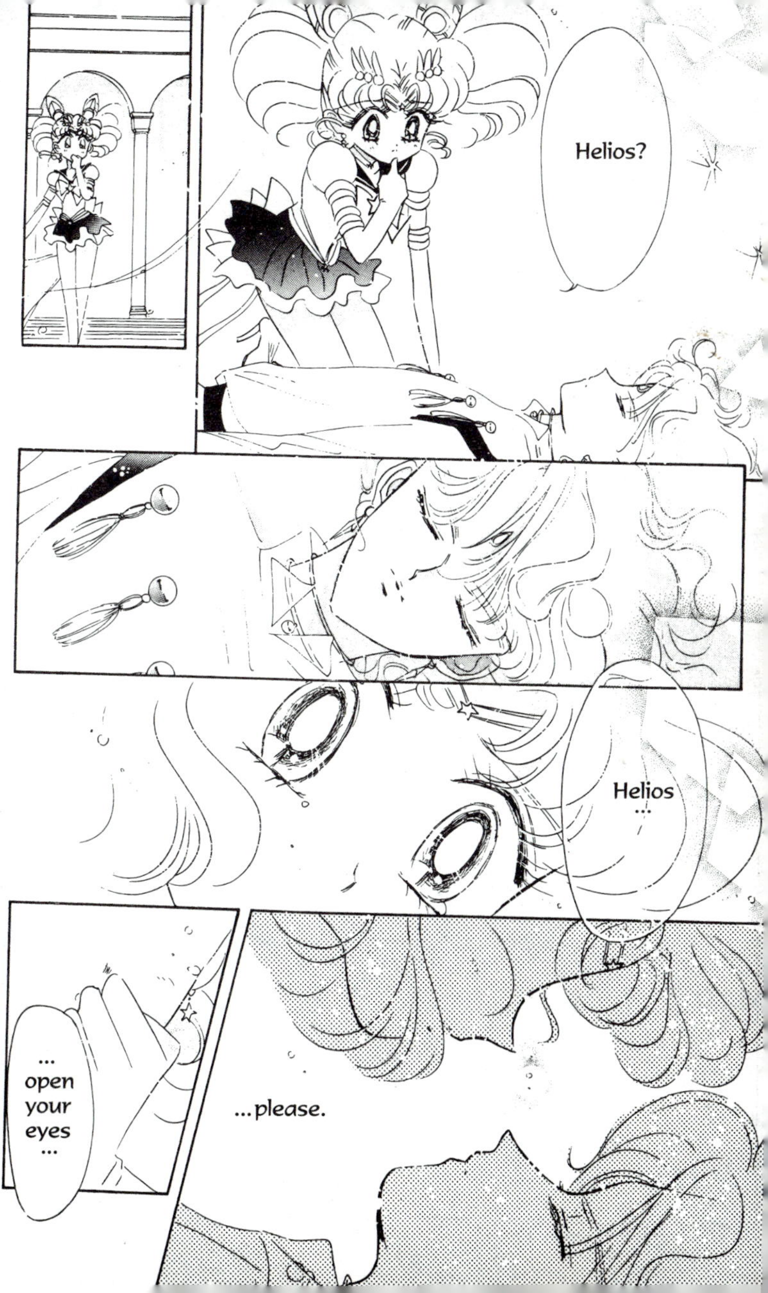

Helios?
Helios ...
... open your eyes ...
...please.

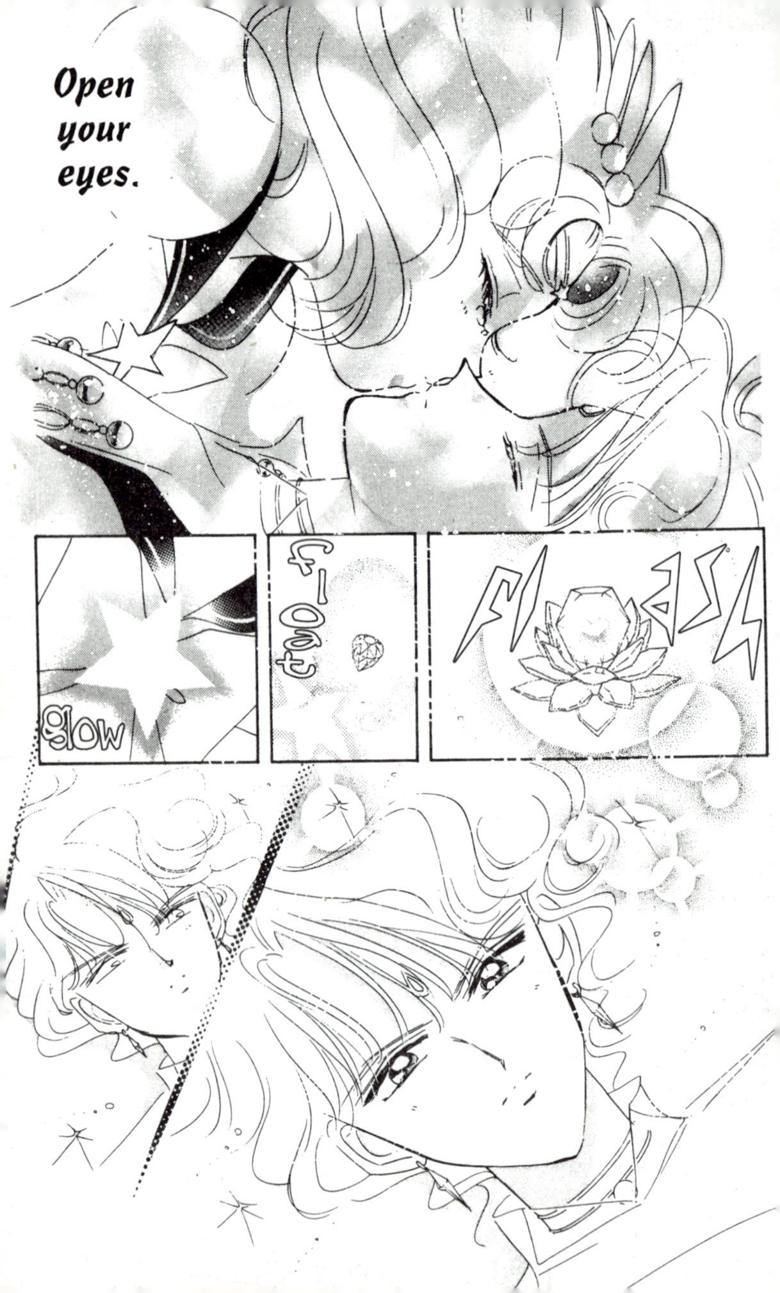
Open your eyes.
glow
float
flash

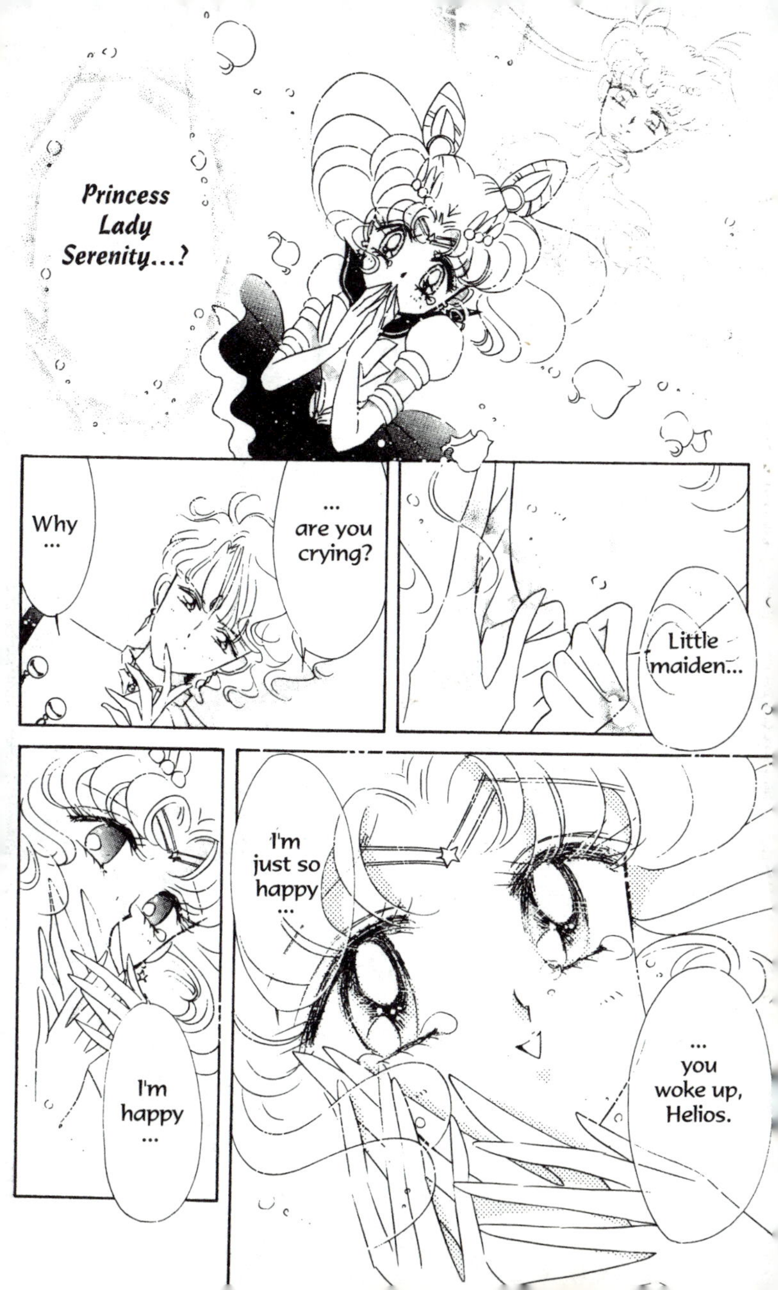
Princess Lady Serenity...?
Why ...
... are you crying?
Little maiden...
I'm happy ...
I'm just so happy ...
... you woke up, Helios.

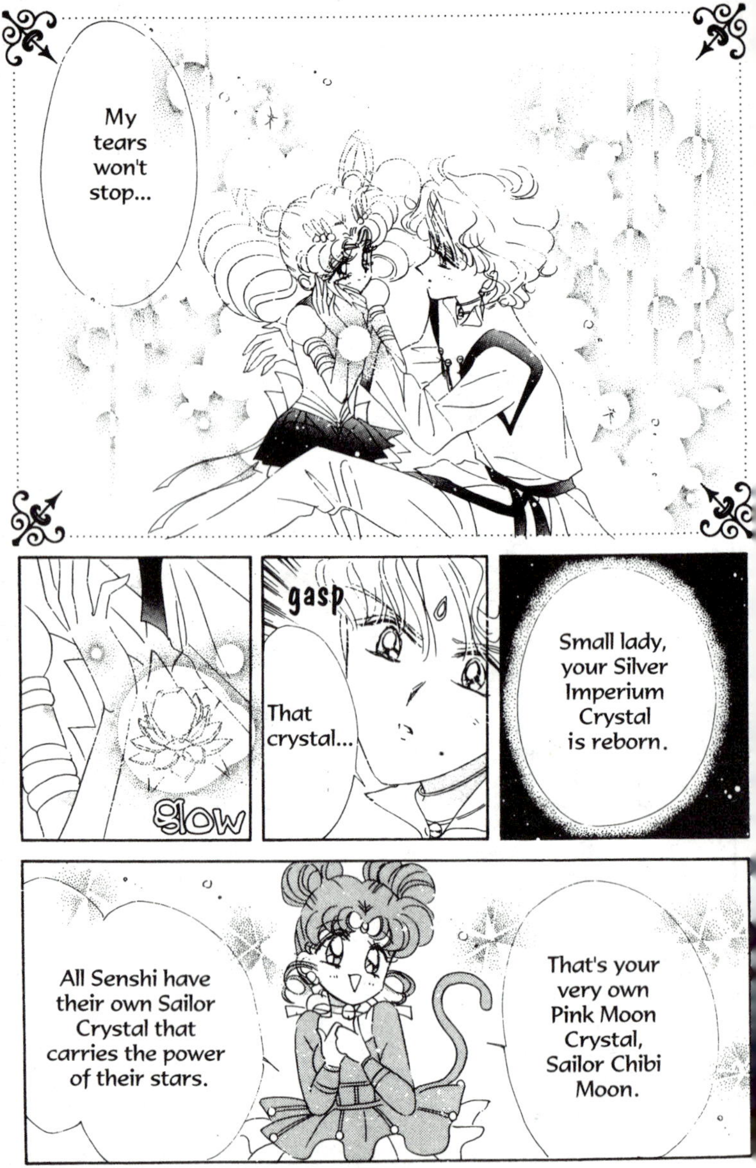
My tears won't stop...
glow
gasp
That crystal...
Small lady, your Silver Imperium Crystal is reborn.
All Senshi have their own Sailor Crystal that carries the power of their stars.
That's your very own Pink Moon Crystal, Sailor Chibi Moon.

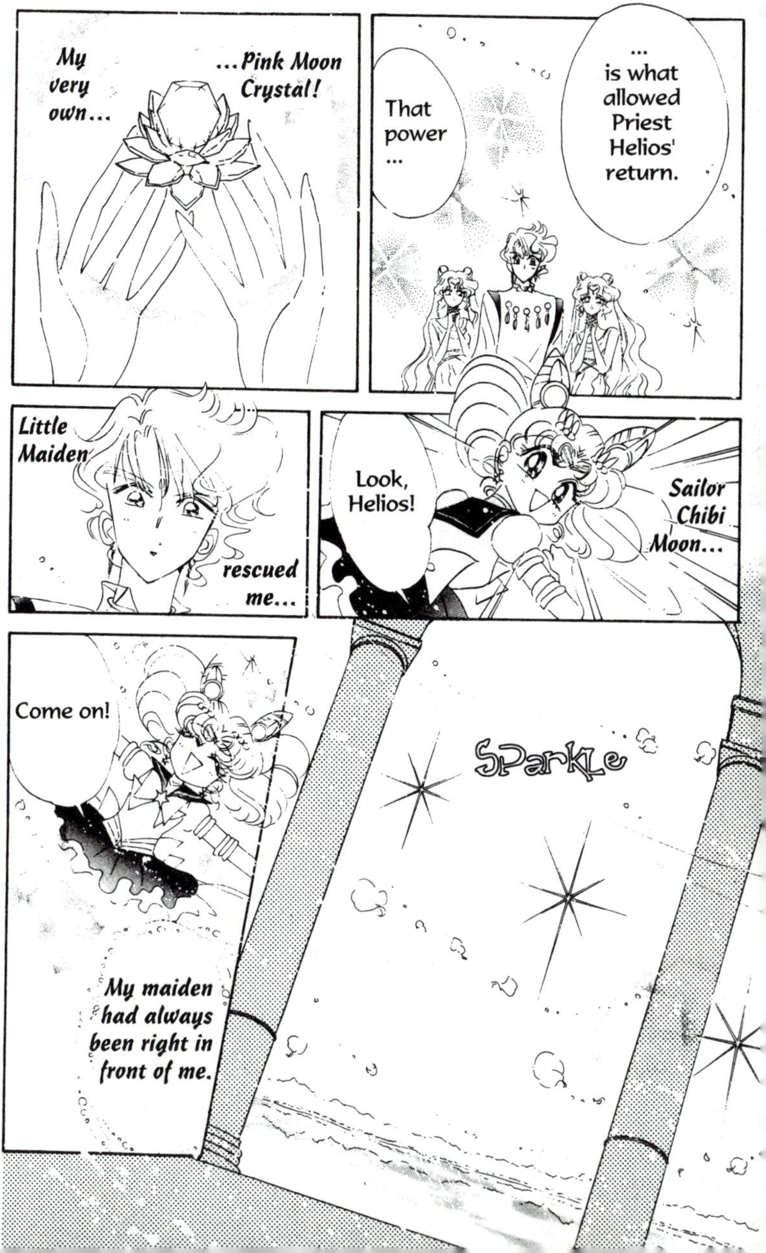
My very own...
...Pink Moon Crystal!
That power ...
... is what allowed Priest Helios' return.
Little Maiden
rescued me...
Look, Helios!
Sailor Chibi Moon...
Come on!
My maiden had always been right in front of me.
SPARKLE

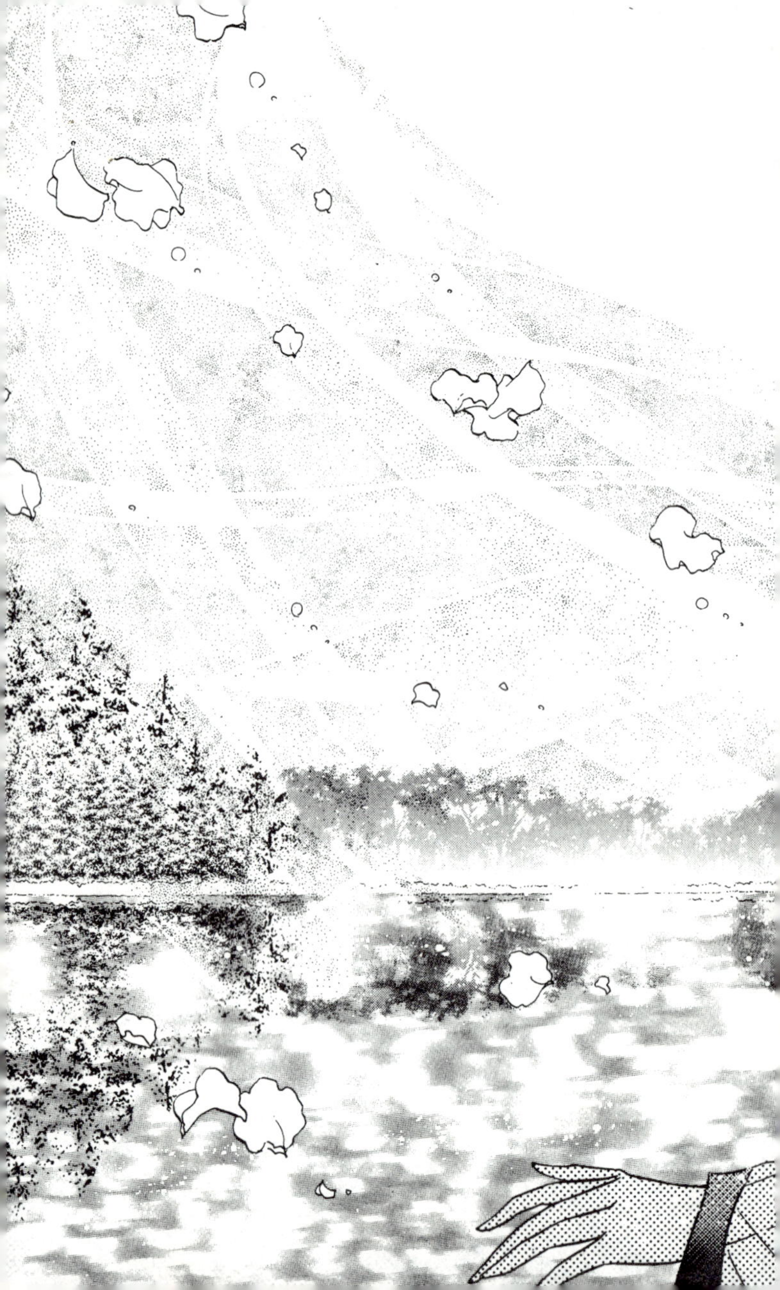

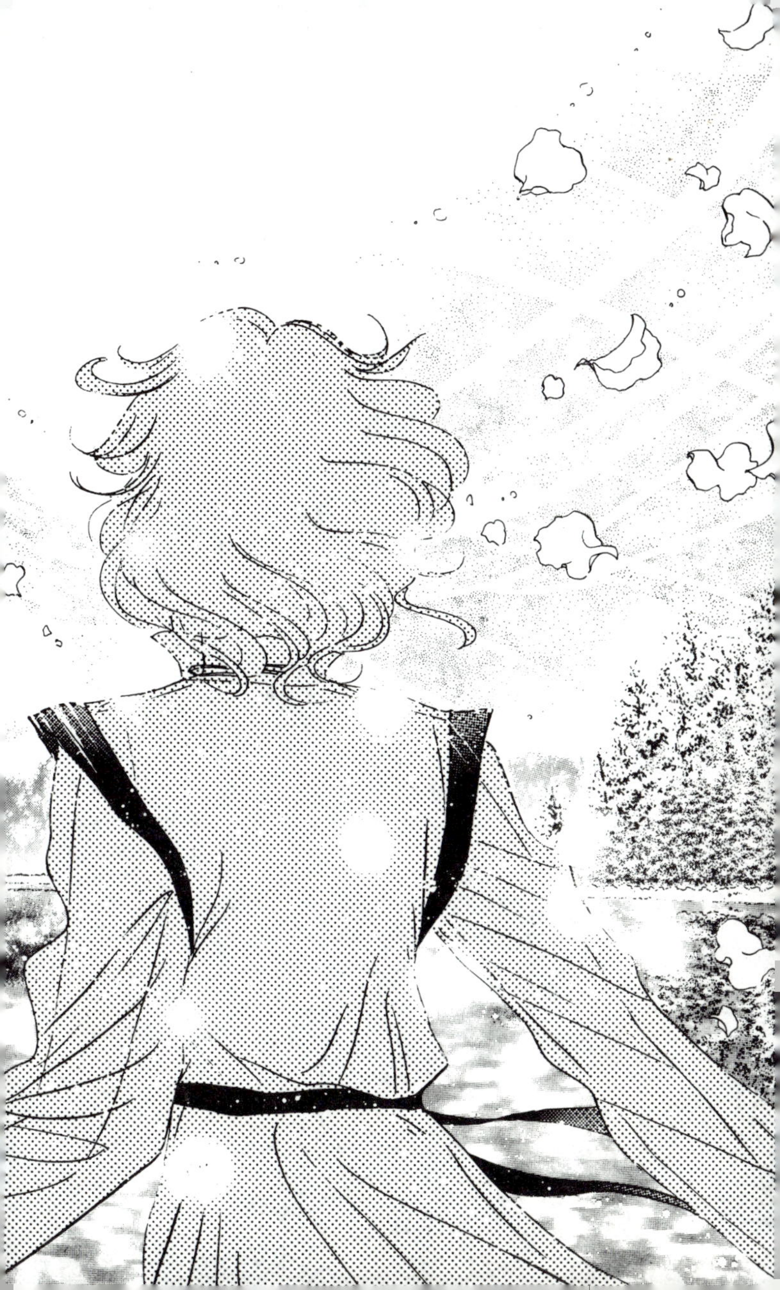

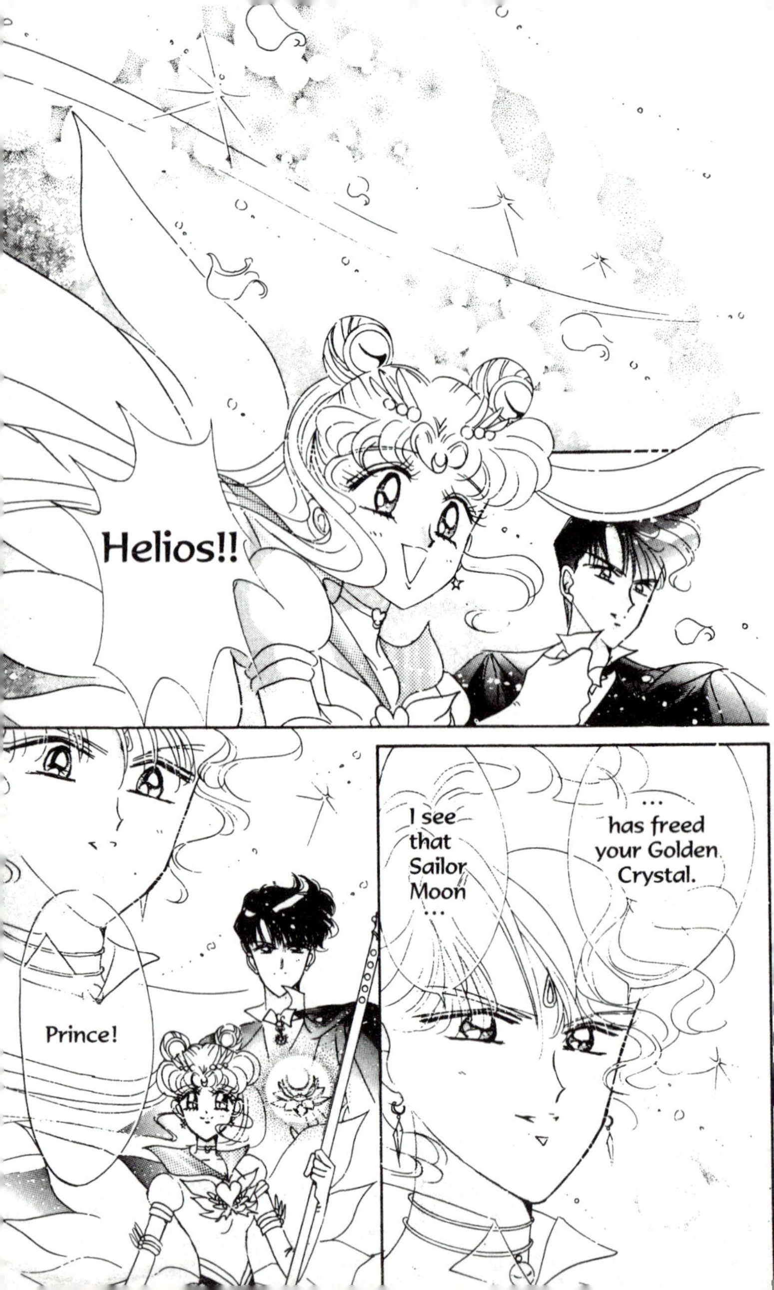
Helios!!
Prince!
I see that Sailor Moon ...
... has freed your Golden Crystal.

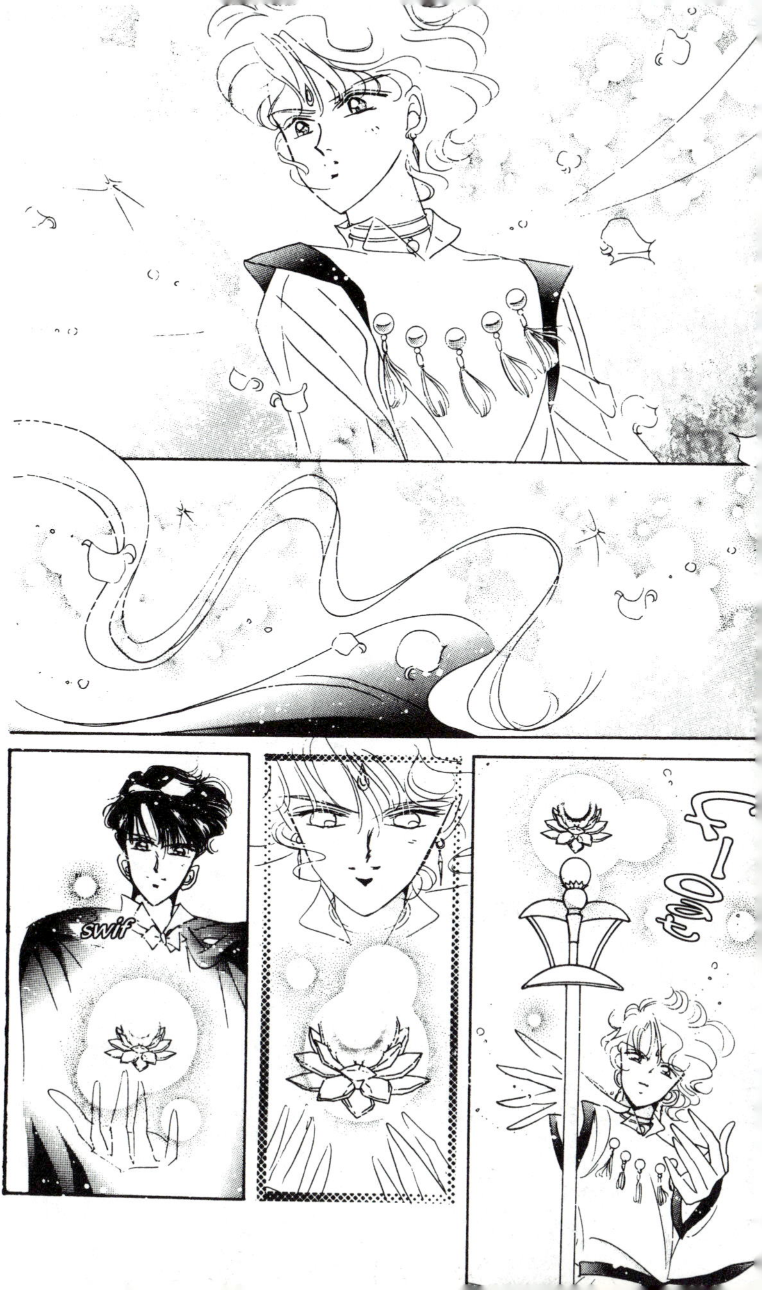
swif

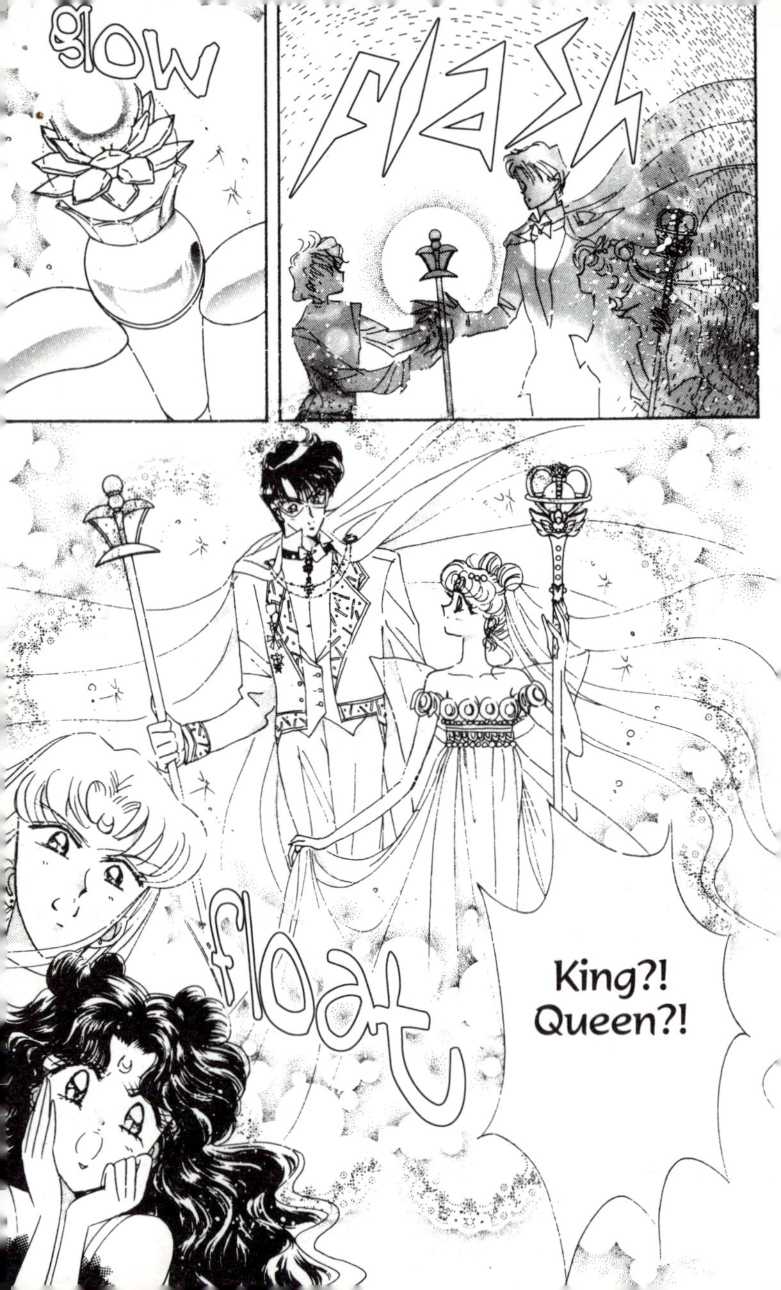
glow
flash
float
King?!
Queen?!

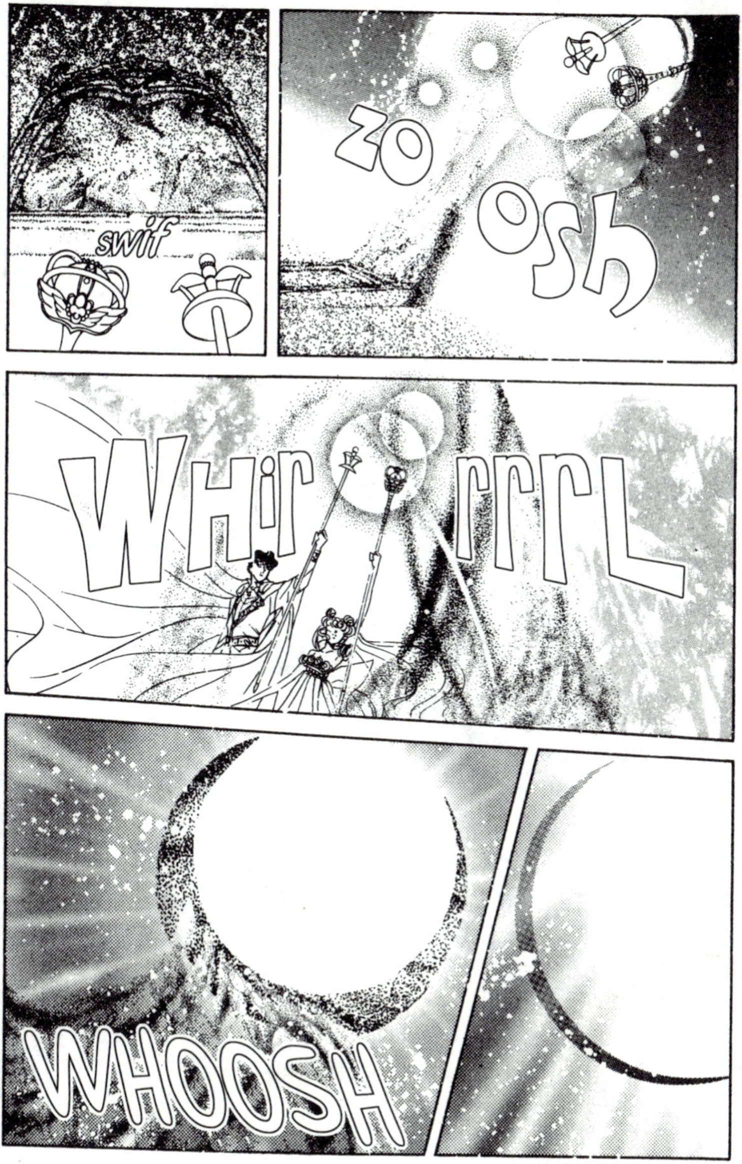

swif
ZOOSH
WHIRRRRL
WHOOSH

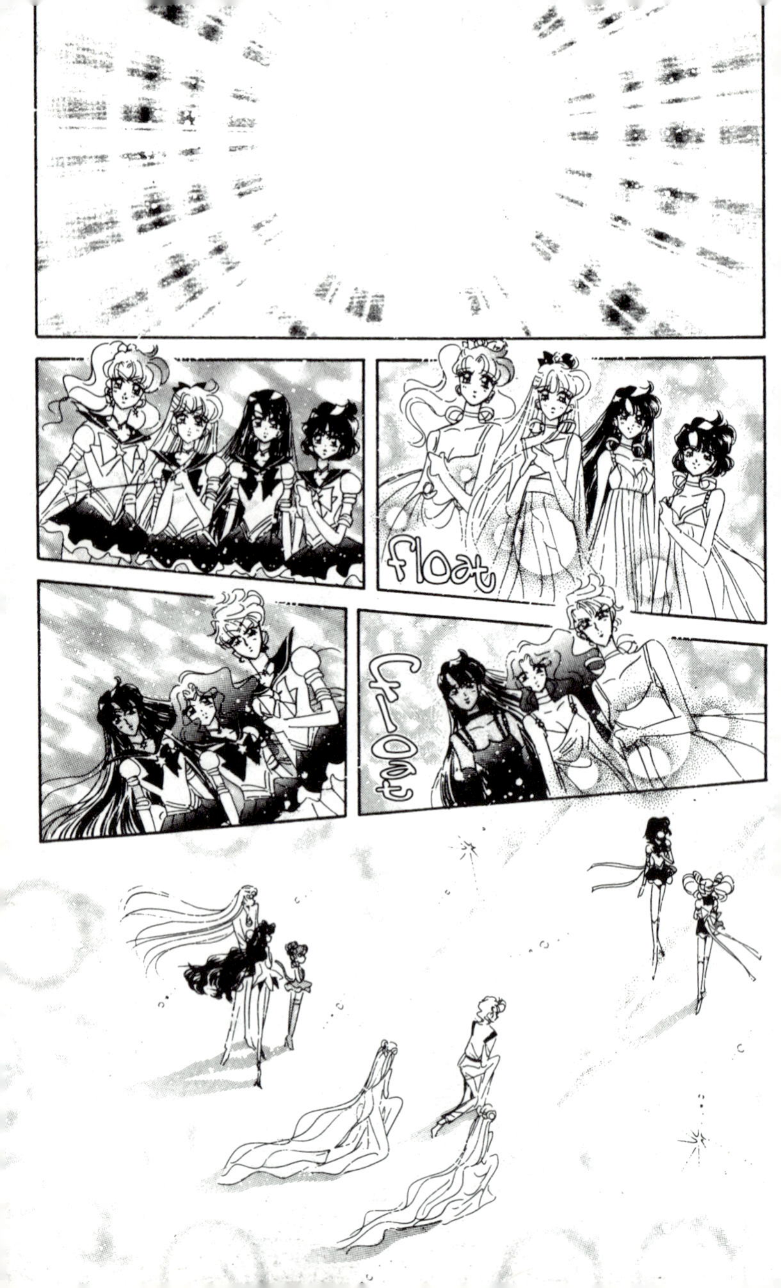
float
float

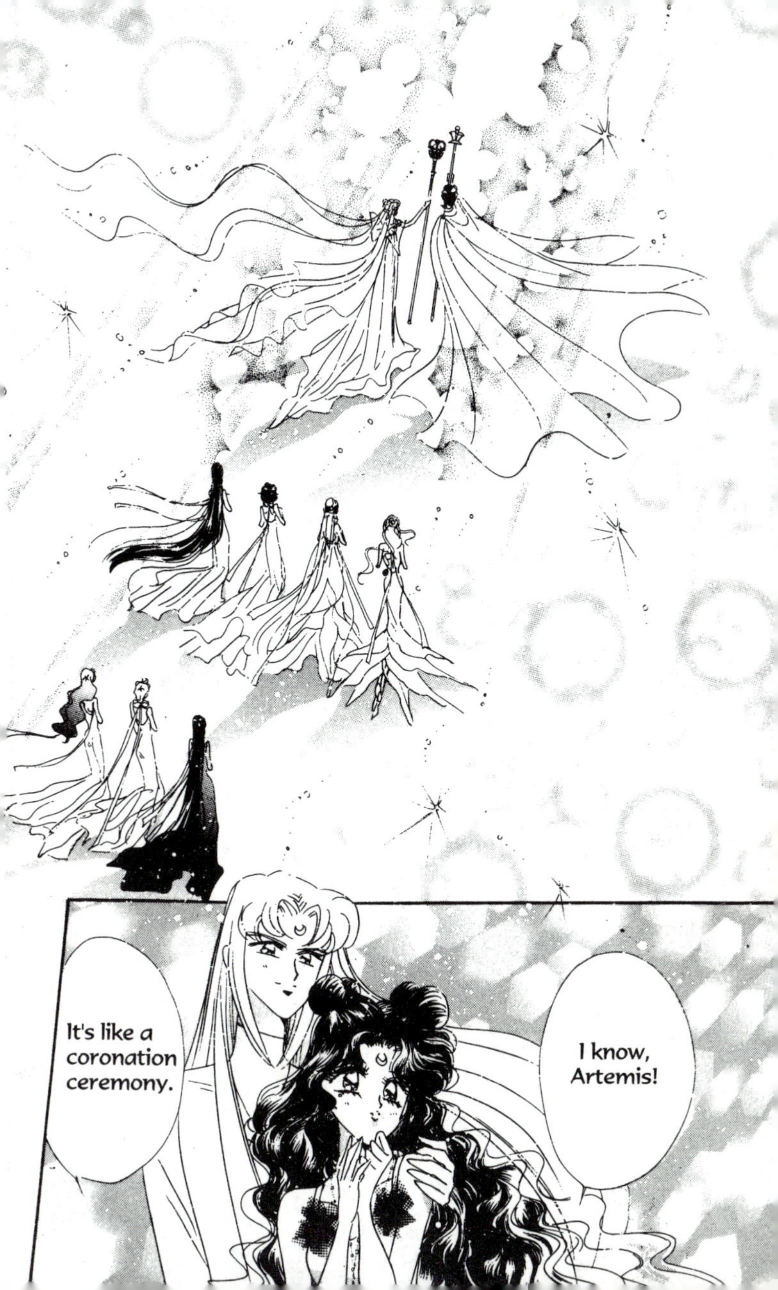
It's like a coronation ceremony.
I know, Artemis!

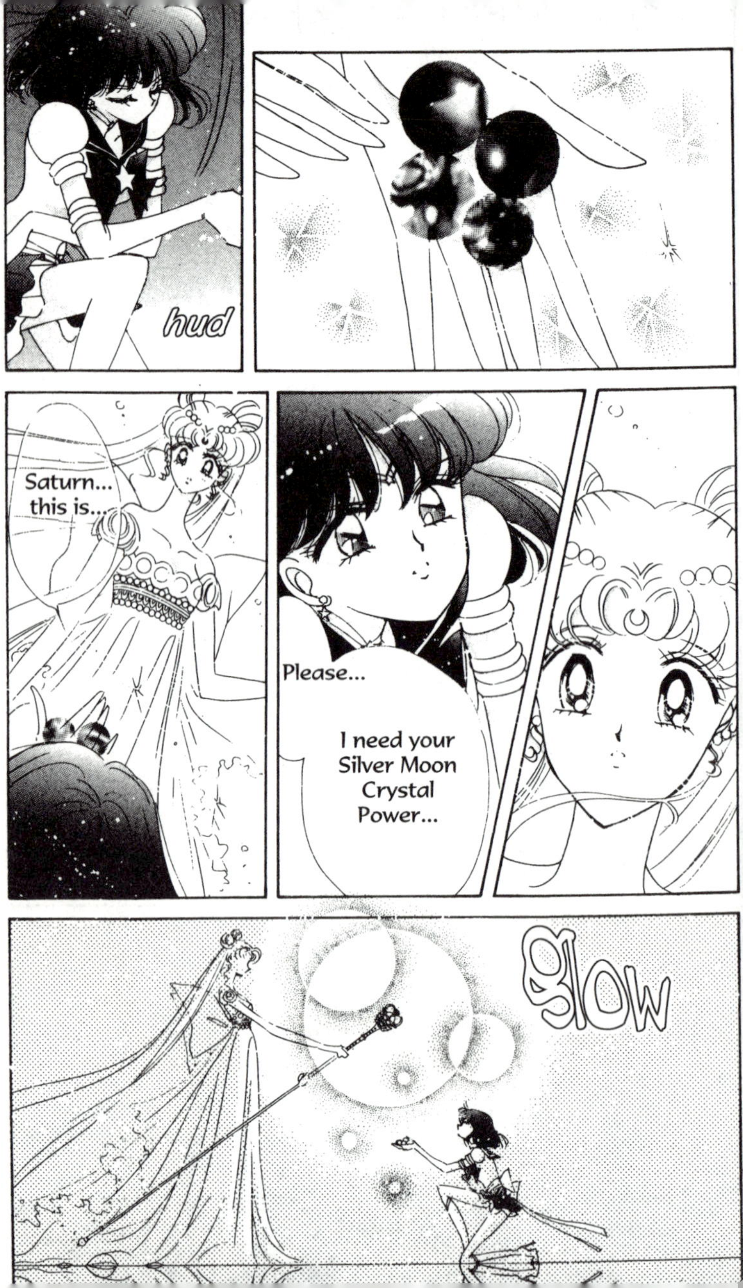
hud
Saturn... this is...
Please...
I need your Silver Moon Crystal Power...
glow

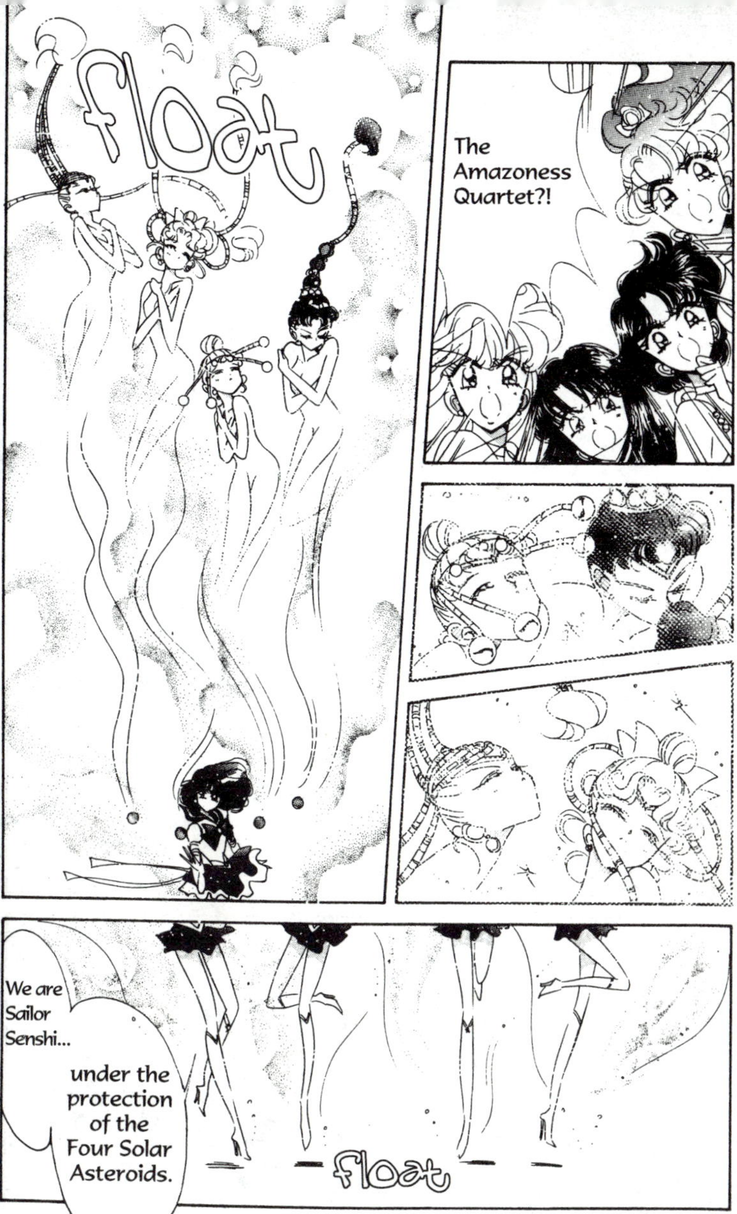
float
The Amazoness Quartet?!
We are Sailor Senshi...
under the protection of the Four Solar Asteroids.
float

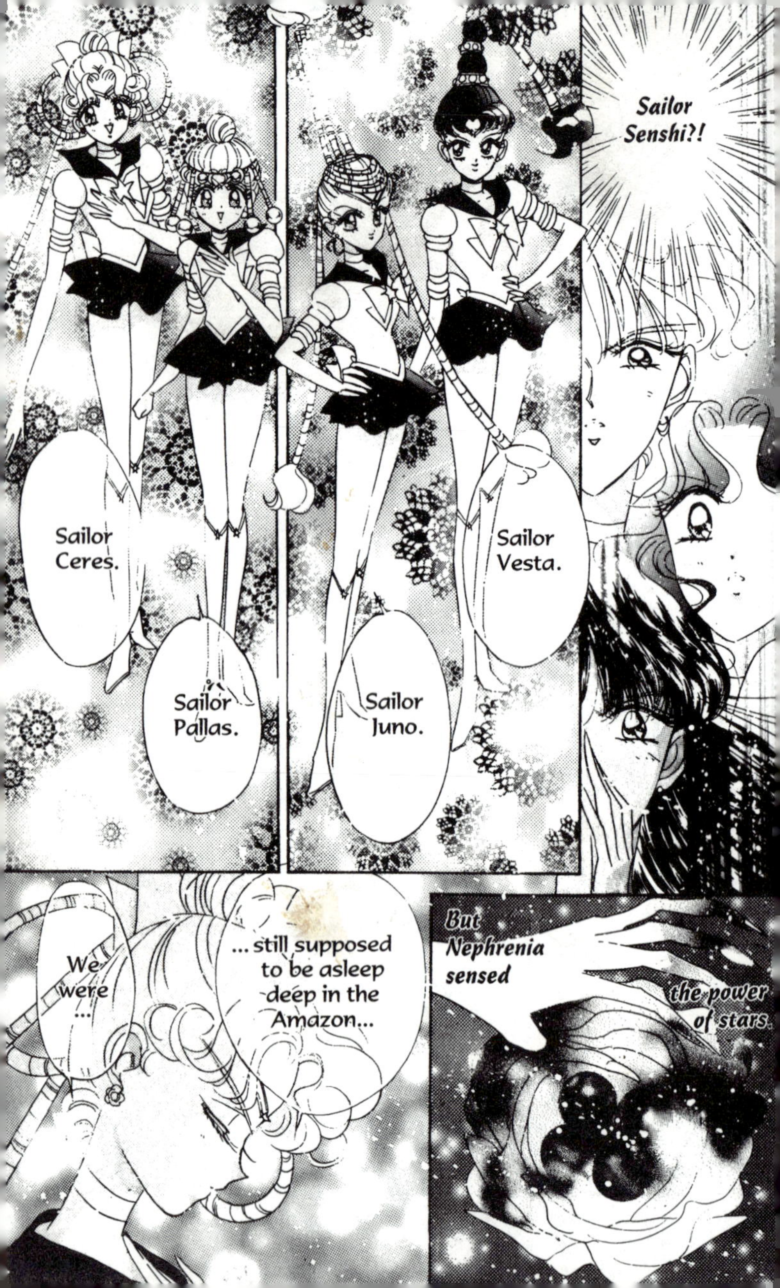
Sailor Ceres.
Sailor Pallas.
Sailor Juno.
Sailor Vesta.
Sailor Senshi?!
We were ...
... still supposed to be asleep deep in the Amazon...
But Nephrenia sensed
the power of stars.

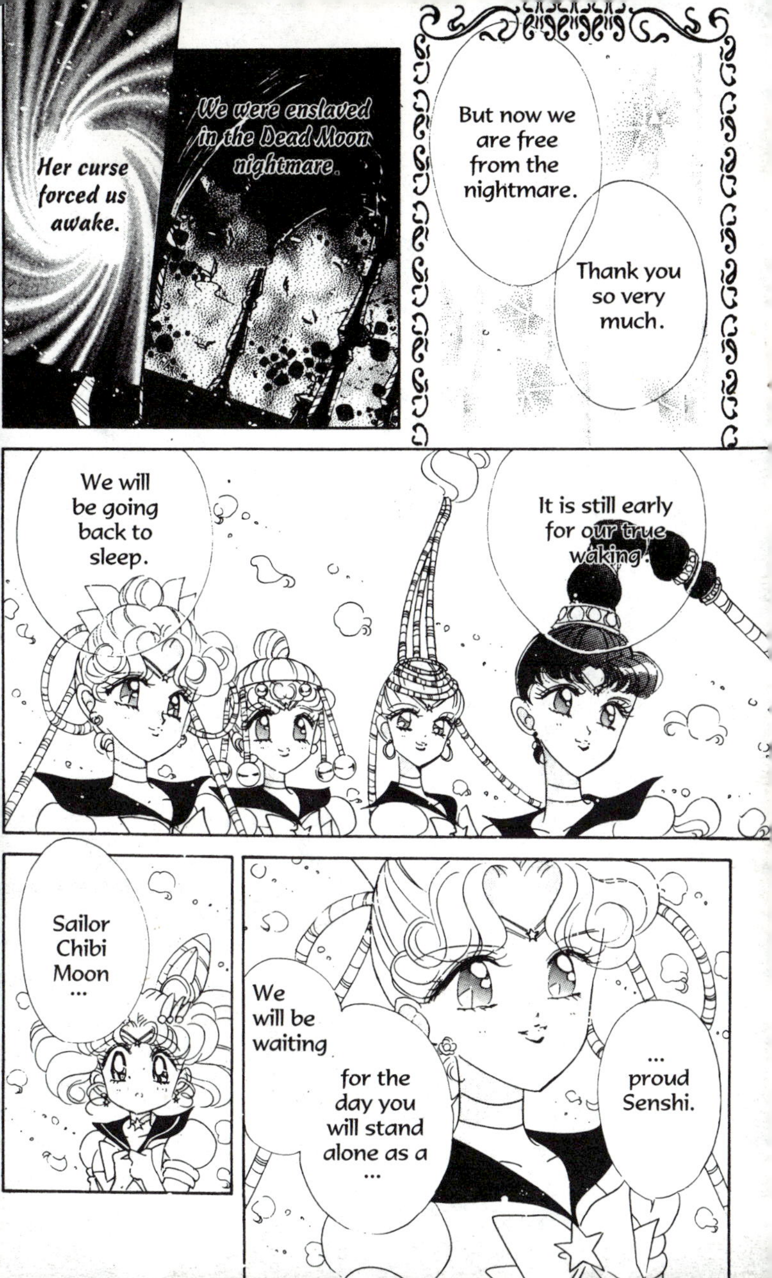
Her curse forced us awake.
We were enslaved in the Dead Moon nightmare.
But now we are free from the nightmare.
Thank you so very much.
We will be going back to sleep.
It is still early for our true waking.
Sailor Chibi Moon ...
We will be waiting
for the day you will stand alone as a ...
... proud Senshi.

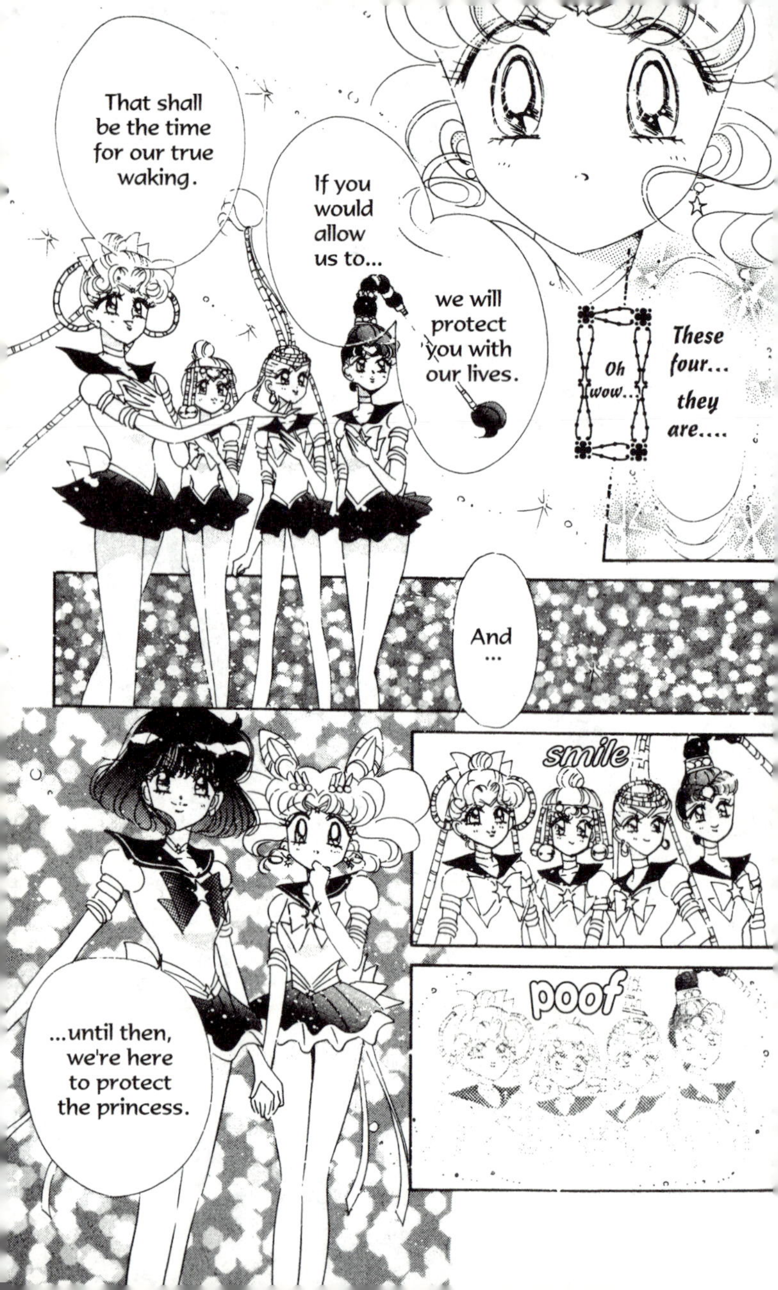
That shall be the time for our true waking.
If you would allow us to...
we will protect you with our lives.
Oh wow...
These four... they are....
And ...
...until then, we're here to protect the princess.
smile
poof

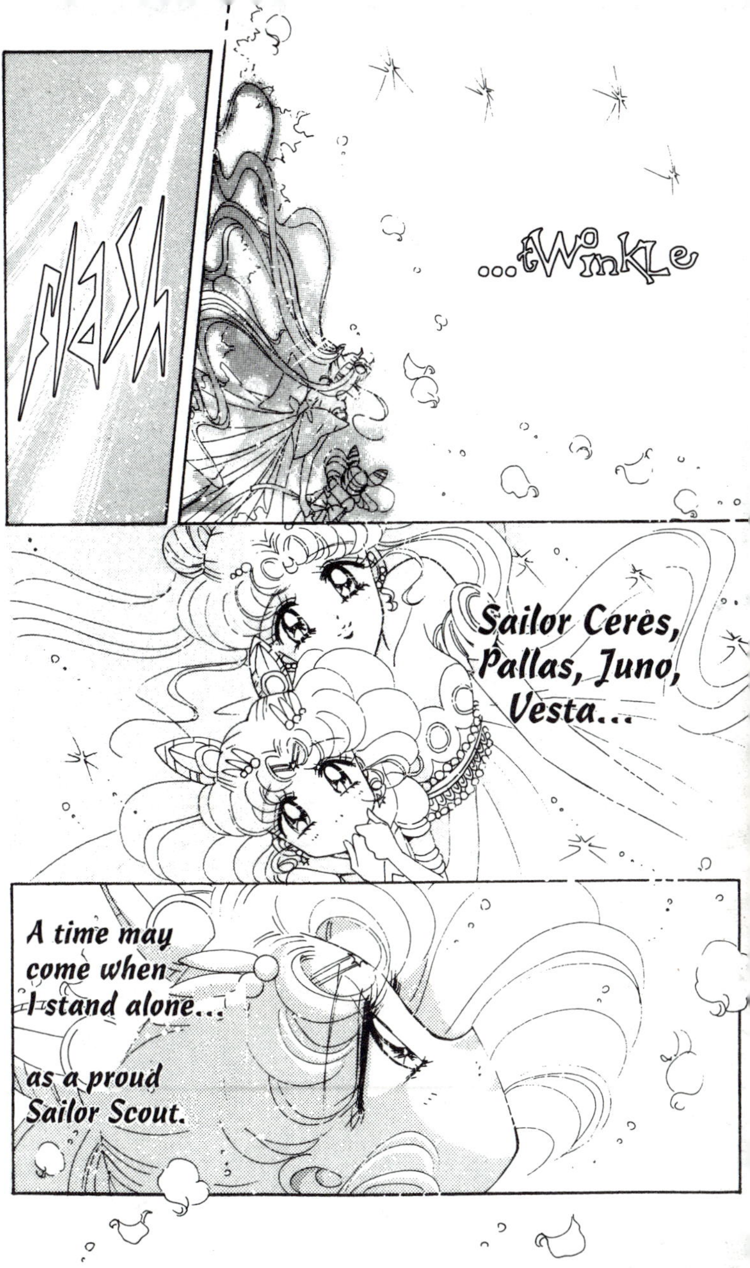
FLASH
...twinkle
Sailor Ceres, Pallas, Juno, Vesta...
A time may come when I stand alone...
as a proud Sailor Scout.

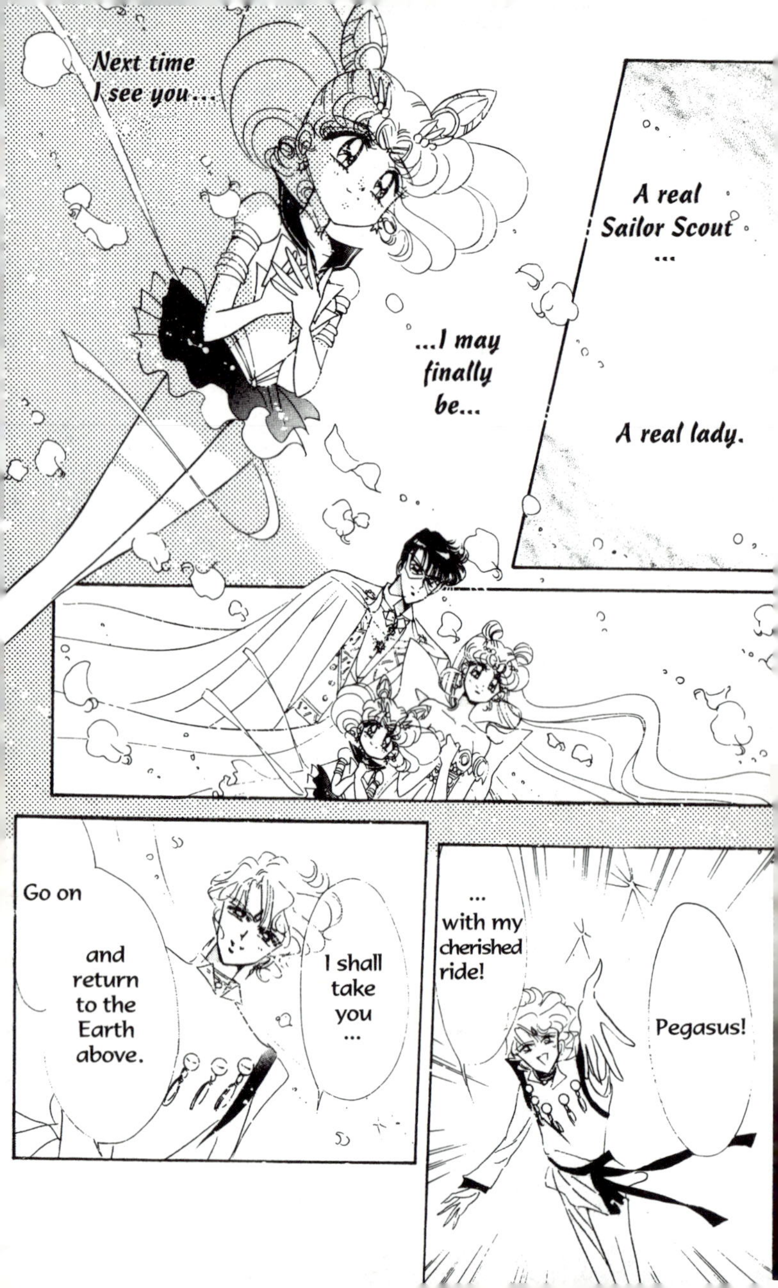
Next time I see you...
...I may finally be...
A real Sailor Scout ...
A real lady.
Go on
and return to the Earth above.
I shall take you ...
... with my cherished ride!
Pegasus!

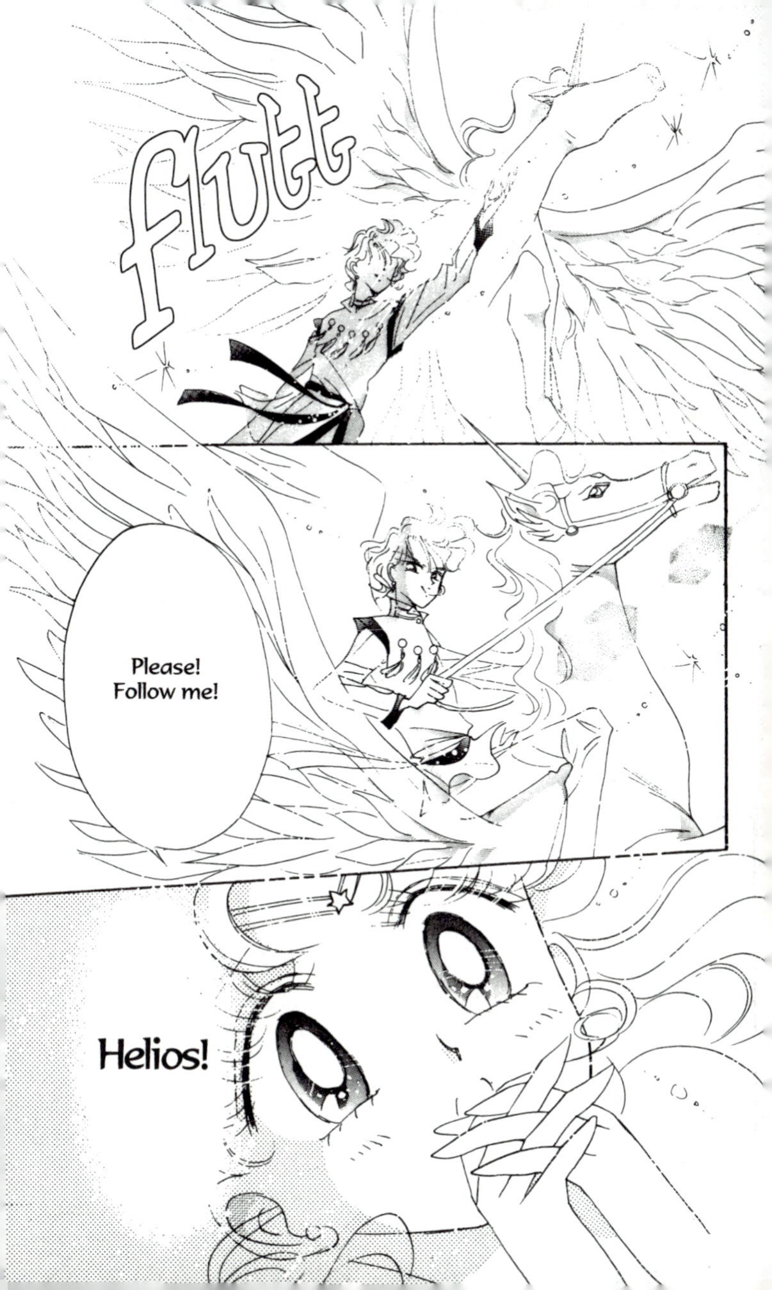
flutt
Please! Follow me!
Helios!

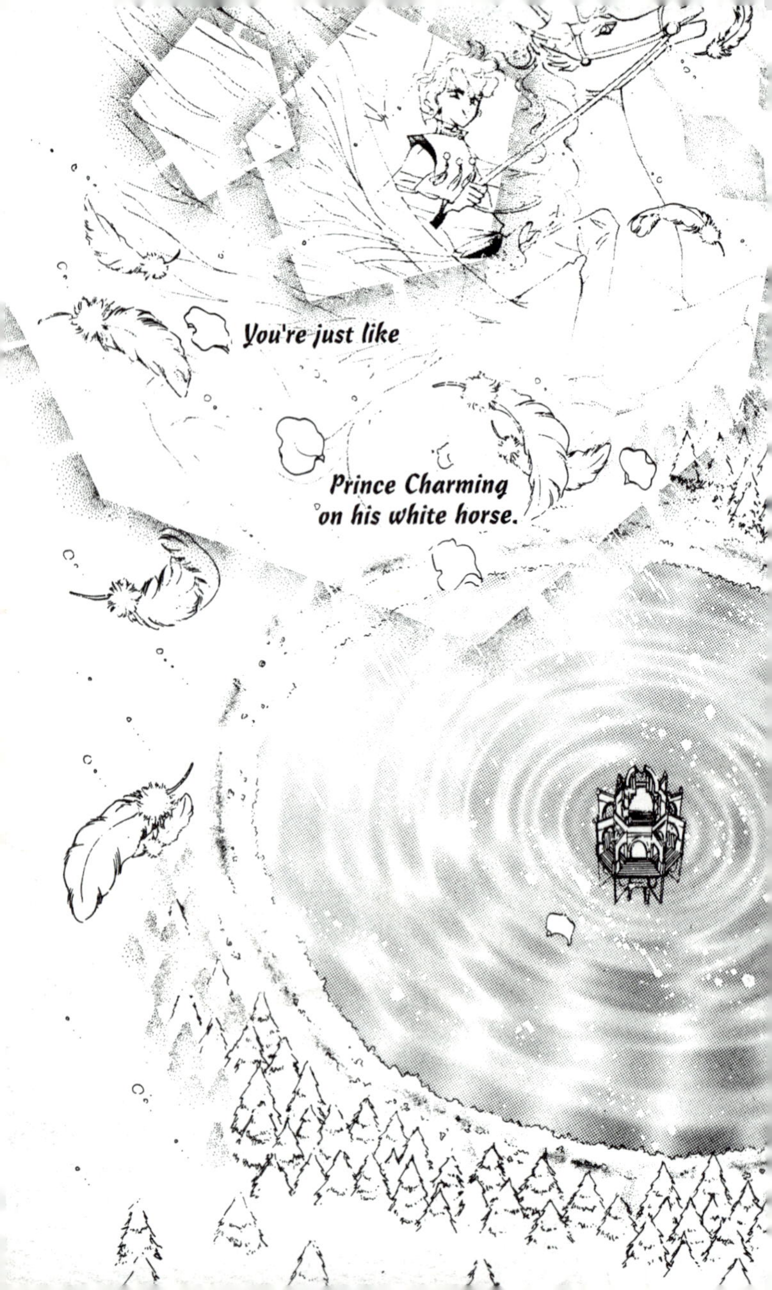

You're just like
Prince Charming on his white horse.

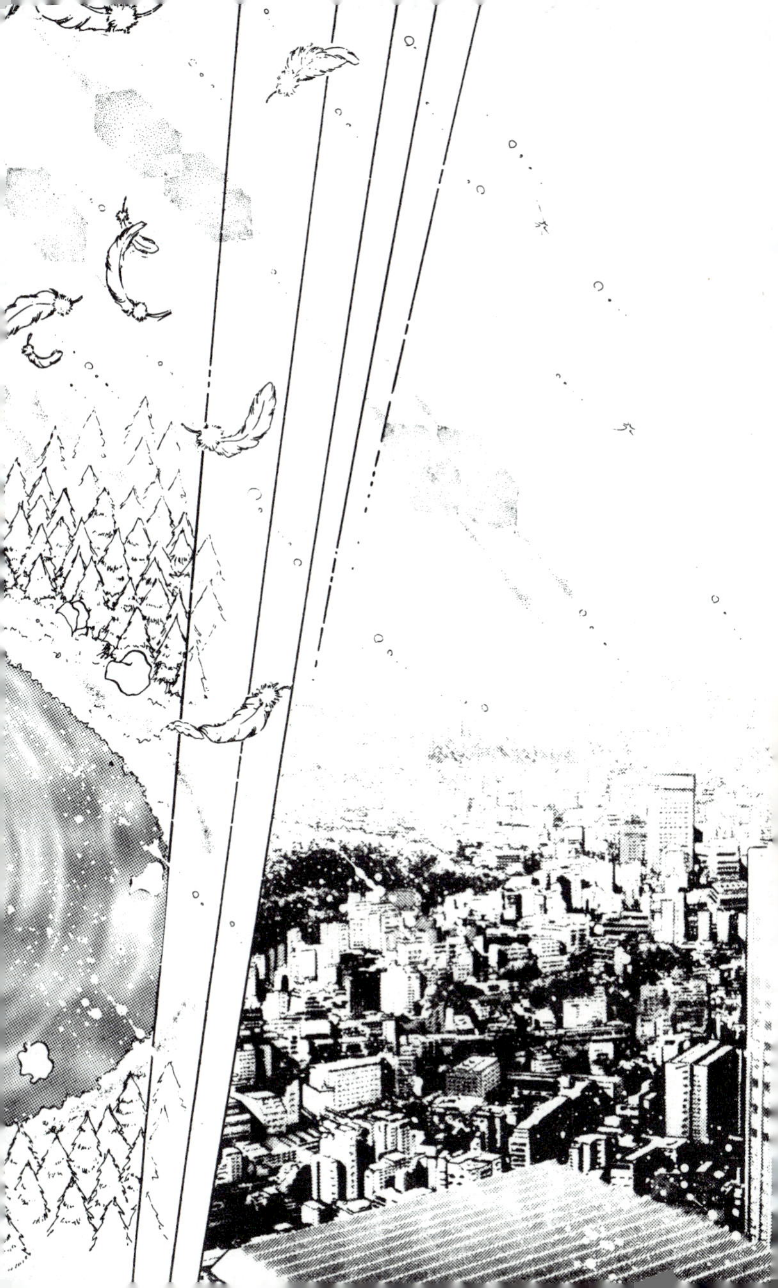

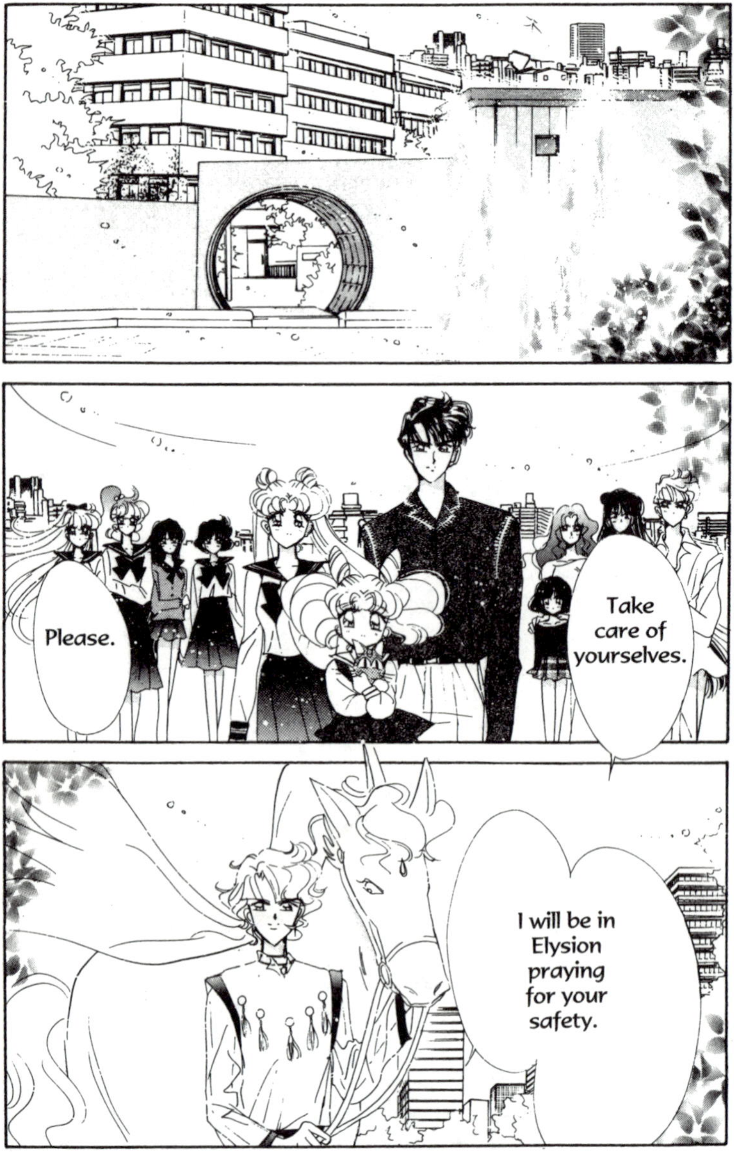
Please.
Take care of yourselves.
I will be in Elysion praying for your safety.

Helios ...

I'll see you again, right?

Of course ...

... Maiden

And for you, Prince ...

I'll be looking forward to it.

flutt

From the bottom of my heart.

Helios! It's a promise!

I'll come see you again.

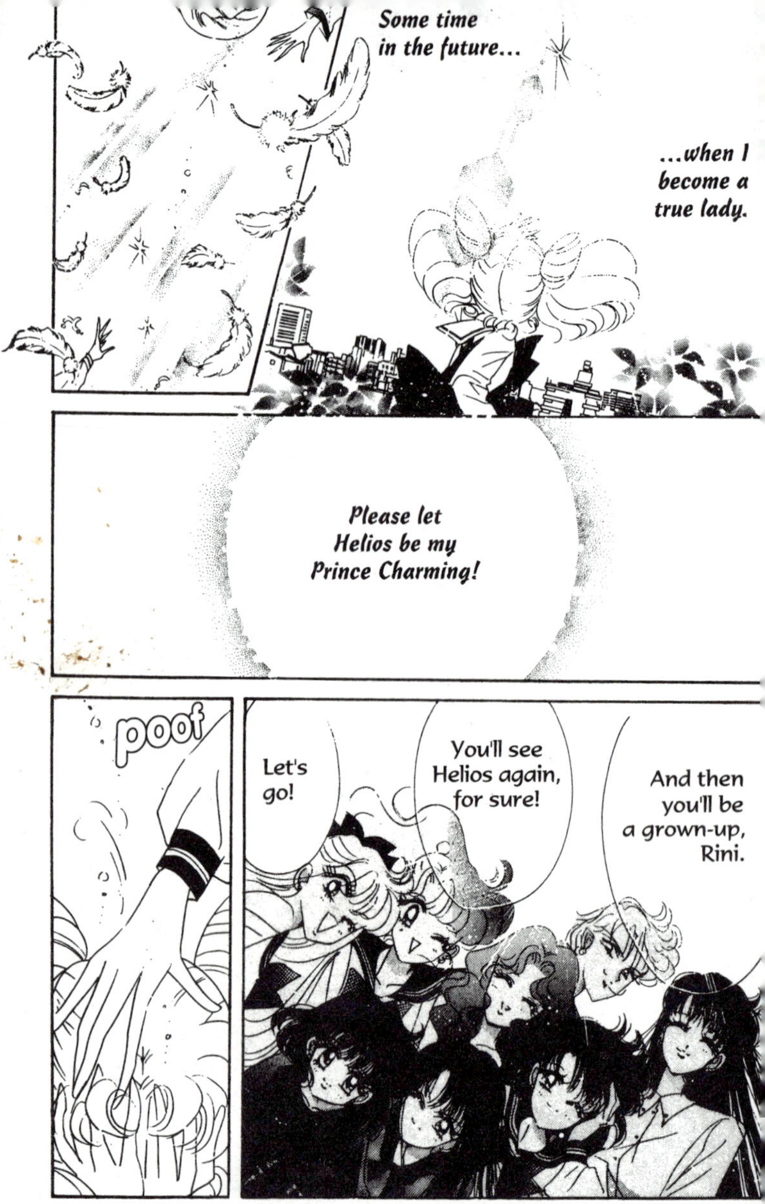
Some time in the future...
...when I become a true lady.
Please let Helios be my Prince Charming!
poof
Let's go!
You'll see Helios again, for sure!
And then you'll be a grown-up, Rini.

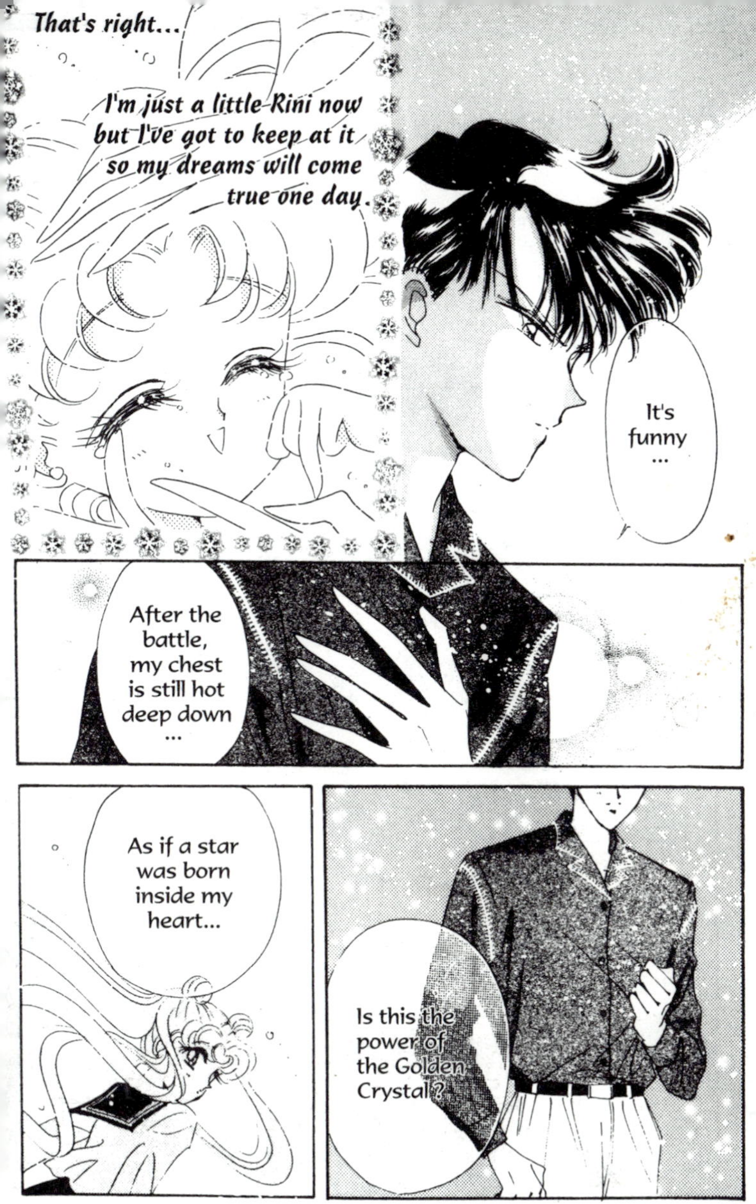
That's right...
I'm just a little Rini now but I've got to keep at it so my dreams will come true one day.
It's funny ...
After the battle, my chest is still hot deep down ...
As if a star was born inside my heart...
Is this the power of the Golden Crystal?

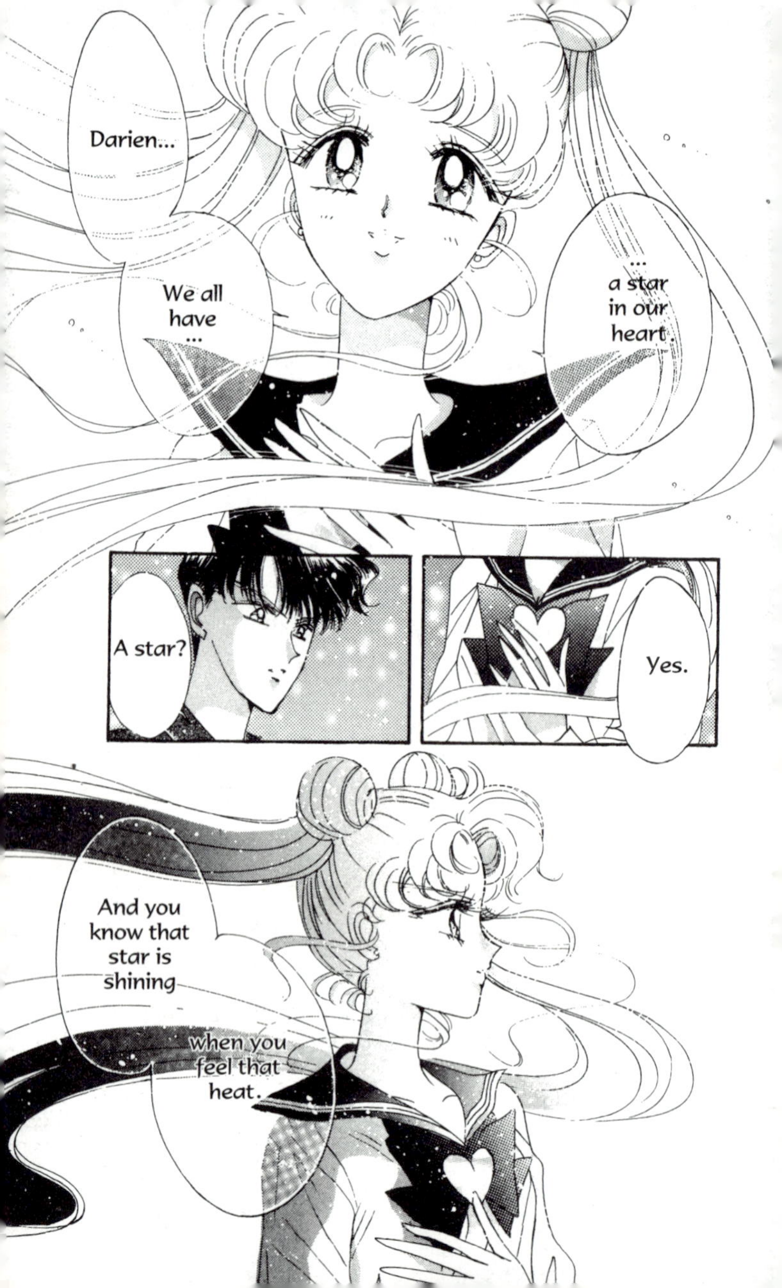
Darien...
We all have ...
... a star in our heart.
A star?
Yes.
And you know that star is shining
when you feel that heat.

To protect
the ones I love.

And to
keep
fighting.

To make my
dreams
come true.

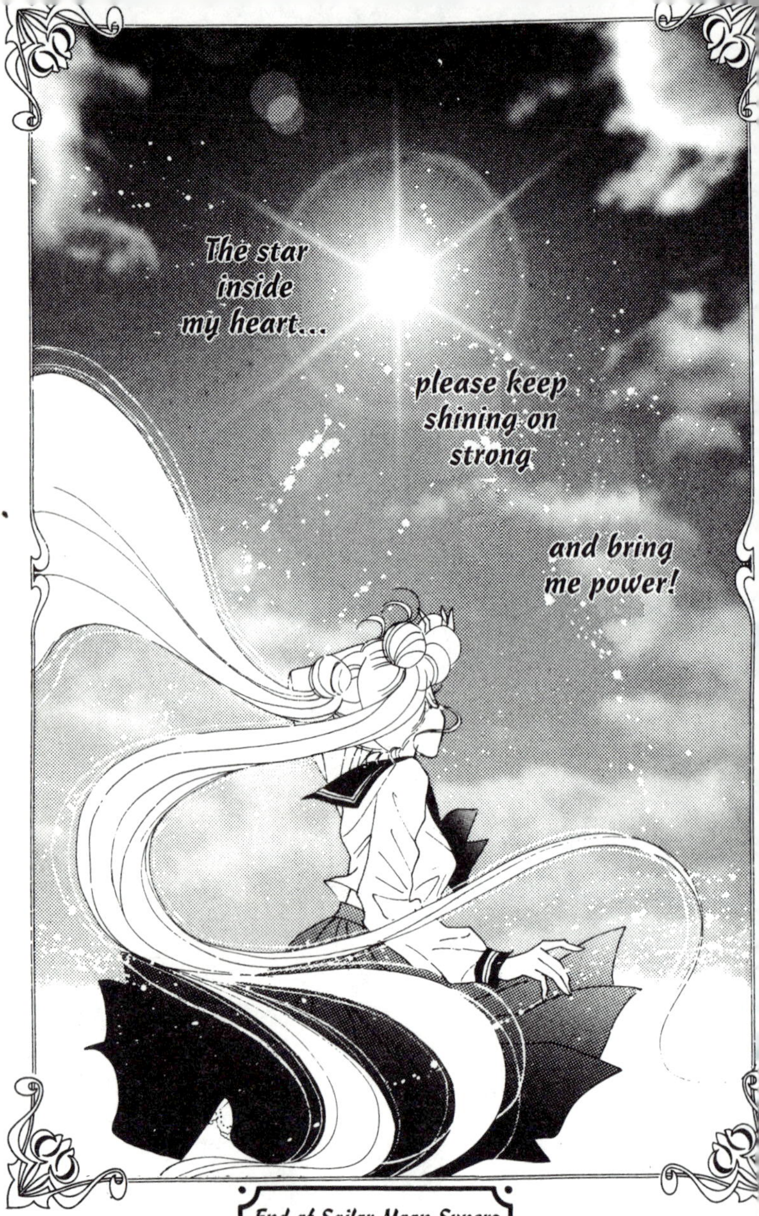
The star inside my heart...
please keep shining on strong
and bring me power!

End of Sailor Moon Supers

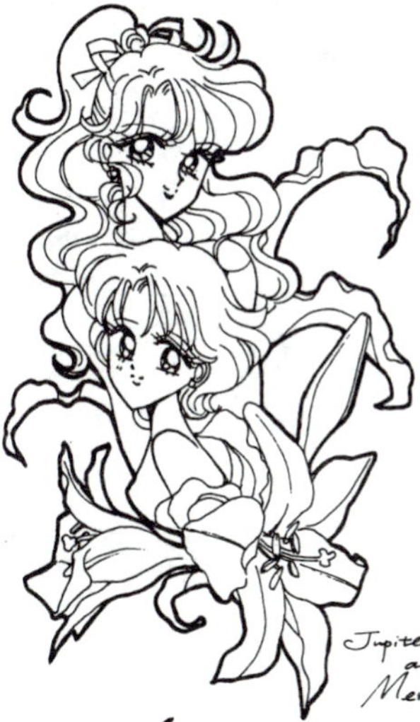

Jupiter and Mercury

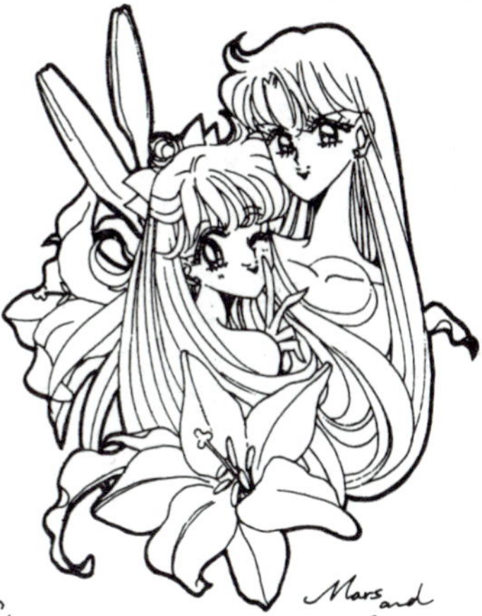

Mars and Venus.

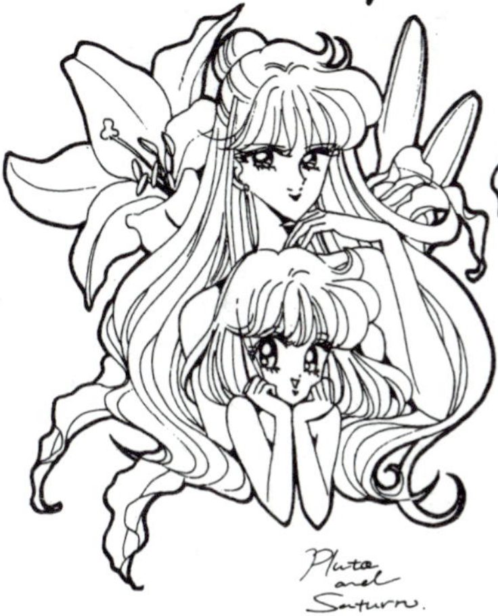

Pluto and Saturn.

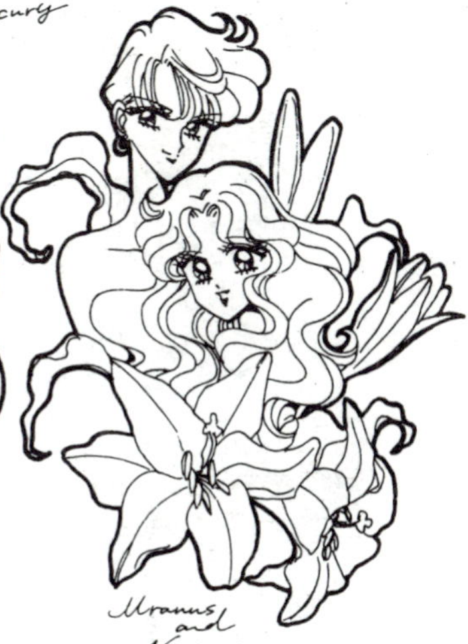

Uranus and Neptune.

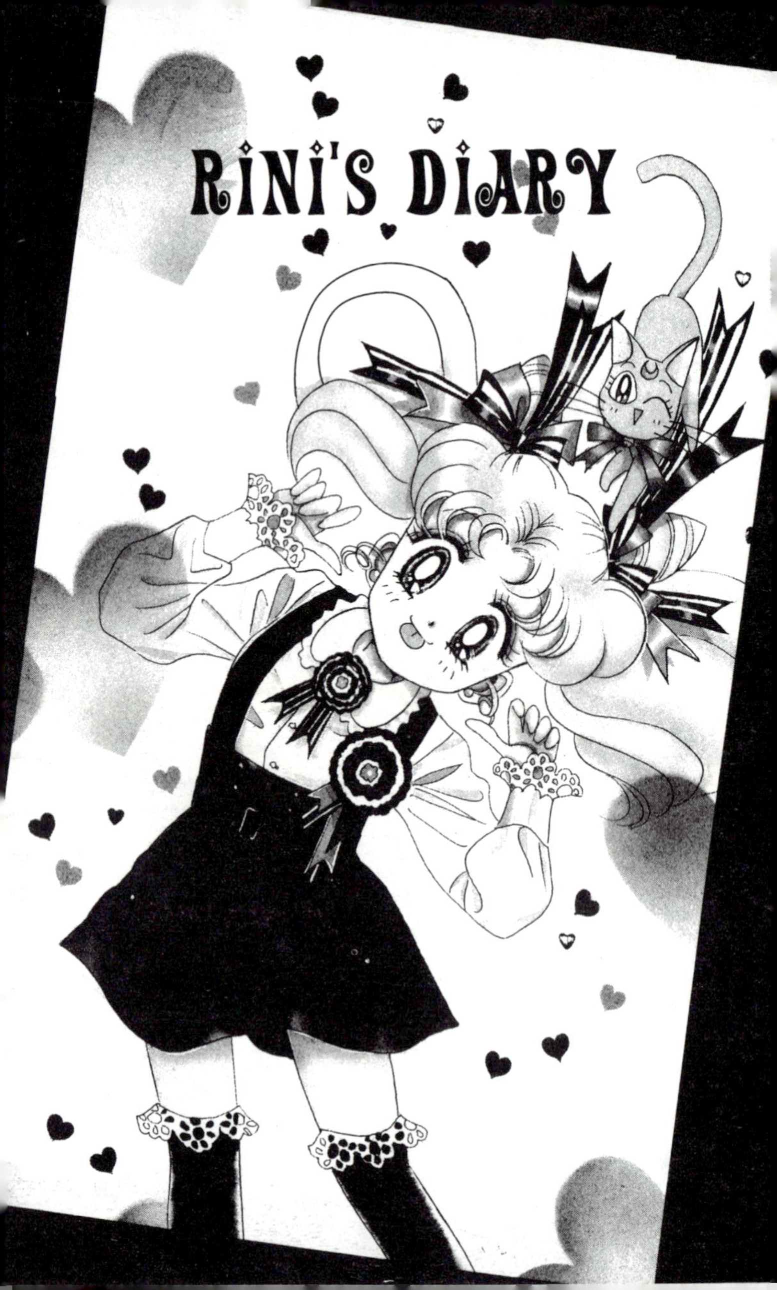
RINI'S DIARY

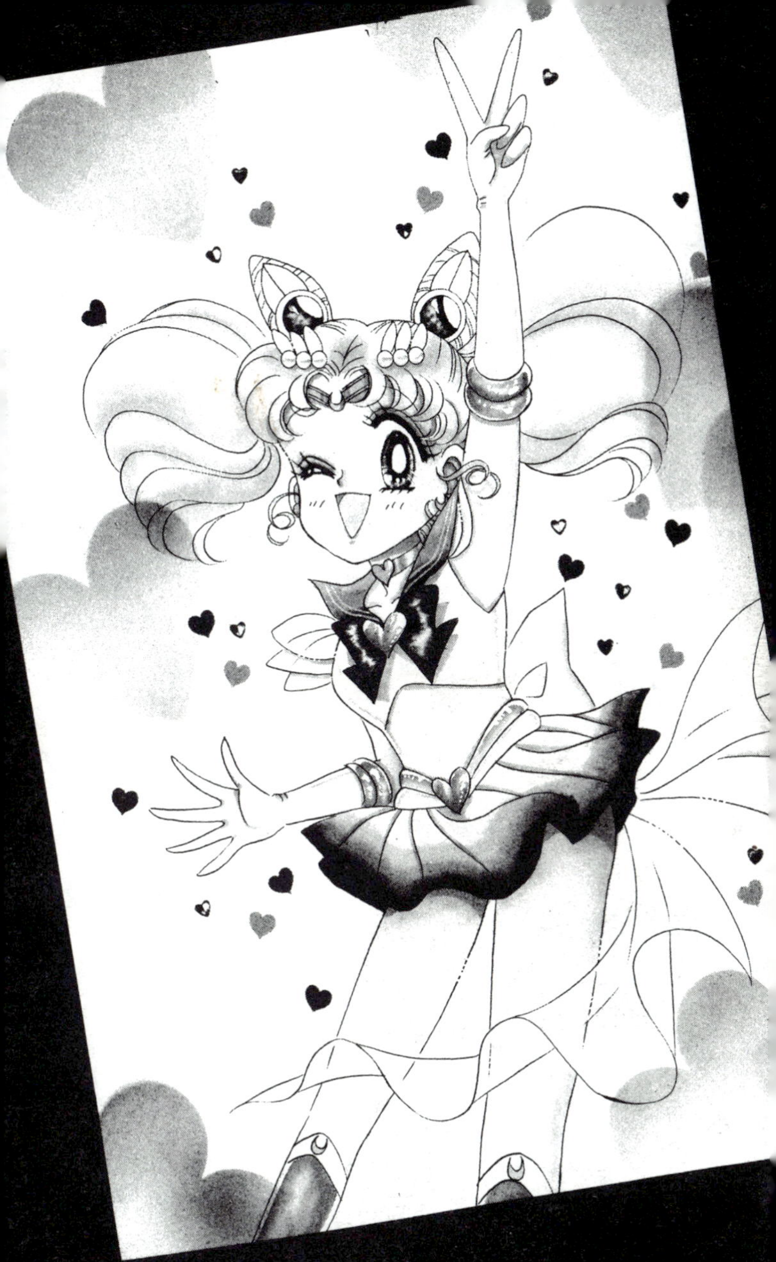

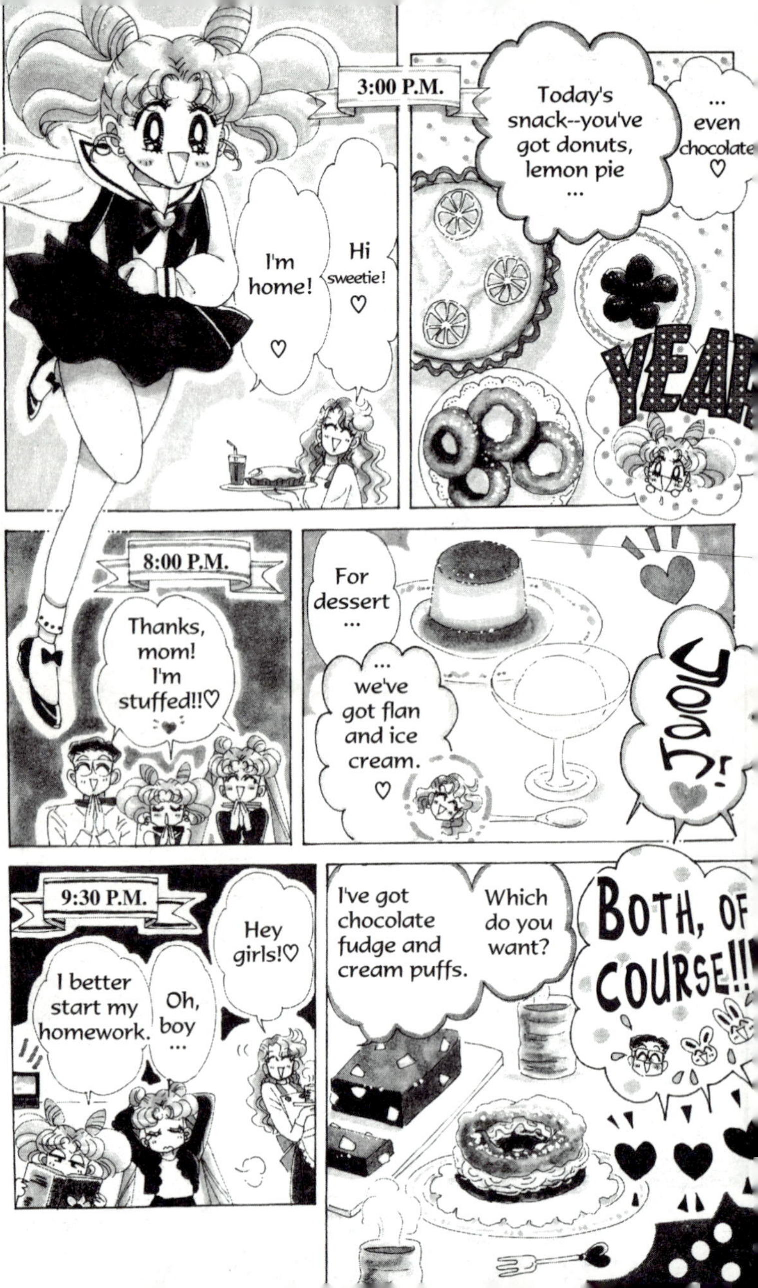
3:00 P.M.
I'm home! ♡
Hi sweetie! ♡
Today's snack--you've got donuts, lemon pie ...
... even chocolate ♡
YEAH
8:00 P.M.
Thanks, mom! I'm stuffed!!♡
For dessert ...
... we've got flan and ice cream. ♡
Joy!
9:30 P.M.
I better start my homework.
Oh, boy ...
Hey girls!♡
I've got chocolate fudge and cream puffs.
Which do you want?
BOTH, OF COURSE!!!

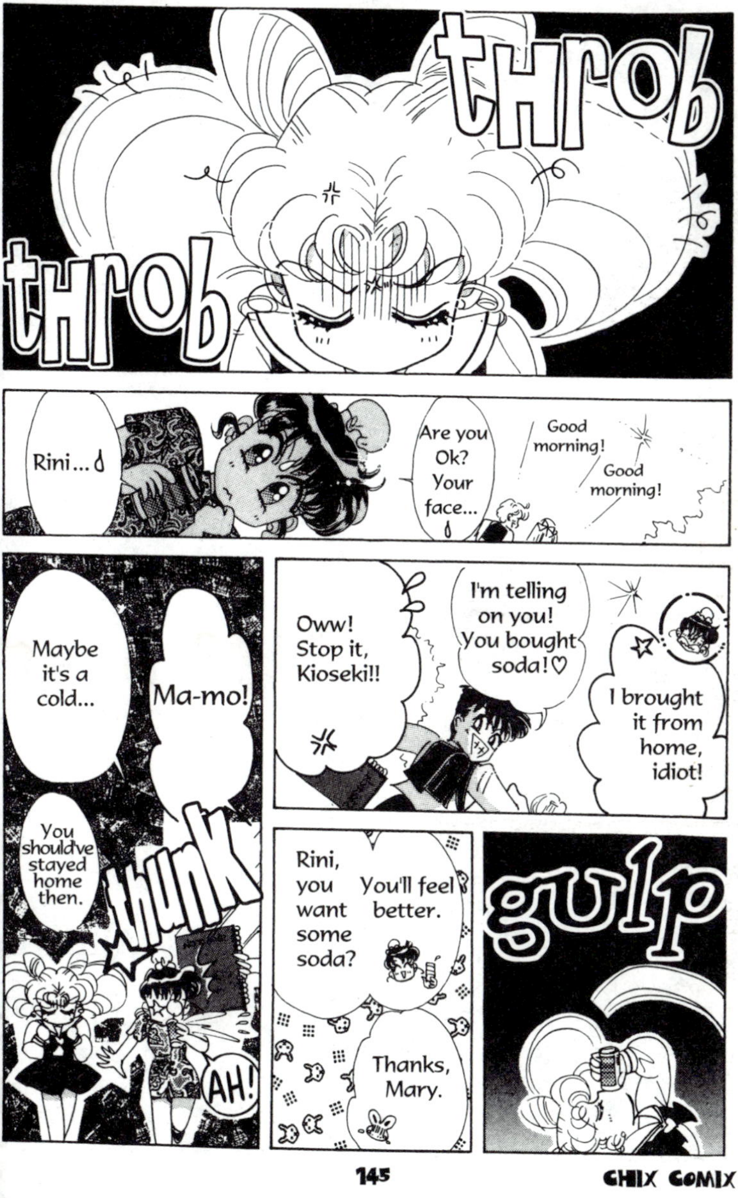
throb
throb
Rini...
Are you Ok? Your face...
Good morning!
Good morning!
Maybe it's a cold...
Ma-mo!
You shouldve stayed home then.
thunk
AH!
Oww! Stop it, Kioseki!!
I'm telling on you! You bought soda!♡
I brought it from home, idiot!
Rini, you want some soda?
You'll feel better.
Thanks, Mary.
gulp

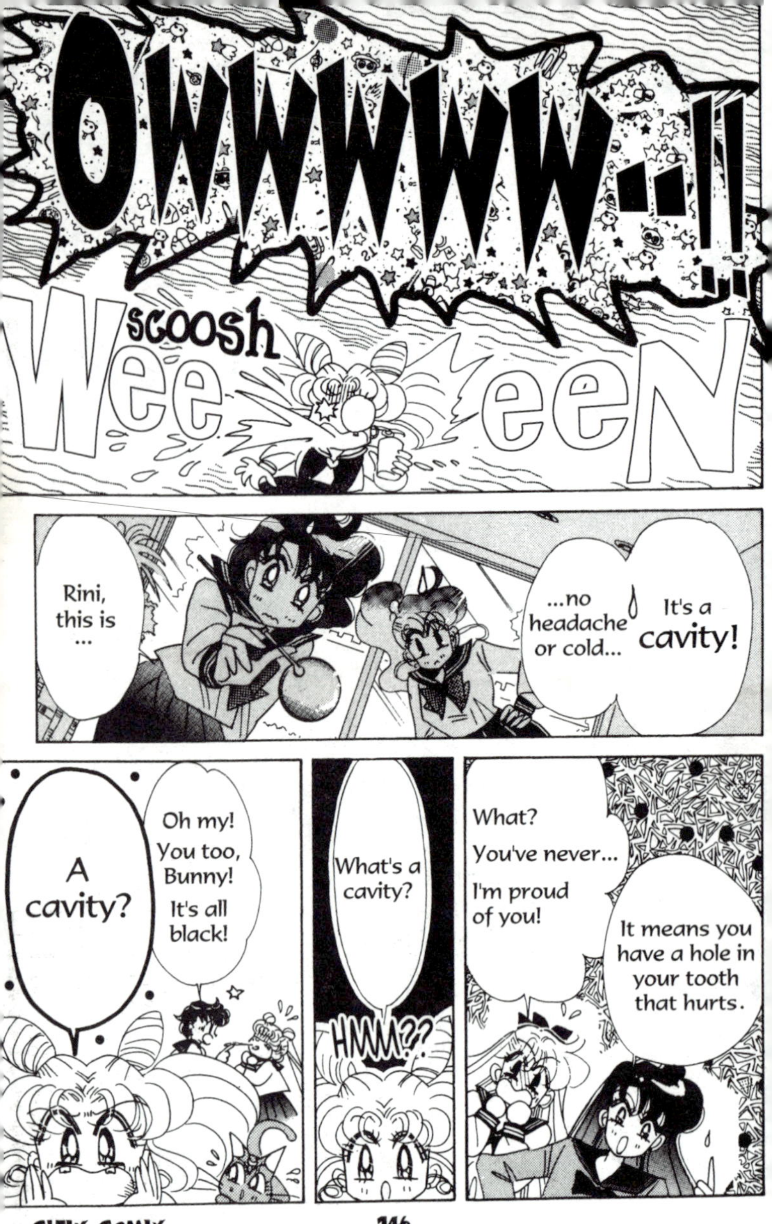
OWWWWW..!!
scoosh
Wee een
Rini, this is ...
...no headache or cold...
It's a cavity!
A cavity?
Oh my! You too, Bunny! It's all black!
What's a cavity?
HMM??
What? You've never... I'm proud of you!
It means you have a hole in your tooth that hurts.

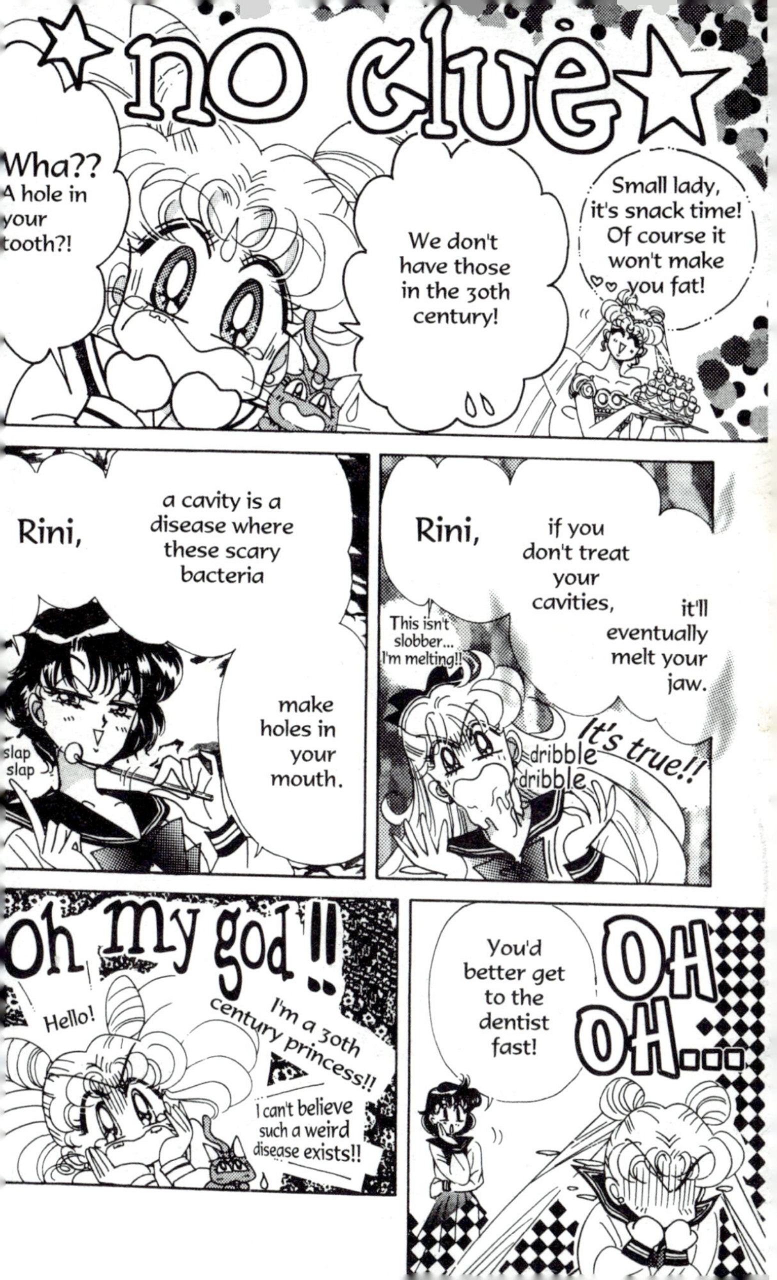
★no clue★
Wha?? A hole in your tooth?!
We don't have those in the 30th century!
Small lady, it's snack time! Of course it won't make you fat!
Rini,
a cavity is a disease where these scary bacteria
make holes in your mouth.
slap slap
Rini,
if you don't treat your cavities,
it'll eventually melt your jaw.
This isn't slobber... I'm melting!!
It's true!!
dribble dribble
Oh my god!!
Hello!
I'm a 30th century princess!!
I can't believe such a weird disease exists!!
You'd better get to the dentist fast!
OH OH...

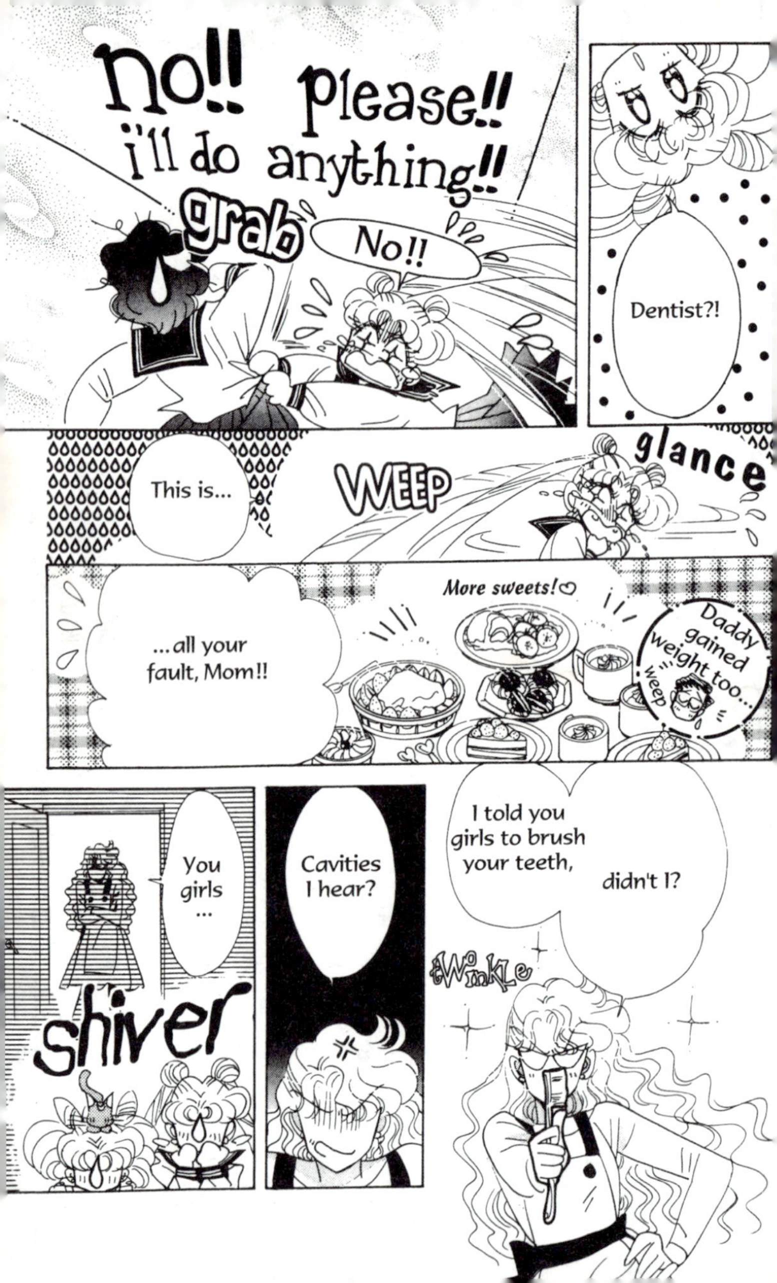
No!! Please!! I'll do anything!!
grab
No!!
Dentist?!
This is...
WEEP
glance
...all your fault, Mom!!
More sweets!♡
Daddy gained weight too...
weep
You girls ...
shiver
Cavities I hear?
I told you girls to brush your teeth,
didn't I?
twinkle

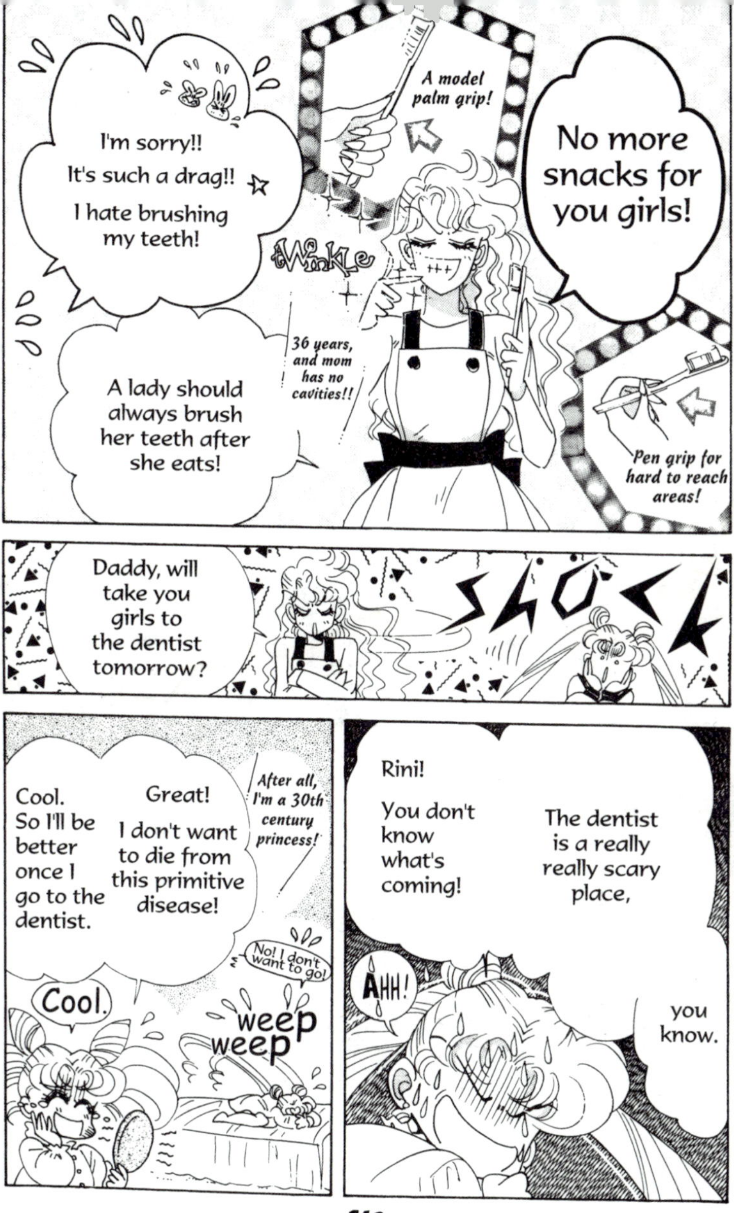
I'm sorry!! It's such a drag!! I hate brushing my teeth!
A model palm grip!
No more snacks for you girls!
Twinkle
A lady should always brush her teeth after she eats!
36 years, and mom has no cavities!!
Pen grip for hard to reach areas!
Daddy, will take you girls to the dentist tomorrow?
SHOCK
Cool. So I'll be better once I go to the dentist.
Great! I don't want to die from this primitive disease!
After all, I'm a 30th century princess!
No! I don't want to go!
Cool.
weep weep
Rini!
You don't know what's coming!
The dentist is a really really scary place,
AHH!
you know.

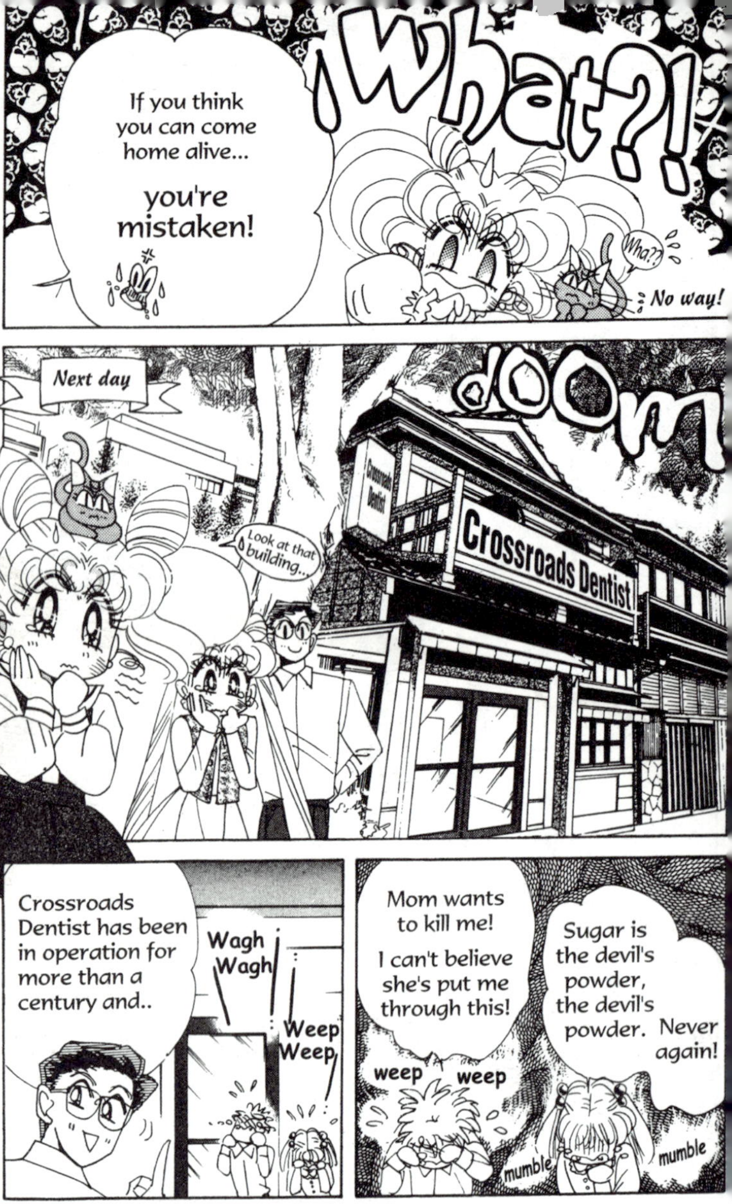
If you think you can come home alive... you're mistaken!
What?!
Wha??
No way!
Next day
dOOm
Crossroads Dentist
Crossroads Dentist
Look at that building...
Crossroads Dentist has been in operation for more than a century and..
Wagh Wagh
Weep Weep
Mom wants to kill me! I can't believe she's put me through this!
Sugar is the devil's powder, the devil's powder. Never again!
weep weep
mumble
mumble

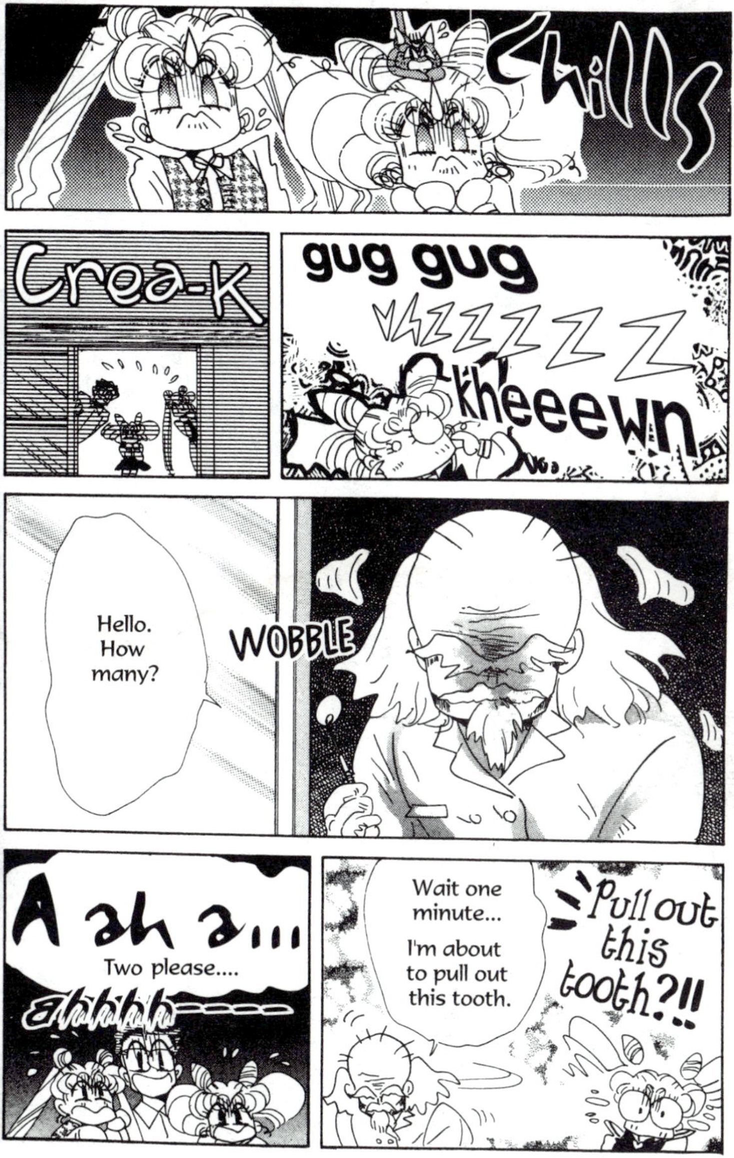

Chills
Crea-K
gug gug
VZZZZZZ
Kheeewn
Hello. How many?
WOBBLE
A ah a...
Two please....
ahhhh————
Wait one minute...
I'm about to pull out this tooth.
Pull out this tooth?!!

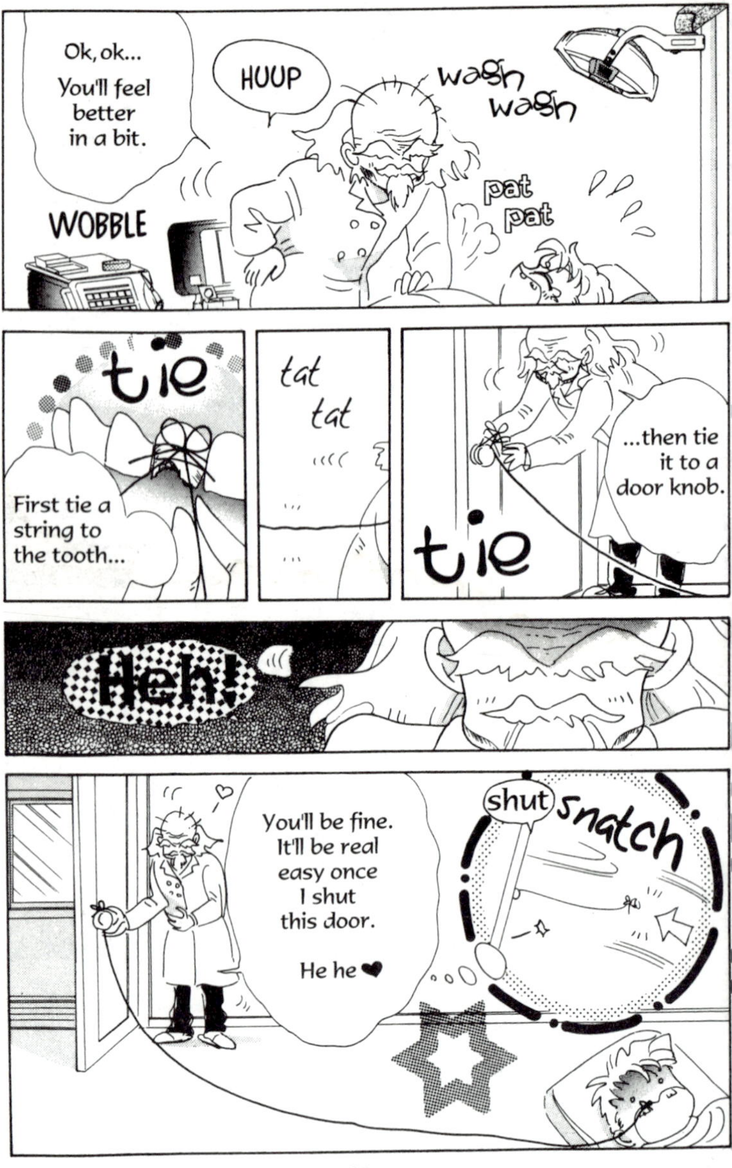
Ok, ok...
You'll feel better in a bit.
HUUP
wagh wagh
pat pat
WOBBLE
tie
First tie a string to the tooth...
tat tat
...then tie it to a door knob.
tie
Heh!
You'll be fine. It'll be real easy once I shut this door.
He he ❤
shut
snatch

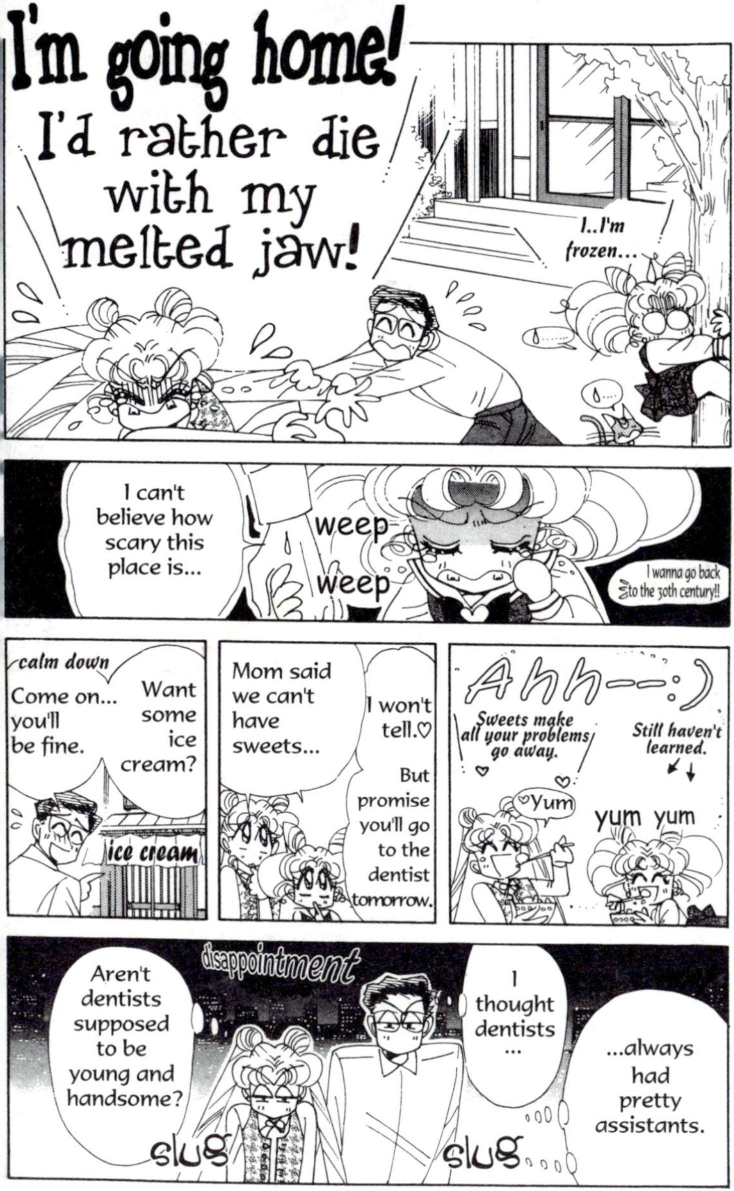
I'm going home!
I'd rather die with my melted jaw!
I..I'm frozen...
I can't believe how scary this place is...
weep
weep
I wanna go back to the 30th century!!
calm down
Come on... you'll be fine.
Want some ice cream?
ice cream
Mom said we can't have sweets...
I won't tell.♡
But promise you'll go to the dentist tomorrow.
Ahh---:)
Sweets make all your problems go away.
Still haven't learned.
♡Yum
yum yum
disappointment
Aren't dentists supposed to be young and handsome?
slug
I thought dentists...
...always had pretty assistants.
slug

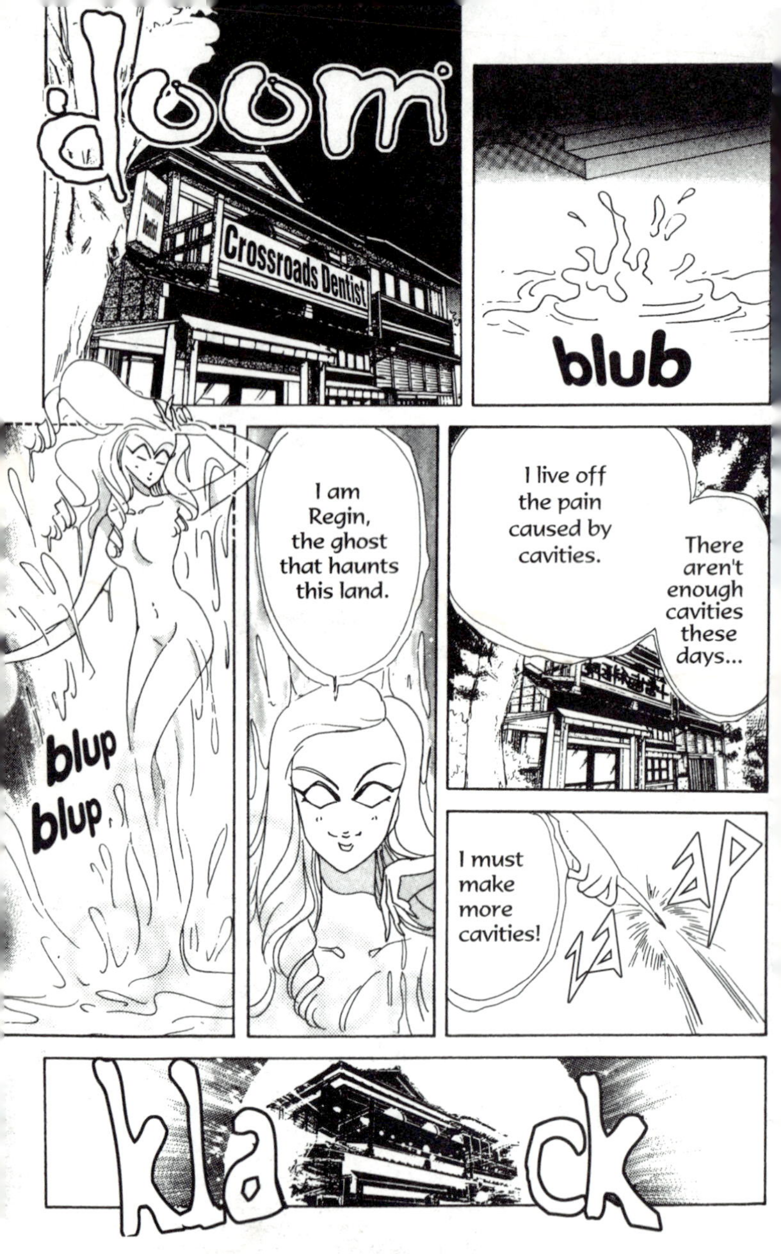
doom
Crossroads Dentist
Crossroads Dentist
blub
blup
blup
I am Regin, the ghost that haunts this land.
I live off the pain caused by cavities.
There aren't enough cavities these days...
I must make more cavities!
zap
zap
klack

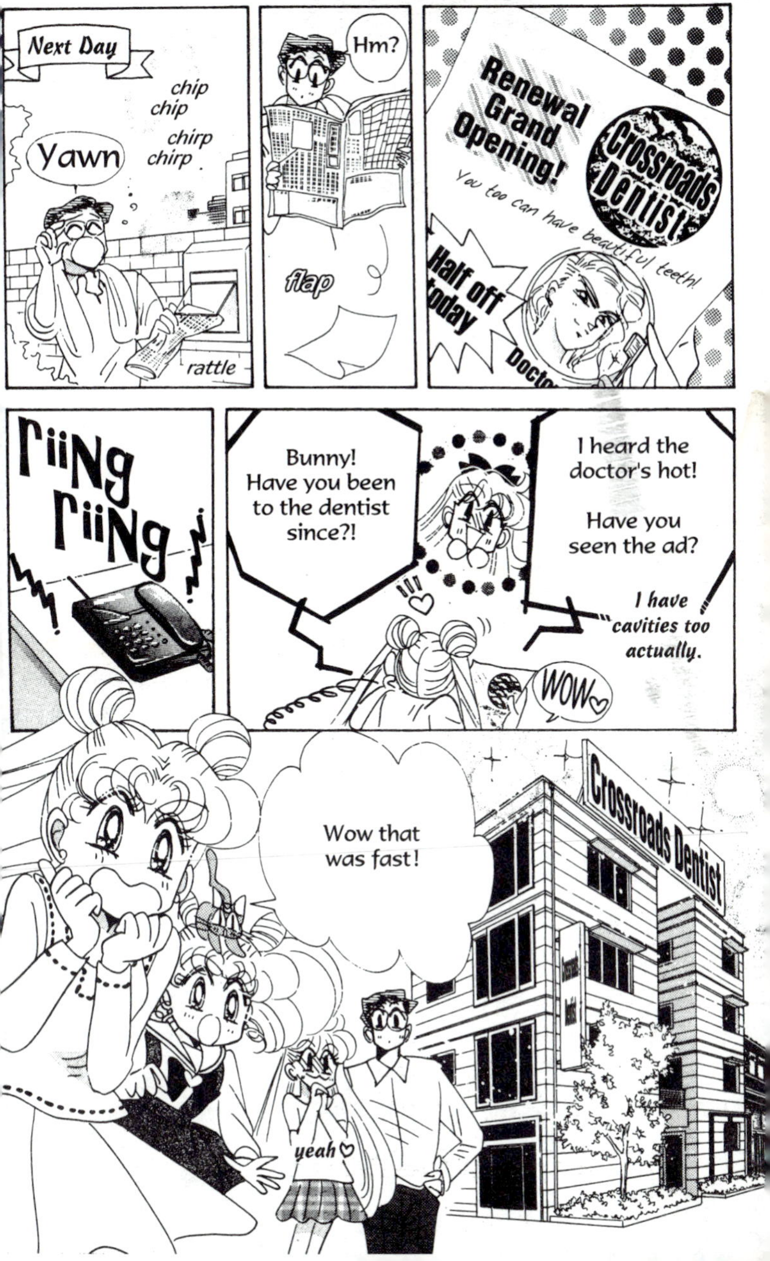

Next Day
Yawn
chip chip
chirp chirp
rattle
Hm?
flap
Renewal Grand Opening!
Crossroads Dentist
You too can have beautiful teeth!
Half off today
Doctor
riiNg riiNg
Bunny! Have you been to the dentist since?!
I heard the doctor's hot!
Have you seen the ad?
I have cavities too actually.
WOW
Wow that was fast!
Crossroads Dentist
yeah

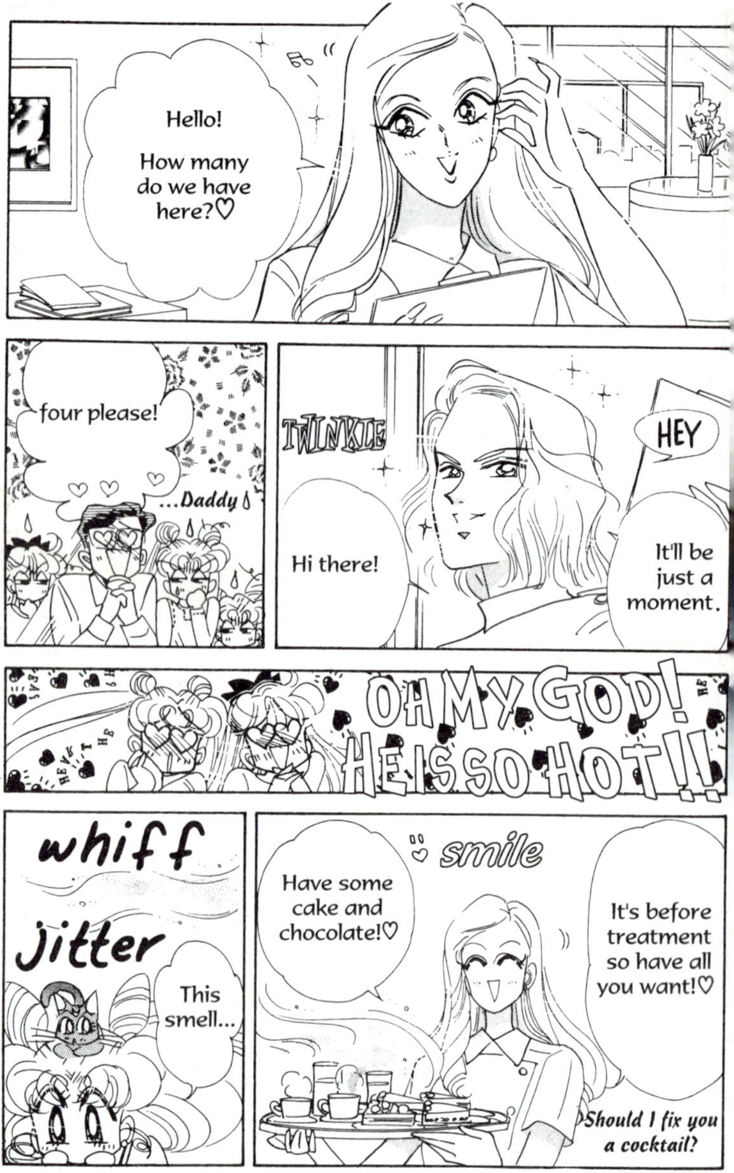

Hello!
How many do we have here?♡
four please!
...Daddy
TWINKLE
Hi there!
HEY
It'll be just a moment.
OH MY GOD! HE IS SO HOT!!
whiff
jitter
This smell...
smile
Have some cake and chocolate!♡
It's before treatment so have all you want!♡
Should I fix you a cocktail?

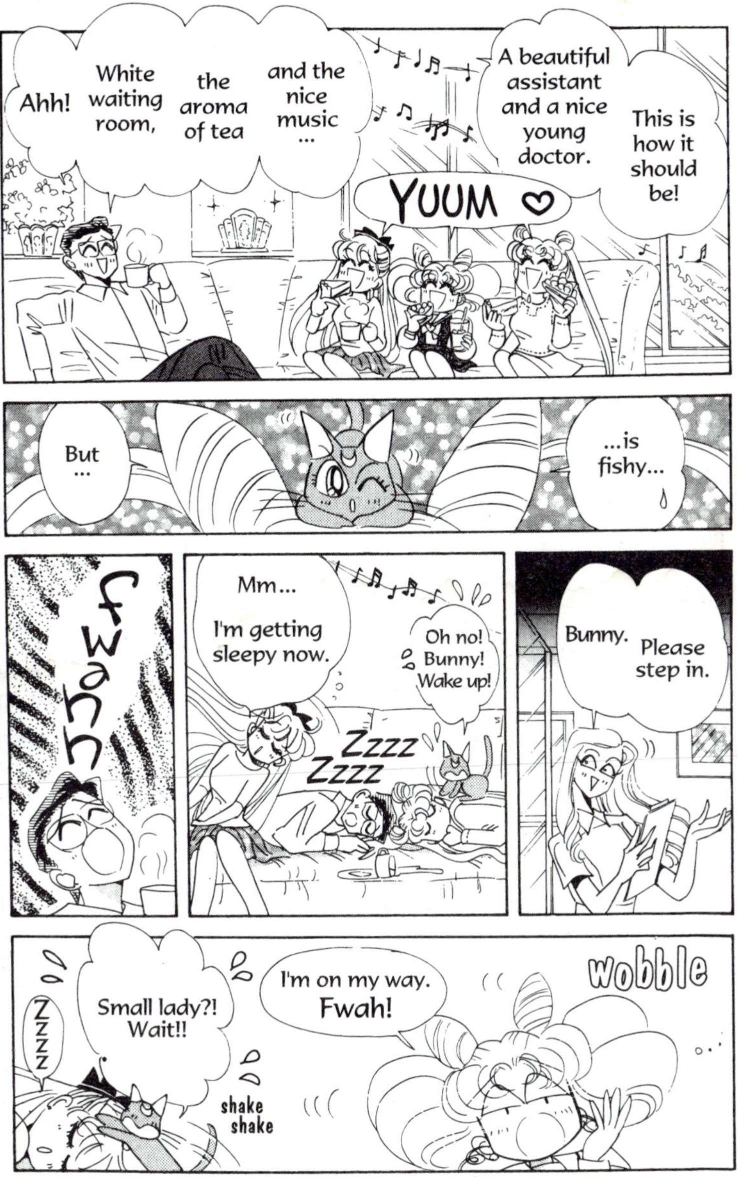

Ahh!
White waiting room,
the aroma of tea
and the nice music ...
YUUM ♡
A beautiful assistant and a nice young doctor.
This is how it should be!
But ...
...is fishy...
fwahh
Mm...
I'm getting sleepy now.
Oh no! Bunny! Wake up!
Zzzz Zzzz
Bunny.
Please step in.
ZZZZ
Small lady?! Wait!!
shake shake
I'm on my way. Fwah!
wobble

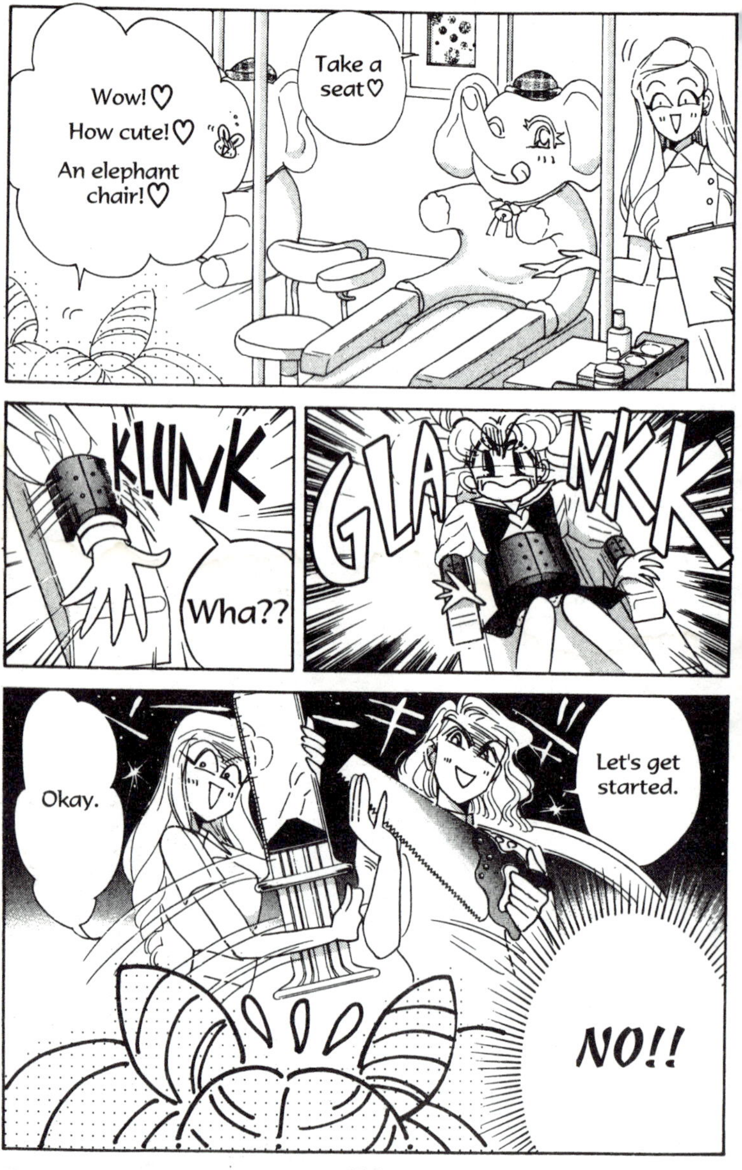

Wow!♡ How cute!♡ An elephant chair!♡
Take a seat♡
KLUNK
Wha??
GLANKK
Okay.
Let's get started.
NO!!

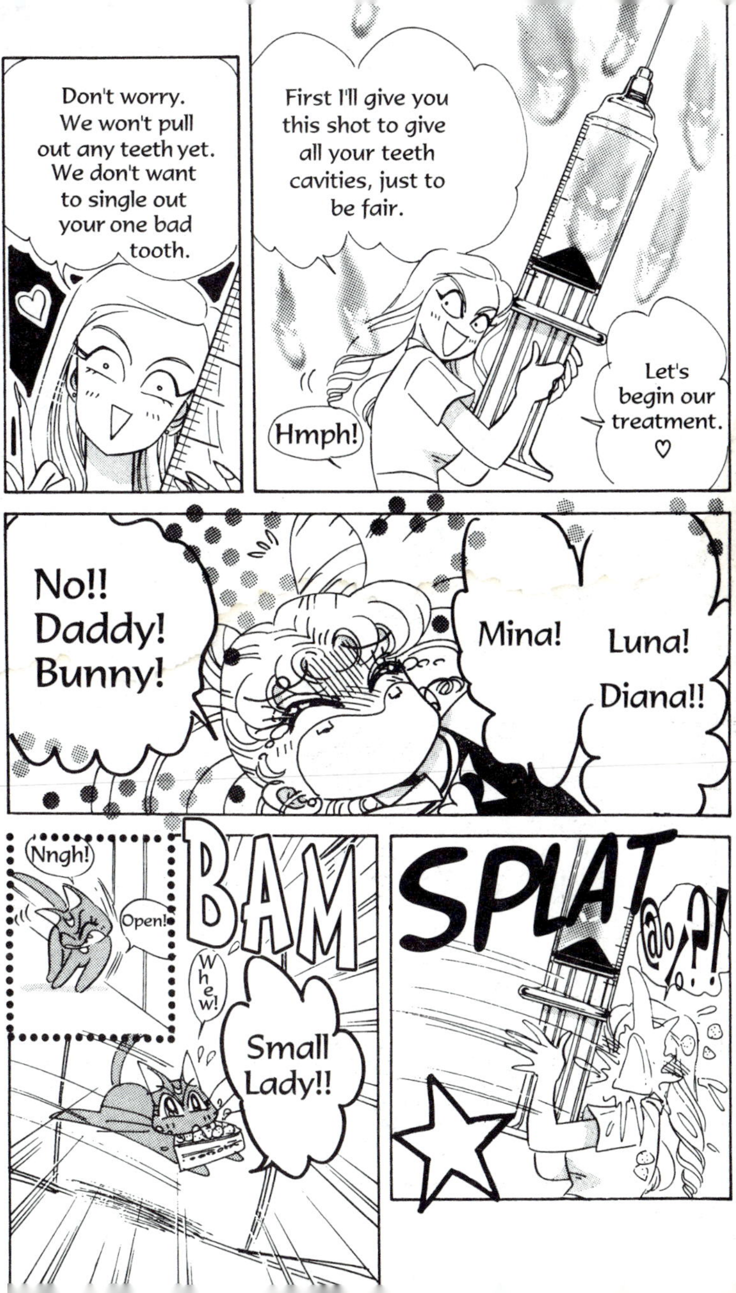
Don't worry. We won't pull out any teeth yet. We don't want to single out your one bad tooth.
First I'll give you this shot to give all your teeth cavities, just to be fair.
Hmph!
Let's begin our treatment. ♡
No!! Daddy! Bunny!
Mina!
Luna!
Diana!!
Nngh!
Open!
BAM
Whew!
Small Lady!!
SPLAT
@%?!

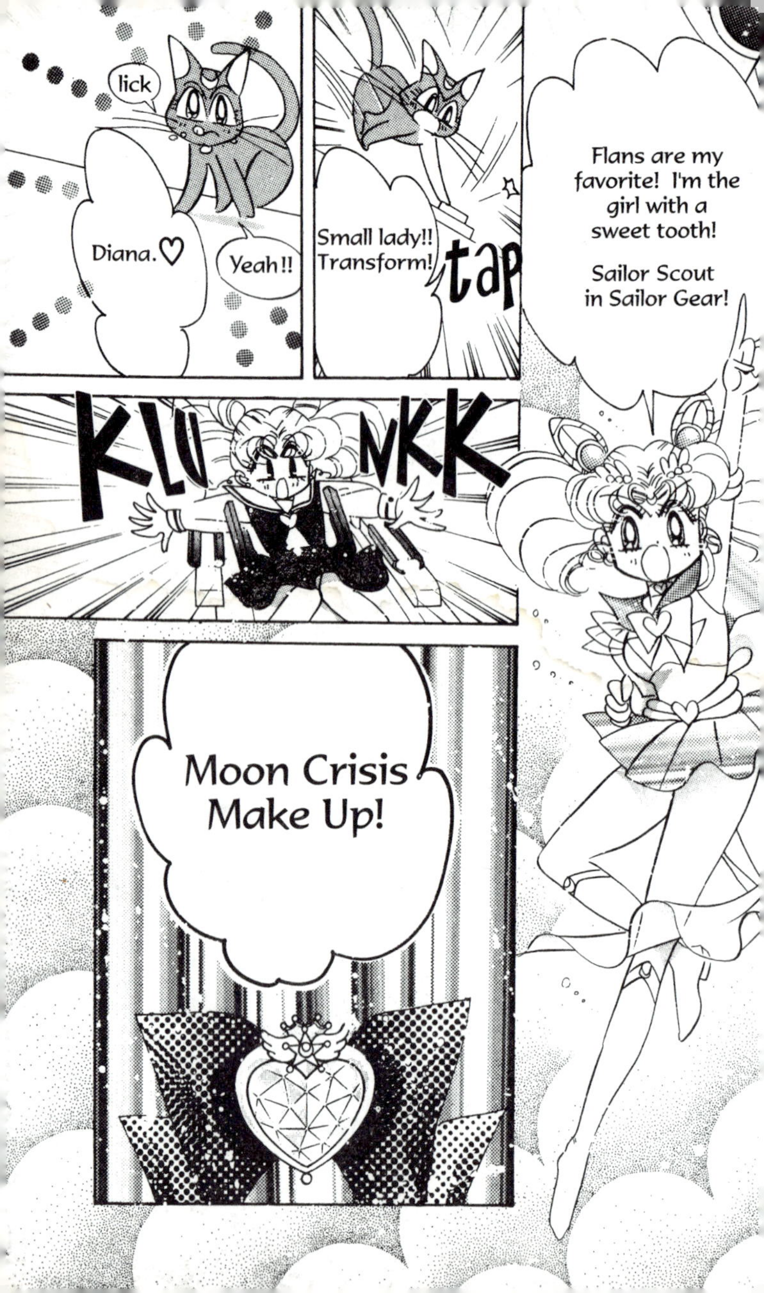

lick
Diana.♡
Yeah!!
Small lady!! Transform!
tap
KLUNKK
Moon Crisis Make Up!
Flans are my favorite! I'm the girl with a sweet tooth!
Sailor Scout in Sailor Gear!

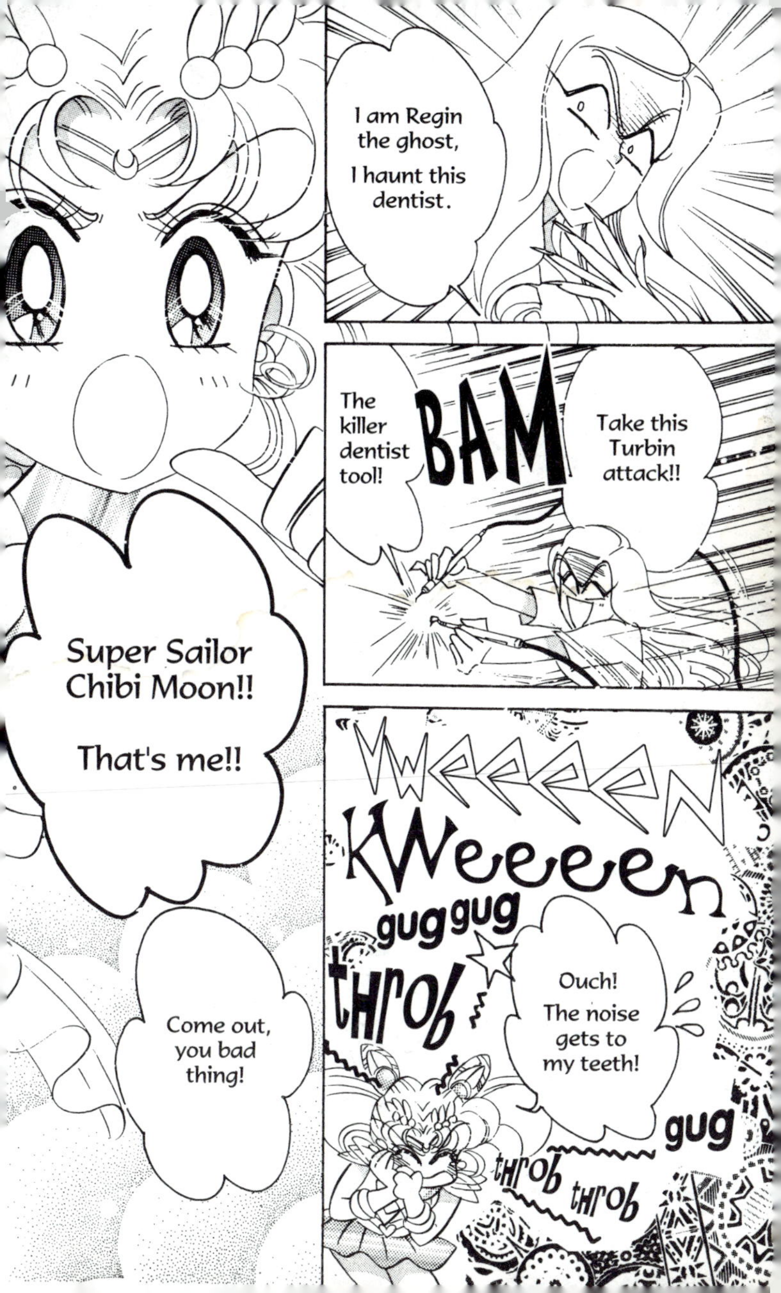
Super Sailor Chibi Moon!! That's me!!
Come out, you bad thing!
I am Regin the ghost, I haunt this dentist.
The killer dentist tool!
BAM
Take this Turbin attack!!
Kweeeeen
gug gug
throb
Ouch! The noise gets to my teeth!
gug
throb throb

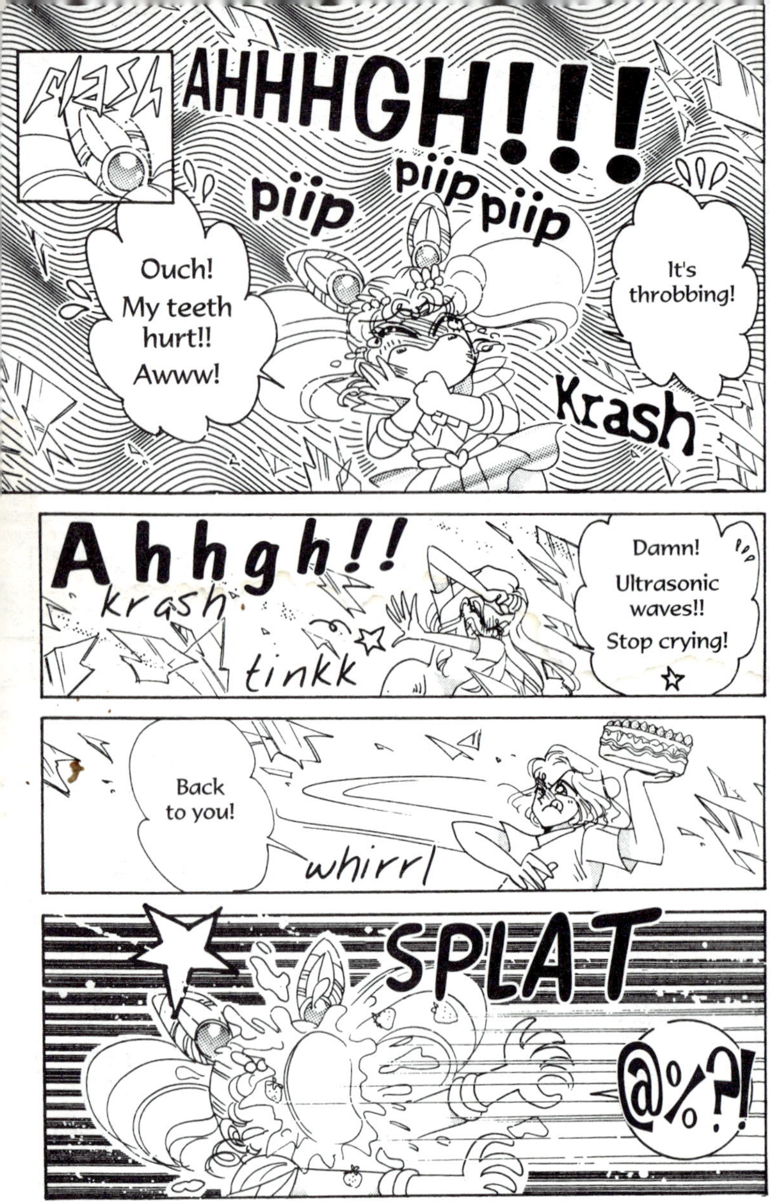
FLASH
AHHHGH!!!
piip
piip piip
Ouch! My teeth hurt!! Awww!
It's throbbing!
Krash
Ahhgh!!
krash
tinkk
Damn! Ultrasonic waves!! Stop crying!
Back to you!
whirrl
SPLAT
@%?!

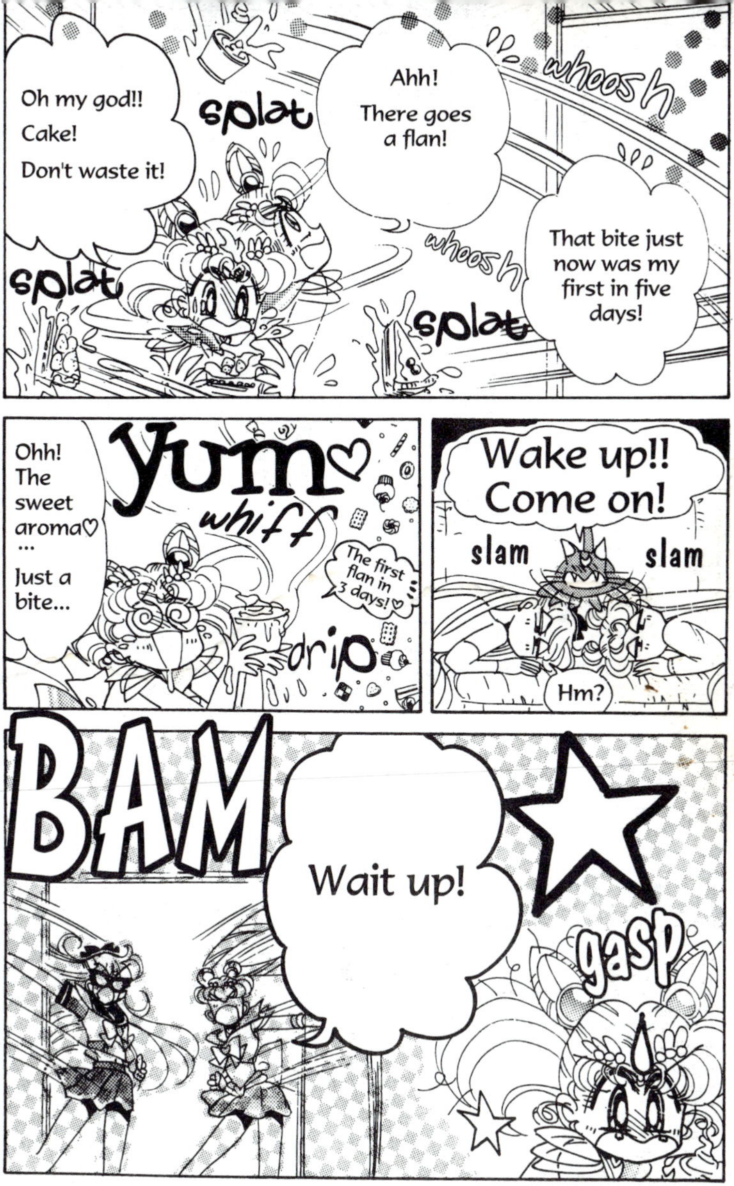
Oh my god!! Cake! Don't waste it!
splat
Ahh! There goes a flan!
whoosh
splat
whoosh
splat
That bite just now was my first in five days!
Ohh! The sweet aroma♡ ... Just a bite...
yum♡
whiff
The first flan in 3 days!♡
drip
Wake up!! Come on!
slam
slam
Hm?
BAM
Wait up!
gasp

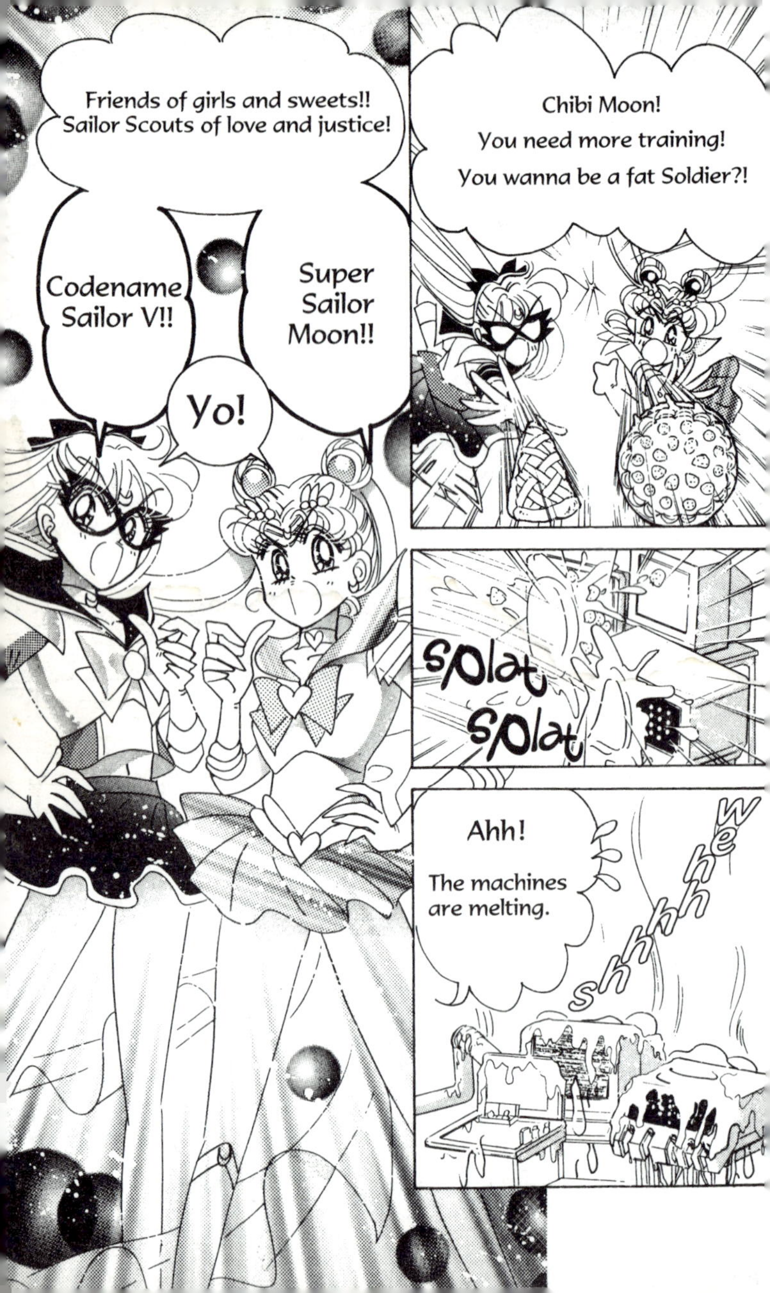
Friends of girls and sweets!! Sailor Scouts of love and justice!
Codename Sailor V!!
Yo!
Super Sailor Moon!!
Chibi Moon! You need more training! You wanna be a fat Soldier?!
splat
splat
Ahh! The machines are melting.
shhhhhew

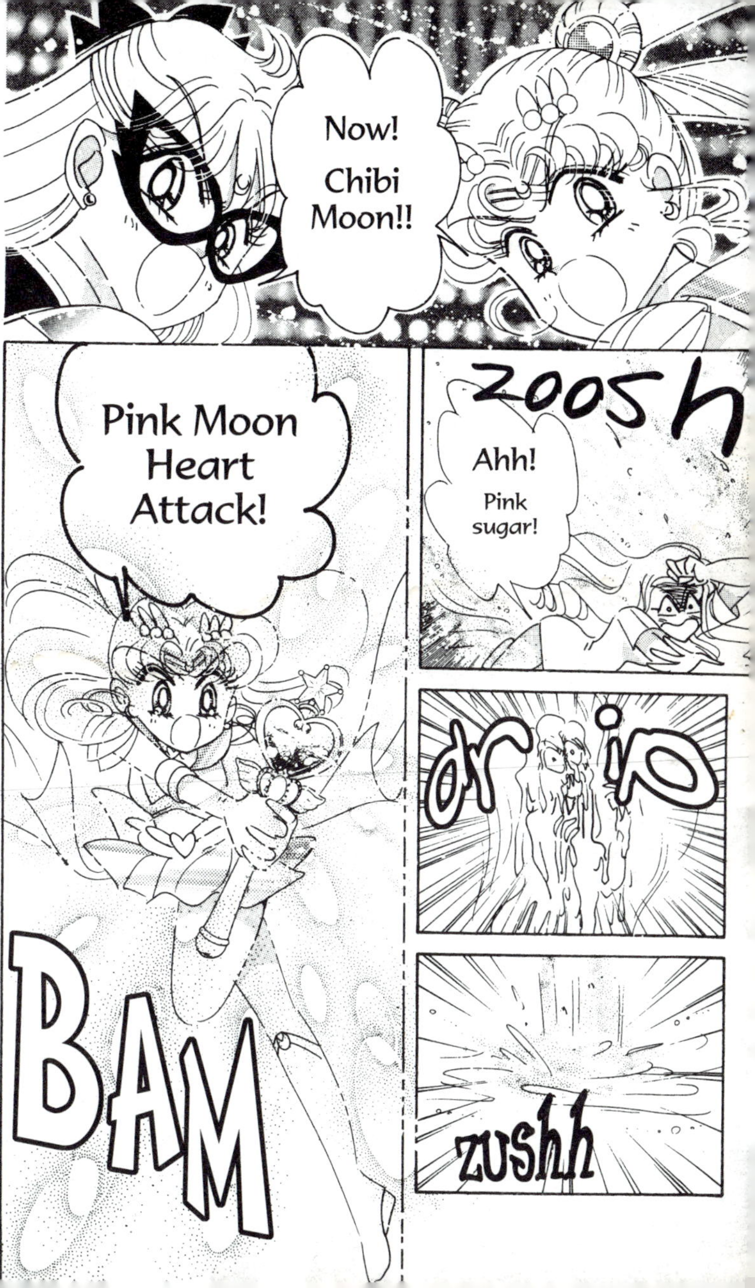
Now! Chibi Moon!!
Pink Moon Heart Attack!
BAM
zoosh
Ahh! Pink sugar!
drip
zushh

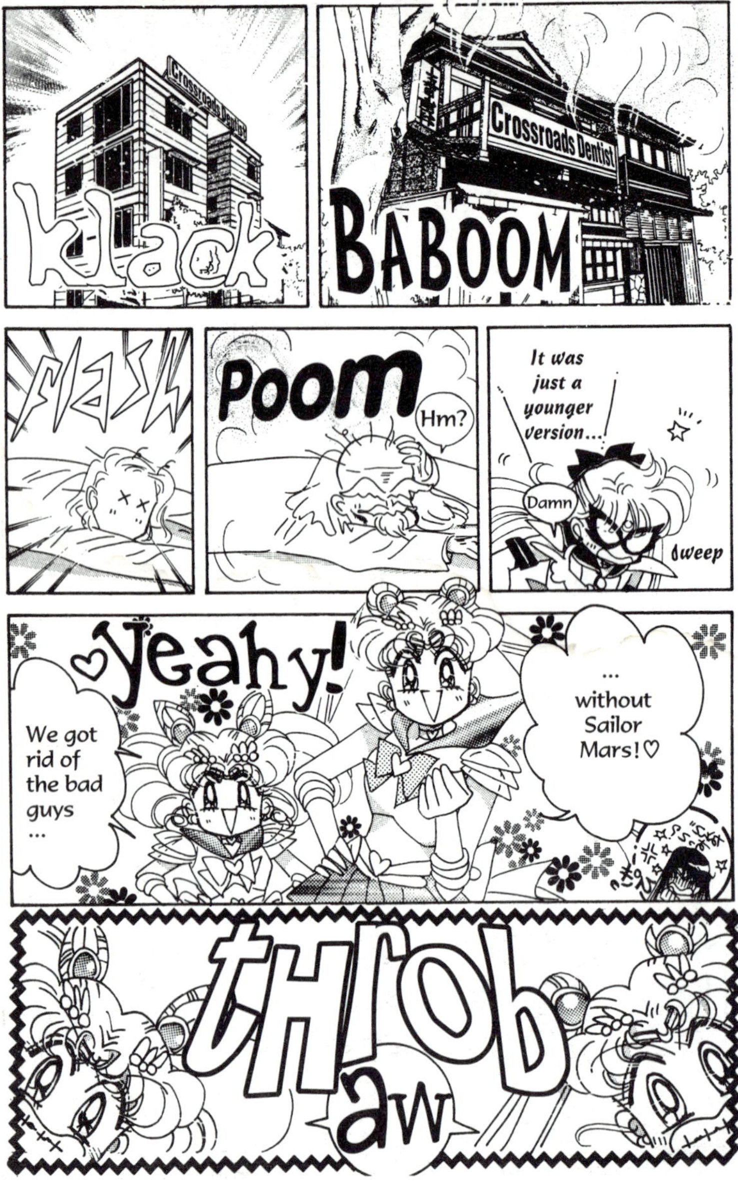
Crossroads Dentist
klack
Crossroads Dentist
BABOOM
flash
Poom
Hm?
It was just a younger version...
Damn
sweep
yeahy!
We got rid of the bad guys ...
... without Sailor Mars!♡
throb
aw

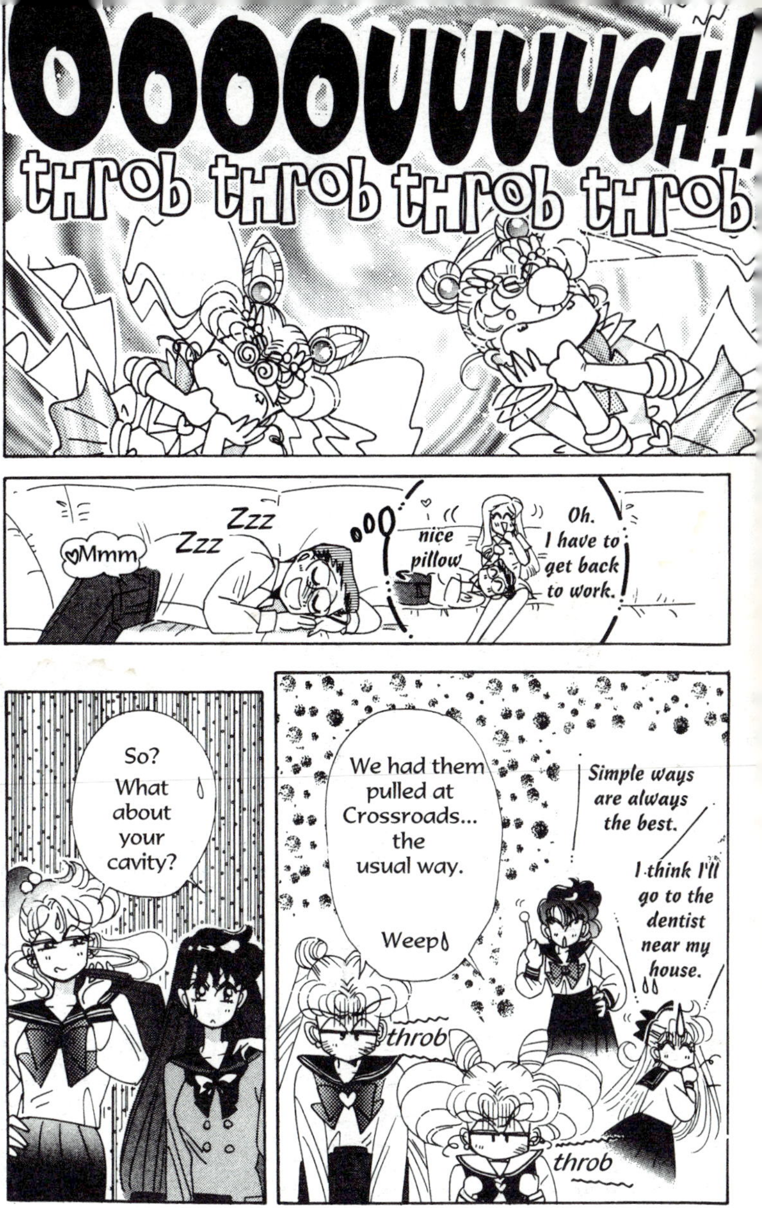
OOOOUUUUCH!!
throb throb throb throb
♡Mmm
Zzz
Zzz
ooo
nice pillow
Oh. I have to get back to work.
So? What about your cavity?
We had them pulled at Crossroads... the usual way.
Weep
Simple ways are always the best.
I think I'll go to the dentist near my house.
throb
throb

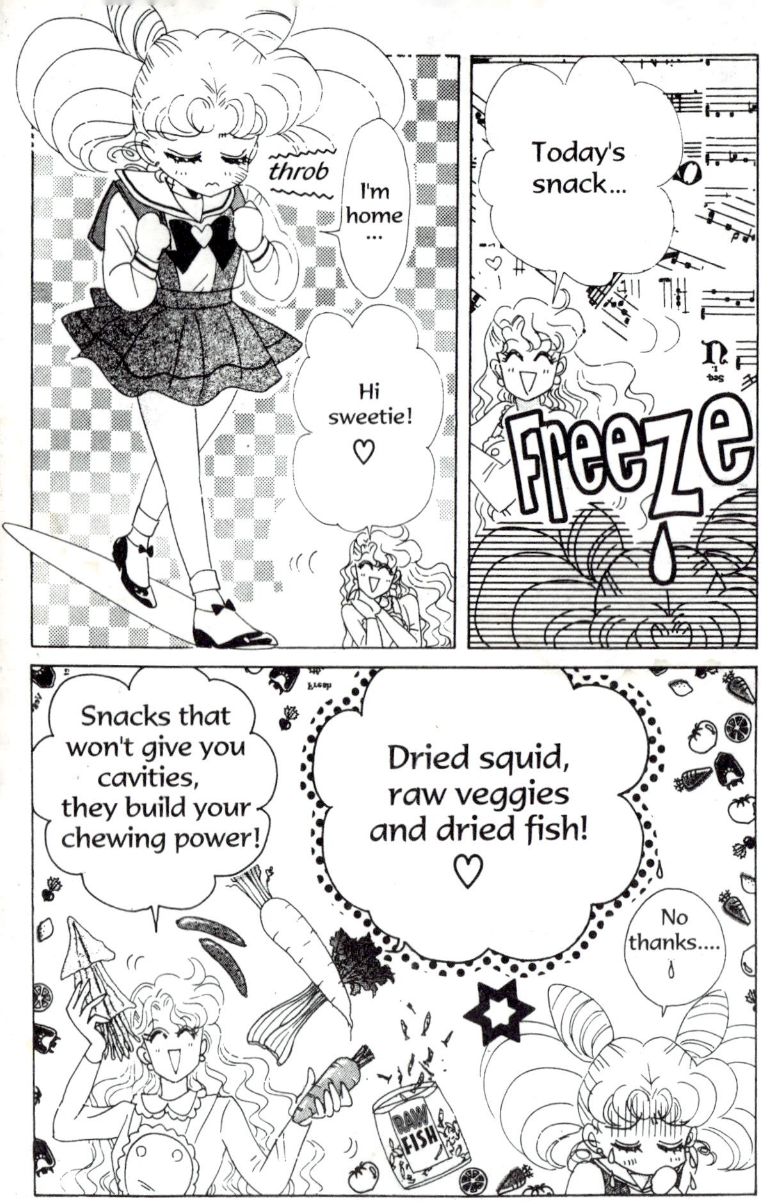
throb
I'm home ...
Hi sweetie! ♡
Today's snack...
Freeze
Snacks that won't give you cavities, they build your chewing power!
Dried squid, raw veggies and dried fish! ♡
RAW FISH
No thanks....

★★ End ★★